Central Works of Philosophy

Central Works of Philosophy is a multi-volume set of essays on the core texts of the Western philosophical tradition. From Plato's *Republic* to the present day, the volumes range over 2,500 years of philosophical writing covering the best, most representative, and most influential work of some of our greatest philosophers. Each essay has been specially commissioned and provides an overview of the work and clear and authoritative exposition of its central ideas. Together these essays introduce the masterpieces of the Western philosophical canon and provide an unrivalled companion for reading and studying philosophy.

Central Works of Philosophy

Edited by John Shand

Volume 1: Ancient and Medieval

Volume 2: The Seventeenth and Eighteenth Centuries

Volume 3: The Nineteenth Century

Volume 4: The Twentieth Century: Moore to Popper

Volume 5: The Twentieth Century: Quine and After

Central Works of Philosophy Volume 2

The Seventeenth and Eighteenth Centuries

Edited by John Shand

McGill-Queen's University Press

Montreal & Kingston • Ithaca

In memory of my parents, Alexander Hesketh Shand and Muriel Olive Shand

© Editorial matter and selection, 2005 John Shand. Individual contributions, the contributors.

ISBN 0-7735-3017-7 (hardcover)
ISBN 0-7735-3018-5 (paperback)

Legal deposit third quarter 2005
Bibliothèque nationale du Québec

Published simultaneously outside North America
by Acumen Publishing Limited

McGill-Queen's University Press acknowledges the financial support of the Government of Canada through the Book Publishing Development Program (BPIDP) for its activities.

Library and Archives Canada Cataloguing in Publication

Central works of philosophy / edited by John Shand.

Includes bibliographical references and indexes.
Contents: v. 1. Ancient and medieval — v. 2. The seventeenth
    and eighteenth centuries.
ISBN 0-7735-3015-0 (v. 1 : bound).—ISBN 0-7735-3016-9 (v. 1 : pbk.).—
ISBN 0-7735-3017-7 (v. 2 : bound).—ISBN 0-7735-3018-5 (v. 2 : pbk.)

1. Philosophy—Introductions. I. Shand, John, 1956-

B21.C45 2005   100   C2005-902037-7

Designed and typeset by Kate Williams, Swansea.
Printed and bound by Biddles Ltd., King's Lynn.

Contents

Contributors   vii
Preface   ix

Seventeenth- and Eighteenth-Century Philosophy: Introduction   1
John Shand

1 René Descartes: *Meditations on First Philosophy*   15
   Janet Broughton

2 Baruch Spinoza: *Ethics*   37
   Steven Nadler

3 G. W. Leibniz: *Monadology*   61
   Douglas Burnham

4 Thomas Hobbes: *Leviathan*   89
   G. A. J. Rogers

5 John Locke: *An Essay concerning Human Understanding*   115
   J. R. Milton

6 George Berkeley: *A Treatise Concerning the Principles of Human Knowledge*   137
   Tom Stoneham

7 David Hume: *A Treatise of Human Nature*   167
   P. J. E. Kail

8 Jean-Jacques Rousseau: *The Social Contract*   193
   Jonathan Riley

Index   223

Contributors

Janet Broughton is Professor of Philosophy at the University of California, Berkeley. Her main philosophical interests lie in the history of seventeenth- and eighteenth-century philosophy. She is the author of *Descartes's Method of Doubt*.

Douglas Burnham is Senior Lecturer in Philosophy at Staffordshire University. He is the author of *An Introduction to Kant's* Critique of Judgement and *Kant's Philosophies of Judgement*.

P. J. E. Kail is Lecturer in Philosophy at the University of Edinburgh. He is the author of *Projection and Realism in Hume* (forthcoming) and a number of articles in the history of philosophy.

J. R. Milton is Senior Lecturer in Philosophy at King's College, London. He has written widely on various aspects of Locke's thought, and has just completed work on an edition of Locke's early writings on religious toleration.

Steven Nadler is Professor of Philosophy at the University of Wisconsin-Madison. Among his recent books are *Spinoza: A Life* and *Spinoza's Heresy*.

Jonathan Riley is Professor of Philosophy at Tulane University. His most recent book is *Mill's Radical Liberalism*.

G. A. J. Rogers is Professor of the History of Philosophy Emeritus at Keele University and, since 1993, the Founder-Editor of the *British Journal for the*

History of Philosophy. His most recent book, with the late Karl Schuhmann, is a critical edition of Hobbes' *Leviathan*.

John Shand is an Associate Lecturer in Philosophy at the Open University and is the author of *Arguing Well* and *Philosophy and Philosophers: An Introduction to Western Philosophy* (Acumen).

Tom Stoneham is Lecturer in Philosophy at the University of York. Prior to that he was a Fellow of Merton College, Oxford, where he still owns the house in Holywell Street where Berkeley died. He is the author of *Berkeley's World*.

Preface

The works in the *Central Works of Philosophy* volumes have been chosen because of their fundamental importance in the history of philosophy and for the development of human thought. Other works might have been chosen; however, the underlying idea is that if any works should be chosen, then these certainly should be. In the cases where the work is a philosopher's *magnum opus* the essay on it gives an excellent overview of the philosopher's thought.

Chapter 1 by Janet Broughton introduces Descartes's *Meditations on First Philosophy*, which is usually taken as marking the beginning of modern philosophy. Descartes takes an intellectual journey, that is both logically rigorous and psychologically convincing, moving from sceptical subjectivity to establishing that there may be objective and certain knowledge. He also seeks to determine the ultimate nature of reality, and concludes that it can be divided into unextended consciousness or thought, and unthinking extended matter. The overall aim is to set aside the contingent aspects of our perspective on the world and so arrive at an objectively true conception of reality.

Chapter 2 by Steven Nadler presents Spinoza's *Ethics*. This work aims to connect at a fundamental level metaphysics and ethics. Spinoza sets out to show that ultimately there can be only one substance: something that includes within itself the full explanation for both its nature and existence. He calls this "God", but it has none of the features of a traditional personal God, and instead God is identified with the universe as a whole. There can only be one possible universe, and occurrences within it unfold with necessary logical inevitability. The appearance of contingency is merely a consequence of our ignorance of causes. Mind and matter are two attributes of this single substance. We are morally responsible and most truly ourselves when we act according to reason, free from immediate external contingent influences, and we act according to reason in so far as our ideas are active and thus adequately reflect the structure of reality.

Chapter 3 by Douglas Burnham discusses Leibniz's *The Monadology*, which condenses and sums up his philosophy. He seeks to identify the nature of true substance. Although Leibniz agrees with Spinoza that substance is autonomous and must appeal to nothing outside itself for an explanation of its nature, he does not include the explanation of its existence as part of its essence. Substances – unextended, simple, purely qualitative, and without parts – he calls "monads". God chooses to bring into existence one of an infinite number of possible universes of monads; the explanation for His choosing this universe is that it satisfies the condition of its being the best. Once created the universe unfolds with logical necessity. What we call appearances, or the physical world, are well-founded phenomena that reflect systematic changes in the monads. The guiding idea of Leibniz and Spinoza is to give an account of fundamental reality, if there is to be, as there must, a complete explanation for why it is as it is.

Chapter 4 by G. A. J. Rogers gives an account of the political philosophy of Hobbes's *Leviathan*. In this work Hobbes presents a view of human nature as fixed: base, brutal and without a natural capacity for mutual trust. The only way to avoid an endless war of all against all in a state of nature – the worst of all worlds – is for individuals to mutually agree to hand over virtually all their rights to a sovereign who will through sanctions impose moral order.

Chapter 5 by J. R. Milton looks at Locke's *An Essay concerning Human Understanding*. The fundamental aim of this book is to set proper limits on what we can be said to know about the world, by arguing that any knowledge we have of the world must be based on ideas that derive from experience. There are no innate ideas from which one could gain an understanding of the world independently of experience. There is a liberal impulse to this, so that we are encouraged to think things through for ourselves and not to rely on mere authority or appeals to innate, supposedly natural, intuitions. Locke also insists that we need not abandon ourselves to scepticism where we cannot have certain knowledge, because in these areas – which in fact constitute most of what we claim to know – we are still capable of probable belief and thus of rationality.

Chapter 6 by Tom Stoneham presents the arguments of Berkeley's *A Treatise Concerning the Principles of Human Knowledge*. The overriding aim of this work is to overcome what Berkeley sees as scepticism caused by the illegitimate and nonsensical positing of a material substance that might exist in some way other than how it can be talked about by reference to our ideas. Whether this constitutes an ontological reduction of the world to ideas and the minds that have them is open to debate. But by closing the gap between our ideas of the world and the world itself existing as a collection of sensible things, he seeks to eliminate any doubt we may have in talking about the existence of the world or its nature as we come to know it in our experience. He also reintroduced a dependence on God through His benign maintenance of an ordered world.

Chapter 7 by P. J. E. Kail explores Hume's *A Treatise of Human Nature*. There is a tension between scepticism and naturalism in Hume's philosophy. On the one hand, he shows that we have no rational justification for our most basic beliefs – such as causality, a persistent self, and the existence of the external world – beliefs that underpin all our other substantive non-trivial beliefs. If we did have such a rational justification in these cases they would either be logical truths or we would find that experience supported our belief in them, but in fact we find neither. Hume does not however conclude that we should abandon such beliefs, or that such beliefs are irrational just because they cannot have a rational justification. Rather, nature through actual experience and the inherent disposition of the human mind takes care that we firmly hold these beliefs; thus such beliefs are impervious to sceptical arguments since our having them is not dependent on argument.

Chapter 8 by Jonathan Riley explores the political philosophy of Rousseau's *The Social Contract*. Although he took the view that man's nature is malleable, and potentially perfectible – in opposition to the view of Hobbes – arguably he comes to similar authoritarian conclusions about the ideal state. Just because human nature may be moulded he does not ascribe the bad aspects of human behaviour to our inherent nature, but to the effects of the wrong kind of society. The aim of the ideal State is not to control the ineradicable brutality and lack of moral responsibility inherent in human nature, but to change human nature through the correct sort of socialization into something more rational, moral, and concerned with the common good.

John Shand

Seventeenth- and Eighteenth-Century Philosophy
Introduction

John Shand

The philosophers in this volume mark what may be argued is the second major watershed in the intellectual development of mankind. If Plato is the father of the coming of age of mankind, then the philosophers gathered around the Enlightenment are the thinkers who spread this more mature intellectual outlook deeply and widely throughout the psyche and institutions of the Western world. Kant was asked in 1784 to say what is Enlightenment, and he replied that:

> Enlightenment is man's emergence from his self-incurred immaturity. Immaturity is the inability to use one's own understanding without guidance of another. It is self-incurred, when it depends on a deficiency, not of reason, but of the resolve and courage to use it without external guidance. Thus the watch word of enlightenment is *Sapere aude!* Have the courage to use one's own reason!
>
> (Kant 1784: 481, translation modified[1])

Maturity of mind is a pretty good definition of philosophy: using one's own reason and understanding to think things out for oneself, and following this through wherever it may lead. Plato began this process, but the battle to complete that process was not won by him, and for the generality of humanity it probably never will be. Many seem all too willing to have others tell them what they ought to think, even as they may strongly claim they are making up their own minds. However, there are degrees of success. From Plato it took another two thousand years for

1

the philosophical spirit to spread as an intellectual outlook throughout the edu-cated portions of mankind and then to begin to have significant consequences for large portions of the human population. Eventually came modern science and huge advances in mathematics, the beginnings of democratic institutions and the emer-gence of the importance of such notions as the rule of law, rights and freedom. In fact, it is from the Enlightenment that the substance of almost everything we take for granted in the modern world emerged. The underpinning of this radical trans-formation of outlook is philosophy and the new philosophical ideas that appeared during the seventeenth and eighteenth centuries. During this period philosophy and science reinforced one another. In fact, it is to a large extent a mistake to mark a sharp distinction between philosophy and science during this time.

The hope characteristic of the Enlightenment, that man may be master of his own destiny, was unprecedented. Thinkers of the ancient world had valued reason and used it to attempt to control and understand their lives. Neverthe-less, through Greek and Roman times there remained a fatalism that many features of reality were overwhelmingly beyond our management; a world full of mysterious portent, uncertainly avoided or placated. The Renaissance, lying between the medieval period and the Enlightenment, was not ready to propose that human beings may be free of the vagaries of incomprehensible chance. Thus, the Prince of Machiavelli guided by *virtu* (usually translated "prowess", encapsulating the combination of virtuoso strength and cunning a Prince requires to rule well) had thereby still only the best chance of defying the uncertain deliverances of fate but could not guarantee to overcome them. With the Enlightenment a truly new sort of optimism arose for mankind, one where we need not be passive helpless subjects of the grinding wheels of fate. There was a growing belief that the efforts of reason to understand and control would be rewarded. There was also as part of this a movement away from mysticism and towards secularism. Man could actually get where he wanted to go on his own, not just hope for the best. In the ancient world he still considered the uncontrollable opposition of mysterious fate overwhelming. In the medieval world uncertain yet inevitable fate combined with the belief that man could not get where he wanted without divine aid was entrenched as the very structure of reality. The Christianity of medieval Europe, which intervened between the ancient world and the Enlightenment world, is seen by some as having com-pounded the passivity, hopelessness and powerlessness felt in antiquity as well as denying the value of this world in relation to the next. This view of the medi-eval period is forcefully described by Gilbert Murray as:

> a rise in asceticism, of mysticism, in a sense of pessimism; a loss of
> self-confidence, of hope in this life and of faith in normal human

> effort; a despair of patient inquiry, a cry for infallible revelation;
> an indifference to the welfare of the state, a conversion of the soul
> to God. (1935: 123)

He sums this up crushingly as a "failure of nerve". The Enlightenment was just the opposite of this, a "recovery of nerve" (Gay 1969: 6). It was a time that signalled the end of the sure belief that the striving for human improvement was futile. Rather, there was a confidence that in science and philosophy such effort would triumph, and in the establishment of a good and just social order that would bring about a better life for man in this world. There was also a rise in secularism. In short, the Enlightenment marked an utterly new view of the human condition.

This view, although not uncontentious, is I think basically correct. It should perhaps be balanced a little by pointing both to the way in which medieval notions still have value in our worldview – much of the work in the philosophy of logic and semantics for instance – and the way in which some Enlightenment philosophers saw themselves as building on, rather than overthrowing and replacing, medieval notions. The much studied notion of substance in the medieval period – substance being the basic building block of reality – although almost unrecognizably different in philosophers such as Descartes, Spinoza and Leibniz, is still in them a pursuit of substance in its most basic meaning, as that which does the explaining of other phenomena and is not itself in need of explanation. The guiding idea of Spinoza and Leibniz is to give a rational account of how reality *must* be fundamentally if it is to have, as it must, a complete explanation for why it is as it is. Descartes thought he needed to posit the mind as a separate non-physical substance in order to accommodate, among other things, the disembodied existence of the soul in accordance with religious beliefs that he doubtless held sincerely. Leibniz's conception of substances as "monads" indeed bears similarities to that of Aristotle. It is not, as in Aristotle, a natural kind at the level of things as they appear to us, but it shares with Aristotle's substance that it is something that captures the notion of an individual: something that can undergo change while remaining the same sort of thing. In Leibniz, however, substance both lies beyond appearances and provides the foundation of those appearances as "well-founded phenomena". God is required to explain the bare existence of monads but not their subsequent states, which arise autonomously according to their essential nature. Nor did Enlightenment thinkers suddenly become atheists (although some did, and some like Hume became at the least agnostic). Galileo and Newton were both profound believers, as was Locke. However, religion rested in an utterly new place when it came to explaining and understanding the reality of the world around us. In that capacity it took second place as a source of knowledge to reason and experience. Belief in God was not usually repudiated. Rather He was placed outside the world as well as outside explanations – beyond His bringing about the bare fact of the world's existence – as to why the world appears as it is and operates in the way it does, rather as a clockmaker stands apart from his clocks. There were remarkable exceptions to this in the shape of philosophical idealists such as Berkeley, who, in a reaction to the mechanical model of reality that placed God in a perilously irrelevant position, made reality more dependent on God than even the most devout medieval theistic philosopher would have contemplated. At the same time as God was pushed aside in theories about reality, attempts at direct understanding of the Godhead too were increasingly regarded as futile. The rise of Protestantism was partly both cause and consequence of this. The metaphysical ambitions of religion, in which it pronounced on the truth about the totality of reality, declined. A premium was placed instead on a direct experiential and moral relationship with God guided by personal experience and Biblical reading without the need of the intervention of a metaphysically empowered priestly class, which was in marked contrast to the ethos of the established church of medieval Catholicism. New philosophical systems were built that tended to avoid direct theorizing about God and placed Him in a peripheral role in the explanation of the workings of reality, but which left a separate realm for Him in a personal faith beyond reason. The same was true in science, so that to praise God was to admire, and hence to understand, the beauty of His creation, an understanding that did not require direct reference to God in order to explain the nature of that creation. Locke was highly influential on non-conformist religion, and this was based largely on his notion that it was every person's duty to make his knowledge his own by checking it against his own personal experience, and not rely on the mere authority of others. Locke was also, it must be said, opposed to what he called religious enthusiasm, which, as he had seen, had caused the shedding of too much blood. With prescience, Erasmus in the Renaissance realized that if religion wished to win people's trust and belief, but insisted on going head-to-head with science in attempting to provide an explanation of the world around us, then religion was only going to lose, and in the process thereby undermine its authority generally. Better to give up the science and restrict religious knowledge and authority to the transcendent realm of the spiritual and that of morality, beyond the grasp of the factual enquiries of natural science and of mere speculative philosophy. This separation becomes firmly established in the Enlightenment thinkers, and it culminates in Kant, heir to the Enlightenment, who, in order to make room for faith, not only refrains (if not consistently) from speculative metaphysics generally and theistic metaphysics in particular, which lie beyond the bounds of experience, but endeavours to show that such speculation is impossible.

The common characteristic of the work of the philosophers discussed in this volume is to ask questions at their most fundamental level and, with great originality, to take ideas fearlessly to their limits; to draw out and explore fully their ramifications come what may. There is a tendency towards wanting to sweep clean, and set ideas finally in order, at long last on their proper path to understanding and truth, and moreover a certainty that such an aim is not merely vain hope. There is an intermingling of what would today be distinguished as science and philosophy in most of the thinkers. Some of the philosophers, such as Descartes and Leibniz, are also significant original scientists and mathematicians in their own right; others, such as Locke and Hume, drew upon science directly or indirectly, as well as in return trying to underpin its presuppositions and methods. With some of the philosophers of this period an underlying idea is to draw the boundaries of what we could properly be said to know and think about, thereby rejecting the copious amount of theorizing directed at matters beyond those boundaries as pointless and possibly even meaningless.

The philosophers of the seventeenth and eighteenth centuries are sometimes divided into rationalists and empiricists. Often the ideas of both are brought under the title of modern philosophy. The rationalists are Descartes, Spinoza and Leibniz, and the empiricists Locke, Berkeley and Hume. The distinction, although helpful to some degree, should not be seen as pure, marking rather tendencies that vary in strength from philosopher to philosopher. The rationalist tendency is to contend that the fundamental nature of what reality necessarily is like can be known by the application of *a priori* pure reason alone, a reality that goes beyond what can be accessed *a posteriori* by experience and may only be known independently of the need to refer to such experience. The empiricist tendency is to deny that we may have knowledge of what reality is ultimately necessarily like by the application of *a priori* pure reason alone, concerning matters that lie beyond our possible experience, and to draw the boundary of what can be known (or perhaps even be meaningful) to those matters that can be referred *a posteriori* to experience, which presents a world whose features are always contingent. The empiricist may go further and deny the meaningfulness of putative *a priori* theorizing about reality. One should beware, however, of concluding that in some crude sense empiricists were concerned only with the solid results of experimental work and the rationalists were fanciful armchair theorizers; in fact the former could not avoid using concepts that failed to have a grounding in experience, despite protestations that they would not, and the latter constantly drew upon, and sometimes contributed to, the limited experimental results of their day.

The chief feature of seventeenth- and eighteenth-century epistemology and metaphysics is a move away from divine authority and revelation in understanding ourselves and the world towards what could be derived from the application

5

of reason and verified through experience. In metaphysics this emerges as a search for the ultimate nature of reality that in the rationalist philosophies of Descartes, Spinoza and Leibniz opens up the gap between how things appear and how they really are. This contrasts with the dominant Aristotelian tradition from which the Enlightenment emerges. Aristotelian metaphysics basically takes things at their face value; the ultimate building blocks of reality and the proper units of explanation are just what they appear to be: horses, mountains, trees, water, human beings and the like. These are the fundamental subjects to which various qualities are ascribed and that undergo change; change either from one substance to another (wine into vinegar, Socrates becoming a corpse) or change within a substance (wine turning into sour wine, Socrates becoming old). In substantial change we have one kind of thing changing into another kind of thing; in non-substantial (accidental) change we have one kind of thing remaining the same kind of thing, but changing its properties.

The ambition of the rationalist philosophers, however, is to establish a complete unification of reality, which will underlie the apparent vast diversity of things. For them such everyday kinds of things as appear to us are not the ultimate building blocks of reality. There must be something more fundamental underpinning the apparent diversity of things beyond appearances of which we can know the nature by intellectual reflection alone, and which gives us the ultimate and necessary explanation for why the diversity of things appears as it does. The Aristotelian units of reality and the explanation as to why things are as they are require an appeal to things outside themselves, and so such entities cannot be true substances. Partly the motivation for this is greater simplicity in explanations. The ideal rationalist aim is to find something – true substance or substances – that requires no further explanation, but may act to explain every-thing else, and in a simplified way. For Descartes, these substances are matter and immaterial (non-extended) mind. For Leibniz, ultimate substance consists of non-extended atomic collations of qualities called monads. For Spinoza (the major Jewish philosopher of this period), true substance is nothing less than the whole of reality; he calls this God, but it bears little relation to the personalized God of established religion, and was sufficiently other to have him dubbed a dangerous atheist, or at best a pantheist. The commonality of these conceptions of substance is that, unlike the diverse array of natural kinds presented as substances by Aristotle and the medieval Aristotelians, these substances fit the bill of substance proper: that of requiring no further explanation beyond them-selves for why they are as they are. Spinoza is the most extreme in his search for substance, for the requirement that there need be no further explanation beyond itself includes its very existence, and so it must in the ultimate and true sense be fully self-caused. As we have reached a unit of existence that requires no further explanation as to its nature – indeed, no explanation of its existence in Spinoza's case – we have something that can act as the explanation of everything else. It also produces huge explanatory power by treating different kinds as common in respect of what is relevant to their explanation. In this way, an explanation referring only to one basic kind of thing can be used to explain what appears as a variety of sorts of thing that previously seemed to each require a separate special explanation. It should be noted that Spinoza's concern is centrally ethical, but an ethics based necessarily on his metaphysics. Spinoza's enemy is uncontrolled passion and its destructive consequences; but rather than propose that it should merely be disciplined by act of will, he thought the problem was one of ignorance, and that once we understood the true nature of reality such control would come from reason overpowering passion. Again, the bringing of control through knowledge and eradication of ignorance, a dissolving of dark mysteries and superstitions, is highly characteristic of the Enlightenment mentality.

Locke's view on substance is more circumspect and ambivalent. As an empiricist philosopher he was concerned that beyond the simple truths of logic and mathematics, if we were to have knowledge, and knowledge of the world in particular, it must be derived from experience, not from the speculations of reason as rationalism supposes is possible. Whereas the rationalists have no philosophical problem with positing the requirement of substance such that it would be beyond the bounds of possible experience, Locke wishes to replace a mysterious something that supports all qualities, and thus becomes itself ineffable, with the merely contingently unperceivable collations of atoms whose structure and operations produce things as they appear to be. This again opens a gap between appearance and reality, and some would say that it means that objects that appear red are not really red, but merely appear red because of the reflective structures of their atoms, atoms that themselves are not coloured.

Berkeley may not have taken Locke to be positing a necessarily unknowable substratum as some have supposed, but even if Locke is taken as proposing atomic structure as substance, Berkeley still thinks this deeply mistaken. He is determined to show up contradictions in the notion of matter itself when it is thought of as some stuff underpinning things as they appear that goes beyond what can be translated into talk of the ideas we have of things. But even Locke's atomic structures suppose this, for his atoms as the causes of colour are themselves without any colour. Berkeley questions whether we can even imagine anything with no colour whatsoever.

Berkeley's motivation for this is to stymie what he sees as the widespread scepticism that would arise from the new materialism. Berkeley is keen to close completely the gap between how things appear and how they really are as a metaphysical distinction, as opposed to one made by referring to qualitative differences in the course of our experiences. This is not to revive the division of the world into Aristotelian natural kinds, with such kinds as substances, the ultimate units of reality. Nor does it mean that we cannot make mistakes as to how things really are as opposed to how they appear to be. The gap he is closing is between our knowledge of the world as based on ideas in our minds and the world being some kind of stuff quite other than ideas. If we never have immediate access to the world – a world that may, it is supposed, exist unperceived – but only have ideas of what we think the world is like, we have in principle no way of checking that our ideas correspond to how things really are, or indeed correspond to anything. In that case, we are locked solipsistically in our world of ideas and prone to irredeemable all-pervasive scepticism. It should be said also that Berkeley thinks that materialism leads to atheism, for it makes the operations of the world in principle independent of the need for divine control. One should note, however, that Berkeley is not returning to revelation and church dogma in the medieval manner to bolster his arguments. Berkeley's solution is to say that the world just is metaphysically a construction out of well-ordered ideas occurring in minds. Although he employs an array of complex arguments, the knockdown argument underpinning his position is his request to say something of what the world is like, if it is supposed that the world is not made up of ideas in minds, in a way that does not in fact still refer to ideas: things we can perceive, hear and touch. Berkeley thus does not reject substance, for there is substance, mental substance in which ideas adhere.

The epistemological counterpart to the metaphysical foundation of substance is the foundation of certainty for knowledge and the refutation of scepticism. We are not talking of particular sceptical doubts, but a corrosive universal doubt that knowledge of reality is possible at all. For how can knowledge be possible if everything we assert may be undermined by denial without contradiction, counter-argument and the possibility of our being subject to systematic illusion? The most determined attempt to settle this matter once and for all is found in Descartes. He imagines a situation where we would be most subject to entertaining false beliefs, one where we are systematically misled by a demon with near God-like powers, who could get us to believe anything he wanted. In this case would there be any beliefs immune from the demon that he could not get us to believe, ones that could not be false? Descartes's answer is that there is one: that he is thinking, and that therefore he must exist. The demon could not get him to believe he did not exist, whatever beliefs, false or true, he puts into his mind, because the very act of thinking them – thinking required even if he were to be deluded by the demon on some subject – requires and confirms that he exists. This gives Descartes the touchstone of certainty from which he builds up all other knowledge, that of clarity and distinctness; beliefs apprehended with clarity and distinctness must only be true beliefs. What is striking about this, as a significant part of the Enlightenment outlook, is how it portrays man as alone and as engaged in an individual odyssey, responsible for getting his own beliefs right, and unable to shift responsibility for doing the thinking that would lead to what he should believe on to others. Descartes needs God, it turns out, to escape his scepticism fully; but God becomes a consequence of the most fundamental argument, not an ultimate premise.

The death of scepticism was not so easily brought about. Indeed, we now tend to take it for granted that we have to live with a rationality that must coexist with a lack of certainty, with fallibility. Hume showed serious cracks in a rationality that might be supposed to be based on unshakable foundations. On the metaphysical side he was much more of a consistent empiricist even than Berkeley, who, after all, posits mental, if not material, substance. Hume rejects the notion of substance as nonsensical and meaningless because it is in principle beyond the bounds of experience. In short, if we cannot find an impression in our experience that some thing we talk about as an idea corresponds to, then we are either talking nonsense or, in fact, mean something quite other than we think we mean when talking about that thing. This leads to a pervasive tension in Hume's thought between scepticism – that we find we have no reason to believe some of the most basic things we take for granted – and naturalism – that there is a psychological explanation for why we believe what we do, and a good thing too that nature takes care that we do, because reason cannot do the job of bringing us to hold these beliefs. The fundamental beliefs Hume has in mind are those to do with causation: what it means to say one event brings about another, rather than their merely happening to occur together; that the way the world has gone on, with water being wet, and fire being warm, will continue in that way; that there exists an external world beyond the ideas in our mind, and that things do not come and go out of existence as we enter and leave a room; that there is something identifiable as who we are, a self that persists through whatever happens to us over our lives. All these things, which form the structure of every particular belief we have, are thrown into doubt by its being shown that we have a reason to believe them, while nevertheless we cannot abandon such beliefs. Hume extends this line of thought into ethics, for here he notes that whichever way we look at an action we take to be evil, we never perceive in the act the impression of evil, from which the idea of evil could be derived, and it must therefore be that we are affected by the act in a certain way, and so strongly, that we project our feeling of abhorrence onto the world in such a way that we mistakenly take a moral quality such as evil to be really in the world. Whether all this makes Hume a sceptic is open to debate, for it could be said, as he sometimes seems to, that all he has shown is that our basic beliefs are not derived from our concluding that they are rationally based. That does not show they are irrational, or indeed false; they could be derived non-rationally owing to facts about the way our minds work, and be true.

While the Enlightenment was a revolution in the way human beings thought they should think about things in the fundamental areas of metaphysics and epistemology, thinkers at the same time were applying themselves in similarly radical ways to how societies should be ordered. Rather than taking for granted the hierarchy of the medieval Great Chain of Being, with the pecking order in society reflecting that divinely ordained in the cosmos as a whole (God at the top, and below, in order, angels, man, animals and so on), the new prevailing mood was towards human beings having equal value, and that it is what you do with your life that merits the standing you have. Again, there is the optimism that if matters are thought through from fundamentals, and not merely derived trustingly from the albeit venerable deliverance of contingent historical accident, we can change things for the better and set them on a proper footing.

Rousseau and Hobbes are the two key thinkers in political philosophy represented in this volume. They are interesting counterparts, both because of how they are similar and how they differ, and what leads to those similarities and differences. Fundamental to their political thought, as to that of most others, is their view of human nature. One can either think human nature is fixed and something to be accommodated as best one can by society, or one can think of it as malleable and thus corruptible or redeemable according to the circumstance, in particular the kind of social order that surrounds it. If fixed, human nature can be thought of as either low and base or high and noble. Hobbes took the view that human nature is fixed and brutal; Rousseau took the view that human nature is malleable and perfectible, which also meant it could be fundamentally corrupted too. For Rousseau, human beings in a state of nature, at a time before civic society, may have been noble, but only in the limited sense of not having yet been corrupted by the wrong kind of socialization. Rousseau's state of nature should not be taken as historical, but rather as a hypothetical contrast to the dire effects on human nature of the ill-ordered society he saw around him. In any case, there is no going back to the state of nature, nor would it be desirable; for with civic society comes the possibility of a true humanity, one where, as opposed to being little more than animals enslaved to our passion and desires in a state of nature, human beings may become morally aware and responsible. The crucial question is what kind of civic society we should have, as it is society that brings the worst out in people. If human nature is malleable, then human beings can be changed for the good by changing the structure of the society in which they live. Rousseau was not, however, optimistic that this could actually be brought about. Hobbes takes a different view. Human nature being fixed and essentially brutal, he sees the greatest danger as man, in a state of nature, living in an anarchy that would be a war of all against all; a desperate fight for survival that would include taking pre-emptive violent action to ward off real and perceived constant threats. Interestingly, Rousseau and Hobbes from these opposing, if not opposite, views of human nature, both end up advocating authoritarian – indeed virtually absolutist in Hobbes's arguments – states; in Hobbes's case this is once and for all to avert the slump back into universal anarchy and a desperate personal war of survival; in Rousseau's case to forge human beings into creatures who would live by the best moral quali-ties, born of the firm idea that the good-life can be etched definitively by the uncorrupted human spirit combining with the application of reason. To what degree Rousseau can be viewed as a liberal is a difficult matter, and would seem to depend on how far the general will – which determines definitively what is in the common interest of all, and may legitimately be imposed on those who dissent – is seen as extending into the particular detail of our lives. Rousseau is certainly concerned with freedom, but it is a controversial conception of free-dom based on self-mastery in accordance with reason brought about by a cer-tain kind of benign socialization, and not the liberal conception allowing for the greatest range of individual personal choice and diverse views as to what consti-tutes the good life. In obeying the general will an individual is free, for in obey-ing it he is doing what is truly in his best interest, and what he would choose if he were fully the rational master of himself, that is to say, free. For Rousseau, freedom and the benefits of society are seen as not necessarily being a trade-off, as they are seen in liberalism. Rousseau is in some ways an archetypal Enlight-enment figure, but in some ways he is not. He is suspicious of the elevation of reason alone as being capable of changing human character, as some Enlighten-ment figures hoped. In addition, unfettered reason creates within us ornate fabulous structures of belief, which because they are unconnected to our feel-ings crumble under the pressure of attack or real life, leaving us with less of sub-stance to believe than we had before. Rather we must not merely point to reason as the solution, but form a society that awakens and improves our best natural sensibilities, and does not corrupt and crush them. This is not, then, a call for a return to a state of nature, which would be impossible, but rather for a society where feeling and reason go hand-in-hand. Nevertheless, Rousseau may set too much store in reason to definitively settle answers to the basic question of how we should live and to determine what it means for us to be free. Some would argue that this leads to the conceit of reason, and the overreaching of what it could determine definitively, resulting in the bloodbath of the French Revolu-tion. In this sense, Hobbes is a counter-Enlightenment figure; he does not share the optimism that our innate reason can control the brutality of our human nature, and he opts instead for its external totalitarian control by the state. So dire are human beings, their brutal natures fixed and unamenable to improvement either by appeal to reason or socialization, that Hobbes thinks it is only by handing over nearly all our rights to an unassailable sovereign who coerces people into obeying the moral law, that we can hope to attain the stability that prevents a collapse into the worst of all things, a lawless violent chaos in which only a fool would act morally. In both Rousseau and Hobbes, however, open argument that is not seriously trammelled by sacred or traditional restrictive assumptions is what guides them to their conclusions, and thus they are both part of the sweep of Enlightenment thought.

One should note that these views are not exhaustive of political possibility. Important thinkers such as Adam Smith and, again, Locke in his capacity as a political philosopher, took a less base view of human nature than Hobbes, while at the same time thinking that self-interested human nature could be harnessed for the good of all in a society radically less authoritarian – free-market economics under the rule of law – than Hobbes had in mind. Rather than try to change people fundamentally through changing the structure of society, because one cannot, the liberal tendency of thinkers such as Smith and Locke is to propose that society should be arranged so as to accommodate people as they are, warts and all, to live peacefully and productively together. Herein lies the liberal tradition of tolerance of moral pluralism, a lack of imposition on people of a sharply defined good-life; a toleration of people coming to their own view as to how they should best live; that what matters is that people live as they wish just so long as they do no harm to others. It is not enough that people have a certain kind of life; they must also, to be full human beings, freely choose the certain kind of life that they have.

This does not clear up at one fell swoop the political problems that bedevil mankind: those of balancing freedom as a right with what seems to be the justice of economic and political equality, or at least not too great an inequality; how far diversity can be tolerated when it might undermine social cohesion; what constitutes harm, and at what point it is proper to limit people's behaviour in the name of its doing harm to others. Nevertheless, a new optimism captured the minds of thinkers: that we do not have simply to fatalistically accept things as they are but, through thought and argument, we could in the social realm bring about improvement to the human lot, just as we could through the same methods open a totally new and accurate understanding of reality. Indeed, the two go together, for the technological innovations – productive machines, scientific instruments, advances in medicine – derived from basic science and philosophy promised wealth and the wondrous alleviation of the terror, pain, drudgery, hardship and misery of human life in a way previously undreamt of in human history. This is the Enlightenment; this is the start of the modern world. The ideas underlying it were forged by the modern philosophy of the seventeenth and eighteenth centuries. Little in the modern world is comprehensible without an understanding of the Enlightenment. This book illuminates key philosophers whose intellectual courage, dedication to argument and imagination, changed the world and our view of the human condition.

Note

1. I am grateful to Michelle Grier, Michael Inwood and Thomas Uebel for advice on the slightly modified translation that appears here.

References

Kant, I. 1784. "*Was ist Aufklärung* [What is Enlightenment]?", *Berline Monatsschrift* 4, 481–91. Translated in J. Schmidt (ed.), *What is Enlightenment?: Eighteenth-Century Answers and Twentieth-Century Questions* (Berkeley, CA: University of California Press, 1996).

Murray, G. 1935. *Five Stages of Greek Religion*. London: Watts.

Gay, P. 1969. *The Enlightenment: The Science of Freedom*. New York: Norton.

1

René Descartes
Meditations on First Philosophy

Janet Broughton

You are an educated person of good common sense who has a healthy dose of curiosity. Imagine yourself as just such a person living in the middle of the seventeenth century, and imagine that you were turning to the most learned people of your day, asking questions about the world around you. Their answers would leave your head spinning. The cutting-edge scientists would be telling you that lemons are not yellow and sugar is not sweet, and that the sun moving across the sky is still but the still earth beneath your feet is moving. The sceptical free-thinkers would be hammering you with a battery of persuasive arguments that always force you to the same conclusion: we can never have rational support for believing either that the world is as it seems, or that it is not as it seems. The scholastic philosophers – the Aristotelians who dominated Europe's universities – would at least be claiming that we have a rational understanding of the world, and that things really are much as they seem to be, but they would be nesting those comfortable claims in a prickly snarl of metaphysical theology about which they endlessly quarrelled among themselves. Faced with these fundamental disagreements, what would it make sense for a person like you to do?

Overview of the *Meditations*

In 1641, René Descartes published a short work intended to show readers how to find their way out of this bind. *Meditations on First Philosophy* narrates the

15

sequence of reflections by which anyone might arrive at the correct basic picture of the world. By the end of these meditations, readers will have given up some of their most cherished beliefs, and they will have learned exactly how and why they can defend others. They will see that the worldview of the new science is correct, and that they must give up their common-sense belief that our senses tell us what the world is like. They will also see that the scepticism of the free-thinkers is incorrect, and that we really can find a rational basis for beliefs about every aspect of reality. And, finally, readers will see that the scholastic philosophers have been quarrelling over the details of a fundamentally mistaken metaphysics, and they will see how to replace the mistaken theory with a proper understanding of the nature of reality.

The book is thus a sort of recipe for revolution. The book's readers are to be transformed by working their way through the same series of meditations as the narrator. If we do this, Descartes believes, we shall no longer be baffled by the sceptics and the scholastics; we shall jettison the confused aspects of our ordinary thinking; and we shall see why we can and must accept the philosophical framework within which we can defend the new science.

First Meditation

Descartes's ambitions in the *Meditations* are large, and to carry them out, he invents a remarkable strategy for the meditator to use. The meditator takes nothing for granted, and the way he takes nothing for granted is to take as seriously as possible the most radical grounds for doubt. He ostentatiously refuses to accept any presuppositions: he will not embrace any claim, no matter how seemingly obvious, if there is any way at all to raise even the slightest doubt about it. That way, if any of his beliefs survive this demanding procedure, he will be able to defend them against all comers, including sceptical free-thinkers and scholastic professors. He will be able to show that he can be absolutely certain his beliefs are true, because he will have shown that he cannot raise doubts about them no matter how hard he tries.

Thus, at the outset of his meditations Descartes proposes to withhold his assent to any proposition for which he can find even the slightest reason for doubt. Now, a person of common sense might think that there is no way at all for us to doubt something when we see with our own eyes that it is so, or perceive it by using our other senses. Of course sometimes we are mistaken – for example, when we are looking at something very small or far away – but that does not cast doubt on all of what our senses tell us. For example, if you are now reading this essay in a book that you are holding, your mistakes about small or distant things do not cast doubt on your belief that you have a book in your hands. It seems that when it comes to beliefs like this, we are immune to sceptical worries.

But Descartes gives a reason for doubting even your belief that you have a book in your hands. Consider the hypothesis that you are at this moment fast asleep with nothing in your hands, and that you are dreaming that you have a book in your hands. If this hypothesis were true, then here is what would be going on: you would really be lying in bed having a dream in which you believe you have a book in your hands, but your belief would be false. There would be no book in your hands. Now, if you see a way to rule out this hypothesis as incorrect, then of course it does not give you any reason for doubting your present belief. But the meditator finds to his surprise that he does not see any way to rule out this hypothesis. He may try to assure himself that he is wide awake and looking at a book by thumping the book or pinching himself, but he realizes that, for all he knows, he is fast asleep and simply dreaming that he is thumping a book or pinching himself. So now he has two ways of thinking about his present belief. One is his normal way of thinking, according to which his belief about a book in hand is true. The other is his sceptical hypothesis, according to which his belief is false. He cannot tell which of these ways of thinking is correct, but if he has no way to choose between them, then even though the sceptical hypothesis strikes him as far-fetched, he must treat it as giving him a reason for doubting whether his belief about the book is true.

Although the dream argument is a very radical one, it does seem to leave intact at least some of our beliefs, for example, the belief that the sum of two and three is five. But Descartes now considers an even more radical sceptical hypothesis: the hypothesis that his mind has been designed by an omnipotent but deceptive creator so that he gets things systematically wrong. On this hypothesis, even the things that the meditator's mind will find completely and transparently true will, in fact, be false. On his normal way of thinking, whenever he finds something to be very simple and obvious, such as "$2 + 3 = 5$," then his belief is true. There is no room for confusion; there is no obscurity; it does not even matter whether he is awake or asleep. But on this new sceptical hypothesis, his creator deceives him by designing his mind so that he *thinks* that "$2 + 3 = 5$" is obviously true when in fact it is false. As with the dream argument, the meditator realizes that he cannot tell which is correct: his normal way of thinking, or the radical sceptical hypothesis. The deceiving creator argument, then, is an argument that leaves the meditator with doubt of seemingly universal scope; it calls into doubt not just his beliefs about the world around him, but also his basic mathematical beliefs.

But *exactly* what is the scope of each of these sceptical arguments? Descartes clearly intends the dream argument to call into doubt any fairly specific belief that I hold about the things I take myself to be experiencing here and now: for example, that I am sitting down. But we might wonder whether the dream argument can call into doubt my general beliefs about what I am currently experiencing: that I have a physical body of some sort, and that it is in the vicinity of other physical objects of some sort. By the end of the First Meditation, Descartes clearly is withholding assent from the proposition that there is anything physical at all; the deceiving creator argument brings that proposition into doubt. But it is not clear how close the dream argument by itself comes to giving him grounds for this sweeping scepticism about the physical world.

There is an important question about the scope of the deceiving creator argument as well. If Descartes thinks it can call into doubt our simplest beliefs in arithmetic, then wouldn't he have to agree that it also calls into doubt our beliefs about other things we regard as transparently true, such as our simplest beliefs about the logical principles that guide our reasoning? Take, for example, the principle of *modus ponens*. This principle says that if some proposition p is true, and if the complex proposition "If p, then q" is also true, then q is true. We all have the basic belief that what this principle says is true. Does the deceiving creator argument call basic logical beliefs into doubt in addition to basic mathematical beliefs? It is not easy to think of a reason for drawing a line between the two kinds of basic beliefs and saying that the mathematical ones are dubitable while the logical ones are not. And yet it seems that Descartes had better be able to draw such a line, because otherwise he seems to have doomed his meditations from the start. If he must withhold his assent from the principles of basic reasoning, then he will not have any way to move his own reasoning forwards through rational meditation.

How real are Descartes's radical doubts? Many of us find that when we think about these sceptical hypotheses "from the inside", we agree with the meditator that we cannot really tell whether the sceptical hypotheses are true or false. Yet when we relax our attention and go about our everyday lives, we may find it hard to take the sceptical hypotheses seriously. They seem either exaggerated and far-fetched or part of some sort of intellectual trick. Descartes thought that the sceptical hypotheses are certainly exaggerated and far-fetched, but he did not think this showed that we can dismiss them. Perhaps we take them seriously only when we are giving our full attention to philosophical enquiry, but the doubts they generate are no less real for that.

Whether Descartes was right about this is one of the most debated questions in epistemology, or the theory of knowledge. Some philosophers argue that he is wrong; they think that when he says we do not "know" that there is a physical world, or that we do not "know" that two plus three equals five, he is illegitimately smuggling in his own idiosyncratic and overly demanding conception of knowledge. If I can claim to know that there is a tall round tower on that distant hill, then most philosophers would agree that there are some hypotheses I must be able to rule out: that it is a square tower, for example, or that it is short and fairly close. But (some philosophers would argue) I do not have to rule out the dream hypothesis in order to claim to know something. Think how odd it would be to say that a witness in a criminal trial didn't really know something – say, that there was a gouge on the table at the crime scene – simply because he couldn't rule out the dream hypothesis. Arguably, we are entitled to claim we know things based on our senses even if we cannot rule out the dream hypothesis. To this, defenders of Descartes might reply that just because raising the dream hypothesis in the middle of a cross-examination would be odd doesn't show that the dream hypothesis is an illegitimate challenge to knowledge claims. For practical reasons there are many remote possibilities we do not concern ourselves with in daily life; we open the refrigerator without wondering whether it is filled with snakes. But, as Descartes himself insisted, if we are not concerned with what to do but are instead concerned with what we really know, then we must take seriously even the most far-fetched possibilities. If this is right, then there may be nothing idiosyncratic about Descartes's conception of knowledge.

Second Meditation

Descartes takes his first step forwards out of the swamp of radical doubt by claiming certainty for his belief that at least he himself exists. *"Cogito, ergo sum"*, he wrote in the *Principles of Philosophy*: "I think, therefore I am." As it happens, that wording does not appear in the *Meditations*, but Descartes's reasoning about his own existence in the *Meditations* is often called the "cogito" reasoning anyway. The intuitive appeal of his claim is obvious, but exactly how to understand it is not. Let us consider several interpretative options.

One is to see Descartes's insight as expressing an inference, one that starts with "I think" and draws from that the conclusion "I exist". But saying that much is not saying enough. After all, if we start with "I walk" we can draw from that the conclusion "I exist", but if we are doubting whether anything physical exists, and if we are asserting only what we cannot doubt, then we are not entitled to start by asserting "I walk". My belief that I am walking is vulnerable to the dream argument and to the deceiving creator argument; it is no more certain than my belief that I have a book in my hands. So part of Descartes's insight here would have to be that somehow I can be certain of "I think" or, in other words, that "I think" is different from "I walk".

19

Descartes clearly does believe that we can be certain about "I think", even in the face of the radical sceptical doubts. But what is not clear is whether he intends this to be a basic starting-point for his reasoning about his own existence, or whether he thinks that his certainty about "I think" is itself a conclusion from some other sort of starting-point. This is not easy to say, but in his argument for his certainty about his existence, he does not give explicit reasons for saying that we can be certain of "I think", nor does he begin by explaining what would count as "thinking". Those are both points he turns to later in the Second Meditation. Partly for this reason, some readers think that in the cogito reasoning, Descartes was not treating certainty about "I think" as a starting-point but was instead trying to bring out some other aspect of our knowledge of our own existence.

One possibility is that there is something peculiarly self-verifying about the thought "I exist". Consider an analogy. If you say out loud, "I am not speaking out loud", then what you say must be false. By the same token, if you say out loud, "I *am* speaking out loud", then what you say must be true. The fact that you are saying it makes what you are saying true. Perhaps Descartes is pointing out, in somewhat similar fashion, that if you say or even think, "I do not exist", then what you say or think must be false, and that, by the same token, when you say or think "I *do* exist", what you say or think must be true. This is often called the "performative" interpretation of the cogito argument. One shortcoming of this interpretation, though, is that it does not explain why one of Descartes's key claims in the cogito passage is that if he is being deceived by his creator, then undoubtedly he exists. Descartes seems to draw some tight connection between his efforts to doubt as much as possible and his claim to know that he exists. But on the performative interpretation, the effort to offer reasons for doubt is irrelevant to the insight Descartes is expressing in the cogito argument.

A different way to interpret Descartes would be to see him as suggesting that he cannot doubt his own existence because his own existence is a condition of the possibility of raising radical doubts about anything. Suppose, for example, that in order to raise a radical doubt about a given belief, we must be able to construct a sceptical hypothesis about it. Well, what does Descartes think has to go into a sceptical hypothesis? If we think about the dream argument and the deceiving creator argument, then it looks as though he thinks a sceptical hypothesis will have to offer a scenario in which *I* am having the belief in question and yet for some reason it is false. (*I* am believing I have a book in my hands in my sleep; *I* am being systematically deceived by my creator.) But then one sceptical hypothesis I cannot coherently construct is a sceptical hypothesis about my belief that I exist. I cannot coherently construct such a hypothesis because I cannot include in it *both* myself having the belief in question *and* that

20

belief's being false. But if I cannot raise a radical doubt about "I exist", then I can be absolutely certain that I exist.

Once Descartes has found his first absolutely certain belief, he goes on to ask himself exactly what sort of thing this "I" is, if he can be absolutely certain it exists. In other words, how is he conceiving this "I" when he is conceiving it as something he can be certain exists? He starts his answer to this question by considering his former conception of himself and stripping away any element of it that involves something dubitable. His former conception was of himself as an organism endowed with life or a soul that enabled him to do the things that organisms can do, like be nourished and move around, and that also enabled him to see, hear and so forth, and to reason. From that, he must strip away anything to do with the existence of physical things: his radical doubts of the First Meditation require him to do so. Thus he cannot include in his conception of himself the idea of a human body, or of functions like eating and moving around. He also cannot include seeing, hearing and so forth, because as he has understood sensing, seeing requires eyes, and hearing ears. That leaves only reason, or intellect. There is no obvious reason why he would have to strip away this aspect of himself from his conception of himself.

But Descartes is not satisfied to leave things there. He seeks a more precise understanding of what it is that stays in his self-conception, and why it stays. Is it just purely intellectual activity that stays, for example, doing mathematical proofs? His answer is "no". He argues that there is a way to understand even sensation so that sensation can stay in his self-conception. The trick is to pare the conception of sensation down. Instead of thinking of seeing a light as something that requires eyes (and a light), he proposes that we think of "seeing" in a new way: as what is happening both when people really see (with their eyes) and when they seem to themselves to be seeing (for example, in dreams). One way to put this is to say that Descartes is claiming that the old notion of seeing had two parts all along: one part involving physical things, the light source and the eyes; the other part a distinctive sort of conscious experience. What he now wants to do is to strip away the part involving the light source and the eyes but retain the other part, the distinctive conscious experience. *That* part, he claims, we cannot doubt; whether I am awake or asleep, I am having that particular "like seeing a light" type of experience.

So the conception of himself as something of whose existence he can be certain is a conception that includes all the kinds of conscious states he can have, as long as he carefully subtracts any physical concomitants. He conceives of himself, then, as a thing that "thinks", where this means a thing that reasons, and wills, and imagines, and senses, provided that all of those activities are thought of in a properly pared-down fashion. In so far as he conceives of himself in this way, he cannot doubt whether he exists or whether he has the various states he ascribes to himself. Forming this conception is an achievement, Descartes believes: it is to conceive clearly and distinctly what until now he had conceived only obscurely and confusedly.

From this line of thought in the Second Meditation flow two of the most debated claims in the philosophy of mind: that we can understand the mental aspects of human beings independently from their physical aspects, and that we can be absolutely certain of the character of our own conscious states. For Descartes, the first claim will eventually serve as a crucial premise in an argument for dualism: the view that each human being is a combination of two fundamentally different kinds of things, one mental and one physical. In the Second Meditation, though, he is not yet ready to produce this argument. For one thing, he needs to be able to defeat the deceiving creator argument before he can take a step from the nature of our concepts to the way things are. For another, he needs to make his idea of physical things as clear as his idea of himself as a thinking thing. We will see later how he puts together an argument for dualism.

The claim that we can be absolutely certain of the character of our own conscious states seems to point towards a broad picture of knowledge. When it comes to our own conscious states, we can be absolutely certain of what they are just by reflecting on them, but when it comes to anything else, we must take some additional step in order to achieve knowledge. This very general way of thinking about knowledge sets up a kind of ideal – self-knowledge – and then represents every other sort of knowledge as somehow riskier. (After all, when we try to take that additional step, something could go wrong.) We will see later that although Descartes does think every other sort of knowledge is riskier for people who have not philosophized, he also thinks we have it in our power to reduce the risks to zero.

The Second Meditation is not entirely taken up with self-knowledge. Descartes also begins the process of clarifying his conception of physical things. He is struck by the fact that his first achievement of certainty has not come from sense-experience of some physical thing; he did not discover his existence with the help of visual or tactile or any sort of sensory experience. Before he started his meditations, he assumed that using his senses was the best way to be sure of something, and yet his senses have not been of any help so far in countering doubt. Descartes now asks himself whether his ordinary, sense-based way of conceiving physical things – for example, a piece of wax – is at least clear and distinct. According to his ordinary way of thinking, this piece of wax is a body that is white, sweet, cold and round, something with various qualities he can see, taste, feel and so forth. But Descartes asks himself a difficult question: is his conception of the wax as a body *just* a conception compounded from his sense-ideas of white, sweet, cold and round? Well, when he puts the wax by the fire, the colour changes, the taste disappears, the cold is replaced by heat and the shape droops, yet he conceives of the *body* as there all along. So the conception that is simply compounded from our ideas of various sensible qualities can change while the conception of the body does not.

Our conception of body must have some sort of content over and above the various sensible qualities of which we can be aware. What is that elusive content? To identify it, Descartes strips away all the sensible qualities from his conception of the wax. What is left, he discovers, is a conception of the wax as something that is extended (has spatial extent) and can undergo innumerably many changes in size and shape. This clarified conception of body is a conception that owes nothing to his senses or even to his imagination: only his intellect could allow him to conceive of *countless* possible changes in size and shape. The most the senses or the imagination can do is to present sequentially a large but finite number of different sizes and shapes. So Descartes is arguing here that his clearest conception of body is not a conception he could have derived from his senses, even with the help of his imagination. It is an innate idea, and what tags it as innate is that it represents physical reality as involving continuous quantity, or quantity that can vary in uncountably many ways. Thus Descartes lays down a central challenge to empiricist philosophers, who claim that every aspect of our ideas of physical things can be derived from what we find in our sense-experience.

Third Meditation

At the beginning of the Third Meditation, Descartes reflects on the Second Meditation, and he says he is especially struck by the clarity and distinctness of his recognition that he exists and is a thing that thinks. He explains that this special clarity and distinctness is not just a matter of having a very persuasive thought: it is instead recognizing that the falsehood of what is thought would involve some sort of contradiction. He wonders whether he is yet in a position to say that he can be certain of the truth of all his clear and distinct ideas. For example, can he be certain that two plus three equals five? That is something he grasps clearly and distinctly, and as he entertains that clear and distinct thought, he wants to say that not even a supremely powerful creator could make him wrong about what he is thinking. But then again, the sceptical hypothesis of a deceiving creator was precisely the hypothesis that our faculty of clear and distinct thought was systematically misleading. So Descartes's next order of business is to investigate the nature of his creator. If he could establish that he is created by God – or, more precisely, by a non-deceiving creator – he would not have any grounds for doubting whether all of his clear and distinct ideas are true.

Descartes's strategy at this juncture is to argue from effect to cause: the effect is an idea that he has; the cause is God. Descartes claims that he has one special idea – his concept of an infinite and perfect being – that could exist only if it were ultimately brought into existence by nothing less than an actual infinite and perfect being. (Arguments for God's existence that point to some effect and claim that only God could be its cause are often called "cosmological" arguments.) Although some good questions could be raised about the precise nature of Descartes's concept of God, the bigger questions concern the underlying principles of causality that Descartes relies upon in his cosmological argument.

The most basic causal principle I think he is invoking may strike you as fairly intuitive: everything that exists has some cause, or reason, or explanation for its existence. (Of course, we might not always know what the explanation for something's existence is, but think how odd it would be to say that something's existence is utterly inexplicable.) Now, if we apply just that extremely general claim to the existence in Descartes of a concept of God, we do not seem to get very far. We seem to learn only that the idea of God must have some cause or other, not that the cause must be God, or even that it must be something outside the mind of Descartes. Descartes explains that his argument will turn on a somewhat more specific principle, the principle that the greater cannot be caused by the lesser. He thinks of this as a straightforward consequence of the more general, intuitive principle. For example, if you claimed that a heat lamp all by itself could heat a stone to a higher temperature than the heat lamp has, then you would seem to violate the intuitive principle, because the extra heat acquired by the stone would have no source.

But even the more specific principle does not seem to allow us to draw the conclusion that God exists, because it does not seem that a mere concept would need much to cause it. For example, the mind of Descartes itself seems like a great enough thing to cause one of its own conceptual states. But Descartes argues that if we understand our ideas properly, this principle *is* enough to support his argument. He says that if we consider an idea just as a state of a mind, then indeed it does not have a very high "degree of reality", or capacity for independent existence. A mere state of a thing has less reality than a thing, and a finite thing has less reality than an infinite thing. But there is another way to consider an idea, not in terms of its "formal" or inherent reality, but in terms of its "objective" or representative reality. (Descartes's terminology here is counterintuitive for many of us.) All ideas have the same, fairly low, degree of formal reality, because they are all just states of someone's mind; but ideas may have different degrees of objective reality, depending on what the ideas are ideas *of*, or what they represent to the mind. Descartes thinks that the principle that the lesser cannot cause the greater has the consequence that the cause of an idea must have at least as much *formal* reality as the idea has *objective* reality. And since his concept of God is an idea with infinite objective reality, its cause must have infinite formal reality, which is to say that an infinite being must actually exist.

Few readers have been fully persuaded of the truth of Descartes's causal principle about ideas, largely because, as we might put it, no matter what an idea is an idea of, it is still just an idea and not something straightforwardly comparable to the real thing. But even if we were persuaded that the causal principle is true, we might still have several serious worries about the argument. First, we might think we can account for our concept of an infinite being simply by treating it as a concept built up out of "not" plus our concept of a *finite* being. Descartes considers this objection and argues that the concept of a finite being is itself somehow built up (or down) from the concept of an infinite being, but this argument is fairly compressed. Secondly, we might worry because Descartes needs to argue not just that an infinite being exists, but also that the infinite being could not be a deceiver. At the end of the Third Meditation he says that deception involves a defect, and that an infinite being could not have defects, but he also concedes that in some sense we, as limited beings ourselves, are unable to grasp fully what it would mean to be an infinite being.

Fourth Meditation

In the Fourth Meditation, Descartes reflects upon what he has learned so far from his meditations, and what this tells him about how he should proceed. Now that he knows that God exists and is not a deceiver, he thinks, he is entitled to dismiss the deceiving creator argument. Because it was the only grounds he had for doubting whether clear and distinct ideas are true, he thus also thinks he can be absolutely certain that all of his clear and distinct ideas are true. The way forwards, then, must be to follow wherever his clear and distinct ideas lead him.

But if we think about Descartes's method of doubt, this step appears to be subject to a charge of circularity. The problem of the "Cartesian Circle" is one that Descartes's contemporaries raised and that many present-day readers have wrestled with. Recall that towards the beginning of the Third Meditation, Descartes said that until he knew whether his creator was a deceiver, he could not be certain that his clear and distinct ideas were true. By the end of the Third Meditation, he has given an argument whose conclusion is that his creator is a non-deceiving God. Now, if he can be certain that is true, then he can be certain

25

all his clear and distinct ideas are true. But to be certain that the conclusion of his argument about his creator is true, he must be certain that its premises are true. Even if we suppose for the sake of argument that he grasps the premises of the argument clearly and distinctly, that is not good enough; he must be able to be *certain* that these clear and distinct premises are true. But certainty about the truth of his clear and distinct ideas is supposed to be the outcome of his argument, not its presupposition.

Descartes felt confident that his argument was not circular, and one of the great challenges for readers is to try to understand the *Meditations* in a way that would make sense of this confidence. Readers have taken two broad interpretative approaches to this challenge. Some begin with the view that, for Descartes, we can be absolutely certain about the truth of at least some clear and distinct ideas even before we know that God exists: for example, "I exist". This interpretative approach has the advantage of making good sense of the Second Meditation, where Descartes does seem to be saying that he is discovering some claims that resist the doubt of the First Meditation. Readers who take this view must then try to explain how this helps Descartes establish with certainty that all his clear and distinct ideas are true. For example, is he somehow certain about each of the premises in the argument for God's existence, even though he is not yet certain that *all* his clear and distinct ideas are true? Other readers would say that Descartes is certain of *nothing* – not even his own existence – before he discovers that God exists and is not a deceiver. Readers who take this view must then explain what he means in the Second Meditation when he says he cannot doubt whether he exists, and how from a position of universal doubt he could hope to achieve certainty about God.

In the Fourth Meditation, Descartes goes on to ask why, if God is not a deceiver, we ever make any false judgements. Descartes's answer to this question is something like a "theodicy": an effort to explain how God's goodness is compatible with the existence of evil in the world that he has created. Some people who offered theodicies claim that God's goodness is responsible for our having free will, and that our free but sinful choices are responsible for the evils in the world. In roughly similar fashion, Descartes argues that in giving us free will, God gave us the power to judge or to suspend judgement about anything. Thus God is not deceiving us if we abuse this freedom by assenting to propositions that we do not understand clearly and distinctly. We have it in our power to assent only to what is clear and distinct, and to suspend judgement about matters that we grasp only confusedly. We may wonder why God did not create us so that the scope of our will and the scope of our clear and distinct understanding coincided; if he had, we could not ever go wrong. But having a limited intellect is just part of what it is to be finite, and having an unlimited will is nothing to complain about. To carry forwards his search for the truth, then, Descartes resolves to be guided by the maxim that he should assent *only* to what he understands clearly and distinctly. If he follows this maxim, then he can completely avoid the risk of error.

Descartes presents a highly idealized picture of how our minds can work. He says that if we stop and ask ourselves whether a particular proposition is true, either we will find upon reflection that we grasp its truth clearly and distinctly, or we will see that it is at best something like a probable conjecture. And he thinks that when we are seeing a proposition as at best a probable conjecture, we are seeing it as not supported by fully persuasive reasons either pro or con. He seems to think that once we give such probable conjectures this kind of careful reflective attention, we will find it natural and easy to suspend judgement about whether they are true. But by contrast, when we grasp something clearly and distinctly, we shall accordingly be very strongly inclined to assent to it.

We may wonder whether this sort of careful reflection is always a good thing. We would surely not want to spend time reflecting about which way to veer if we were trying to avoid a traffic collision; if we wanted to stay alive, we would be rational to ignore the maxim of clarity and distinctness and risk making an erroneous judgment. At the very end of the Sixth Meditation, Descartes himself seems to concede that life does not always allow us to follow the maxim of clarity and distinctness. But this concession may be problematic for Descartes. After all, it is God who made us embodied creatures in a world that can destroy our bodies unless we sometimes risk error and make quick and unreflective judgements. If it is indeed rational for us to try to stay alive, then it seems God has created us so that some risk of error will be unavoidable for a rational person. This may conflict with the Fourth Meditation, where Descartes seems to say that God has created us so that a rational person can reduce his risk of error to zero.

We might also wonder whether it is natural and easy to suspend judgement when we recognize a proposition as a probable conjecture. Take, for example, the proposition that there once was water on Mars. Until recently, there was little evidence available one way or the other about whether this proposition is true, and any reflective person would have agreed that suspending judgement was the right thing to do. Now there is some good evidence in favour of saying that there once was indeed water on Mars, although this evidence is not entirely conclusive. "There once was water on Mars" is still merely a probable conjecture, and yet we might well think that our new evidence makes this proposition far more deserving of our assent, rather than still deserving only of suspended judgement. Depending on exactly what Descartes means by clarity and distinctness, perhaps he would agree. Here is a place where study of Descartes's scientific works might be helpful: for example, they would tell us more about his evidentiary standards for assenting to scientific hypotheses.

Fifth Meditation

Armed with the maxim of clear and distinct ideas, Descartes now turns to the clear and distinct idea of physical things that he had extracted from his confused idea of the piece of wax. This is the idea of continuous quantity, or extension in three dimensions. Packed into this are ideas of the possible sizes, shapes, positions and motions that extended things could have. What sort of knowledge do all these clear and distinct ideas allow us? If we assent to the truth of these ideas, exactly what are we asserting?

Descartes argues that these ideas entitle us to assert propositions of pure mathematics, but not any propositions about the actual existence of anything. Take the clear and distinct idea of a triangle. If we assent to its truth, we are assenting to such mathematical truths as the proposition that the sum of the angles of such a figure is 180 degrees, but we are not entitled to assert the existence of any physical thing that is or could be triangular in shape. We grasp truths about the mathematical "essence", extension, but that does not entitle us to assert that anything exists having such an essence. Indeed, Descartes goes on to say, only in the unique case of God can we infer existence from essence.

Here he gives a brief "ontological" argument for God's existence, an argument that is different from the cosmological argument of the Third Meditation. He begins his ontological argument with the premise that he has a clear and distinct idea of a being whose essence includes all perfections. Next, he says that existence is a perfection. Then he concludes that the essence of an all-perfect being includes existence, that is, that God exists. Descartes thinks we can reach this conclusion in exactly the same way we reach the conclusion that it belongs to the essence of a triangle that the sum of its angles is 180 degrees. Some of Descartes's contemporaries objected to this argument by constructing an exactly parallel argument that starts with our idea of an existing lion and concludes that a lion exists. But, these critics said, obviously we cannot prove the existence of a lion simply by reflecting on our own thoughts, so something must be wrong with the ontological argument.

Sixth Meditation

Descartes's reconstruction of the framework for knowledge has gone fairly slowly so far. He has argued that he can be certain that he exists, that God exists, that his clear and distinct ideas are true, and that he has genuine knowledge of mathematical truths. He has also clarified his idea of himself as a thinking thing, and his idea of physical objects as extended things. But he has not yet found clear and distinct grounds for believing that the physical world exists at all, much less that it contains the sorts of things that his five senses tell him it contains. The Sixth Meditation is where Descartes finally takes up basic questions about the physical world and his relation to it. As he answers these questions, he will be using his clear and distinct ideas in new ways; he will not just continue unpacking their contents, as he did in the Fifth Meditation.

After a long review of his progress so far, he launches into an argument for dualism. Cartesian dualism is the view that the mind is a fundamentally different kind of thing from the human body, or indeed from any physical thing. (As I explain this doctrine, I shall help myself to the temporary assumption that there *are* physical things, just for ease of exposition.) More broadly, reality comprises two entirely different sorts of entities: thinking things (for example, God and human minds), and extended things (the whole of the physical world and everything in it, including our bodies). This dualism has implications both for how we think of the subject matter of natural science, and for how we think of ourselves. The job of the scientist, Descartes believes, is to study the extended world and to explain natural phenomena by constructing and confirming hypotheses about the interactions among the basic components of physical things, including everything from stars to living organisms. The proper realm for "natural philosophers" is simply matter in motion, and this realm does not include minds or anything mental. Human beings, though, are not simply matter in motion. Each of us is made up of two fundamentally different things: a body, which *is* matter in motion; and a mind, an entirely non-physical, conscious thing that is the subjective centre of our understanding, experiencing and willing. One important implication of this view is that when we die it is at least possible that our minds outlive our bodies.

Descartes argues for dualism by considering his clear and distinct ideas of mind and body. As he had argued in the Second Meditation, he can form a clear and distinct conception of himself by attributing to himself nothing but thinking. Perhaps less controversially, he now makes the additional claim that he can form a clear and distinct conception of physical things like his own body by attributing to them nothing but extension. He then says that his forming these two conceptions is really equivalent to his forming these clear and distinct ideas: one of the possibility of a mind existing without any body existing, and the other of the possibility of a body existing without a mind existing. Because he knows that God exists and is not a deceiver, he knows that if he has a clear and distinct idea that something is possible, then it is *really possible*. So it is really possible for the mind (a purely thinking thing) to exist apart from the body (a purely extended thing), and vice versa. But that is just to say that the mind and body are distinct things, not the same thing.

Descartes rests this argument on ideas about what is and is not possible, ideas he is confident are clear and distinct. But people sometimes *think* they have a clear and distinct idea of something even when the idea is of something that isn't true, and even *couldn't* be true. For example, a novice geometer may think he has a clear and distinct idea of a triangle that meets this description: it is inscribed in a semi-circle, and the square on its hypotenuse is unequal to the sum of the squares on its sides. (In fact any triangle inscribed in a semi-circle must be a right-angled triangle, and the Pythagorean equality must hold of any right-angled triangle.) The novice might conclude from his supposed clear and distinct idea that it is *really possible* for a triangle inscribed in a semi-circle to exist even if no triangle with the Pythagorean equality exists. But of course he is wrong about that. Descartes does not deny that people sometimes think they have clear and distinct ideas when really their ideas are confused, but he insists that in the case of the basic attributes of things, there is just no room for the sort of confusion the novice geometer gets himself into. He insists that in the Second Meditation he showed how to think in the most scrupulous way possible about the mind, and there (he claims) he found that if he conceives of himself simply as something of whose existence he can be certain, he can conceive of himself while excluding everything from his conception except for thought itself.

Descartes's dualism raises many questions about what human beings are, but before we turn to them, we must see how Descartes at long last establishes that a physical world exists. He starts by noting that he has sensations: experiences of colours, sounds, odours and the like. In having these experiences, he is passive or receptive; it is not up to him what sense-experiences he has. What, then, causes them to occur? We are naturally inclined to answer that physical objects are what cause us to have sensations, but of course Descartes is not accepting natural inclination as an adequate basis for belief; nothing short of clear and distinct understanding is good enough for him. Well, perhaps by using clear and distinct reflection we can establish that physical things are the only possible candidates for the cause of our sensations. But Descartes does not think that is true, because the clear and distinct understanding of causation that he developed in the Third Meditation leaves it entirely open that some non-physical thing should be the cause of his sensations. Certainly, God is great enough to be the cause of our sensations, and at least theoretically there might be other powerful non-physical beings out there great enough to cause human beings to have sensations. So our intellectual resources alone cannot help us narrow down the possibilities to the one we naturally suppose is the right one.

At this juncture Descartes makes an elegant use of something else he knows clearly and distinctly: that God is not a deceiver. He reasons that God would be a deceiver if he left us in the following three-part predicament: first, naturally inclined to believe our sensations come from physical things; secondly, lacking the intellectual resources to correct our natural inclination; and thirdly, living in a world where our sensations actually come from non-physical things. But since we know that God is not a deceiver, and we know that the first and second parts of the predicament actually hold, we can be certain that the third does not: our sensations must come from physical things. Hence physical things exist, or (to be cautious) things exist that have the properties like size, shape and motion that we understand when we clearly and distinctly grasp the idea of continuous quantity. This means that all our clear and distinct ideas in mathematics also afford us insight into the nature of physical reality.

We cannot use similar arguments to show that *everything* we are inclined to believe is true. The kind of argument Descartes gives about the existence of physical things works only when we have no intellectual resources for correcting our inclination if it is wrong. Descartes himself goes on later in the Sixth Meditation to ponder such cases as those of people suffering from dropsy who are very thirsty – strongly inclined to believe they should drink – yet for whom drinking would be fatal. Such people have the intellectual resources to correct their inclination; indeed, the point Descartes makes about all such deceptive experiences is that once we understand the relation between the mind and the body, we shall clearly and distinctly understand that appearances will inevitably sometimes deceive us, and that we would thus be wrong to follow our inclinations wherever they may lead.

But Descartes believes that we can extend the kind of argument he gives about the existence of physical things in at least some directions. First, we can each say that our mind is united with a particular piece of the physical world: a unique human body. We can say that we live among a variety of physical things; that some things will harm us and some will benefit us; that what is disagreeable will usually harm us and what is agreeable will usually benefit us; and that there are correlations between the types of colours, sounds, odours and so forth, that we sense and the types of physical states that are out there in the physical world.

There is at least one additional thing most of us would say we are naturally inclined to believe: that our sensations present us with the kinds of qualities that physical things actually have. For example, we see colours, hear sounds, smell odours; and we would say we are naturally inclined to believe that physical things actually have colours, sounds and odours as their qualities, along with size, shape and motion. Even if we are sometimes deceived about exactly what colour something is, still we are strongly inclined to believe that the things we perceive have *some* colours, *some* sounds and *some* odours. Can we then conclude that these beliefs are true? Descartes's answer is "no". He recognizes that most people do hold such opinions, but he thinks if we use our intellectual resources to examine them, we will find that they do not hold up to scrutiny. For example, he says, we feel heat near a fire and pain when we get too close. We hold the opinion that the heat is a quality in the fire, but we do not think the pain is a quality in the fire. If we stop to reflect on this, we will see that we have no more reason to attribute heat than pain to the fire. Really, if we reflect on our sensations, all they allow us to say is that both the experience of heat and the experience of pain are caused in us by something or other in the fire.

By itself, this line of thought may not seem entirely convincing. For one thing, even if we find the argument about heat persuasive, it is hard to see how we would find similar arguments that would work for all the other sensed qualities. Nor is it clear why we could not construct an argument like the one about the existence of physical things: because we have an inclination to believe physical things have sensible qualities, and yet we have no intellectual resources to show that our belief is wrong, God would be a deceiver if it *were* wrong. Descartes tries to block this line of thought by distinguishing between strong opinions and the inclinations that God gives us as part of what it is to be human. But, at least in the *Meditations*, he does not make this distinction fully compelling.

Descartes's argument that our sensations are caused by physical things shows that although he regards minds and bodies as fundamentally different kinds of things, he is far from thinking they have nothing to do with one another. In fact he thinks that the human mind interacts with the human body throughout our lifetimes, and indeed that the mind and the body together form a united being. States of a person's mind can cause changes in the state of the person's body, as when I will my arm to rise: my mental act of volition is the cause of the physical event of my arm's going up. And states of a person's body can cause changes in the state of the person's mind, as when I experience visual, tactile, olfactory and other sensations when I examine a rose. Bodily sensations like hunger and thirst testify to the unity of the mind and the body. Descartes famously remarks that I am not in my body as a sailor is in his ship. If the side of his ship is bashed in, the sailor learns of the damage by seeing it, or noticing its effects; but if the side of my body is bashed in, I know it by feeling it. It is as if my mind is somehow intermingled with my body.

This account of the relation between the mind and the body is highly controversial. First, most of us think that every state of the physical world is fully determined by other physical states according to general laws of nature. But if the position of every particle in my arm is fully determined according to the laws of matter in motion, then there seems to be nothing about the position of my arm that could instead be caused by a state of my non-physical mind. Secondly, if my mind is non-physical, we might wonder what it could mean to

32

say that my mind is somehow intermingled with my body. When ink intermingles with water, the particles of ink distribute themselves throughout the space occupied by the particles of water, but my mind is unextended and cannot literally be distributed among the particles of my body, because it cannot be divided into extended parts that could be distributed spatially. Thirdly, we might wonder how two such different things as the mind and the body could have effects upon one another. Descartes would agree that we know how one physical thing can move another: by colliding with it. But the mind cannot collide with the body, nor can we envisage a mechanism by which the body could bring about changes in the mind.

Although the *Meditations* does not contain answers to the first two questions, it does contain a response to the third. Descartes suggests that when we think about the causal connections between the mind and the body, we should not expect to discover mechanisms that make these connections possible. Rather, we should simply recognize that there are general laws – we might call them psychophysical laws – that govern mind–body interactions in much the same way as the laws of motion govern body–body collisions. These psychophysical laws are not, for example, rose-sensation laws, or even eyeball-sensation laws. Rather, they are brain-sensation laws: laws stating correlations between various types of brain states and various types of sensory states. (In other works, Descartes identifies the pineal gland as the particular structure within the brain whose states fall under psychophysical laws.) Although Descartes does not claim to know what exact state of the brain is correlated with seeing red, he does claim to know that every time my brain is in that kind of state (call it kind A), my mind will have the visual experience of red. He also claims to know that God has ordained a very great number of such laws in order to help us preserve the health of our bodies in a dangerous world, and in order to help us gain knowledge of the world's various physical phenomena. (Descartes would not, however, want to claim that there is a psychophysical law governing every sort of mental state; he apparently believes that volitions and episodes of purely intellectual reflection do not fall under psychophysical laws.)

When I have a visual experience of red, then, my mind is in the state that is correlated with brain states of kind A, and such a brain state, Descartes claims, is typically caused by a distinctive kind of ocular state (call it kind B), which in turn is typically caused by the pattern of light rays that results when light bounces off a particular kind of surface of a physical object (for example, a rose petal). But seeing red does not give me grounds for saying that the rose petal's surface is red; at most it gives me grounds simply for saying that the rose petal's surface has a feature similar to a feature of the surfaces of apples and fire engines. The job of the scientist is then to make and test hypotheses about the nature of this surface feature (along with the nature of light and of the eye) within the limited but clear and distinct vocabulary of matter in motion.

If I dream of a red rose, my brain is being caused to be in a state of kind A, but the cause of that brain state is something other than my eye's being in a state of kind B. God has, however, set up the psychophysical laws so that *usually* my brain's being in a state of kind A is the effect of my eye's being in a state of kind B. Thus although our experience will occasionally be misleading, we can be sure that on the whole it is not. Descartes draws upon this fact to explain why he thinks we do not need to worry about the dream argument once we have grasped the correct framework for knowledge. The stretches of experience that are orderly and coherent are the waking experiences; the ones that we cannot readily integrate with these are the dreams. If we reflect carefully on our experience, drawing upon all our intellectual resources, we will be able to tell when we have been dreaming; God would be a deceiver if that were not true.

Many readers have felt that this does not quite dismantle the dream argument. After all, part of our careful reflection will have to include remembering stretches of our past experience, and we seem able to raise the question whether we are really remembering our past experience or only dreaming that we are doing so.

Conclusion

The *Meditations* is a compact and tightly structured book. The first three meditations move us from universal doubt to certainty about clear and distinct ideas by building up a reply to the deceiving creator argument. The second three meditations move us from the maxim of clear and distinct ideas to a framework for knowledge by building up a reply to the dream argument concerning sense-perception. The first three meditations reach their goal via a causal argument that bridges the gap between the mind and God; the second three reach theirs via a causal argument from the mind to physical world. There are other rhythms in the *Meditations*. For example, the middle meditation in the first trio of meditations explores the knowledge that our clear and distinct ideas of ourselves allows us; the middle meditation in the second trio explores the knowledge that our clear and distinct ideas of extension allows us. And the first pair of meditations concerns the doubting self; the second pair, the self's relation to God; the third pair, the self's relation to extension.

The work as a whole presents us with a powerful picture of ourselves both as knowers and as things known. We must move from a position in which we know with certainty only our own minds; on that basis we must somehow build up absolute knowledge of a world that lies beyond the horizons of our subjective experience. Yet our minds themselves are objects too: objects of a kind distinct from anything physical, and thus objects that might outlast the dissolution of our bodies when we die. Few subsequent philosophers have agreed that Descartes was right to see philosophy in this way, but few would deny the power of his vision.

Bibliography

Broughton, J. 2002. *Descartes's Method of Doubt*. Princeton, NJ: Princeton University Press.

Chappell, V. (ed.) 1997. *Descartes's "Meditations": Critical Essays*. Lanham, MD: Rowman & Littlefield.

Cottingham, J. 1986. *Descartes*. Oxford: Blackwell.

Curley, E. M. 1978. *Descartes Against the Skeptics*. Cambridge, MA: Harvard University Press.

Doney, W. 1987. *Eternal Truths and the Cartesian Circle: A Collection of Studies*. New York: Garland Press.

Frankfurt, H. 1970. *Demons, Dreamers, and Madmen*. Indianapolis, IN: Bobbs-Merrill.

Hatfield, G. 2003. *Descartes and the "Meditations"*. London: Routledge.

Kenny, A. 1968. *Descartes: A Study of his Philosophy*. New York: Random House.

Rodis-Lewis, G. 1998. *Descartes: His Life and Thought*. Ithaca, NY: Cornell University Press.

Rozemond, M. 1998. *Descartes's Dualism*. Cambridge, MA: Harvard University Press.

Williams, B. 1978. *Descartes: The Project of Pure Enquiry*. Atlantic Highlands, NJ: Humanities Press.

Wilson, M. 1978. *Descartes*. London: Routledge & Kegan Paul.

Further reading

The *Meditations* was published in 1641 (first edition) and 1642 (second edition), along with objections by various contemporaries of Descartes and his replies to their objections. To follow up on questions about the "cogito" argument, look at the Fifth Objections and Replies. For the problem of the Cartesian Circle, try the Second and Fourth Objections and Replies. For some surprising developments in Descartes's account of essences, look in the Sixth Replies at what he says about God's creation of the eternal truths. For questions about the argument for dualism, try the Fourth Objections and Replies.

Descartes's prose in the *Meditations* is lucid, and if you know even a little Latin, you would probably get a lot from looking at the original alongside a translation. The *Meditations* was translated into French in 1647, and the French version contains various small additions and modifications to the original. Although the translation had Descartes's general approval, we cannot be sure which (if any) of the changes he actually proposed.

There are many translations of the *Meditations* available, and quite a few include at least parts of the *Objections and Replies*. C. Adam & P. Tannery (eds), *Oeuvres de Descartes* (Paris: Librairie Philosophique J. Vrin, 1996) is the standard edition of Descartes's complete works in French and Latin. The *Meditations* appears in Latin in Volume 7 and in French in Volume

9. J. Cottingham, R. Stoothoff, D. Murdoch & (vol. 3 only) A. Kenny (eds), *The Philosophical Writings of Descartes* (Cambridge: Cambridge University Press, 1984) is the standard English-language edition of Descartes's philosophical writings. The *Meditations* appears in Volume 2. G. Heffernan (ed.), *Meditationes de Prima Philosophia: Meditations on First Philosophy* (Notre Dame, IN: Notre Dame University Press, 1990) has the Latin text and a very literal English translation on facing pages. It does not include the *Objections and Replies*.

2

Baruch Spinoza
Ethics

Steven Nadler

Baruch (or Benedictus) Spinoza was perhaps the most original and radical philosopher of his time. He was also, for just those reasons, the most vilified thinker of the early modern period. Even during Spinoza's own lifetime, the term "Spinozism" became synonymous with atheism, as political and religious authorities issued numerous and highly agitated condemnations of his ideas. Despite this formidable opposition, Spinoza and his followers exercised a good deal of influence upon the Enlightenment and modern philosophical, political and religious thought.

Biographical sketch

Spinoza was born in Amsterdam in 1632 to a prominent merchant family in the city's Portuguese–Jewish community. As a boy, he had undoubtedly been one of the star pupils in the congregation's Talmud Torah school. He was intellectually gifted, and this could not have gone unremarked by the congregation's rabbis. It is possible that Spinoza, as he made progress through his studies, was being groomed for a career as a rabbi. But he never made it into the upper levels of the curriculum, those which included advanced study of Talmud. At the age of 17, he was forced to cut short his formal studies to help run the family's importing business.

And then, on 27 July 1656, Spinoza was issued the harshest writ of *cherem*, or excommunication, ever pronounced by the Sephardic community of Amsterdam;

it was never rescinded. We do not know for certain what Spinoza's "monstrous deeds" and "abominable heresies" were alleged to have been, but it is quite easy to make an educated guess. There is good reason to believe that he was, even as a young man, already giving utterance to just those ideas that would later appear in his mature philosophical treatises. In those works, Spinoza denies the immortality of the soul; strongly rejects the notion of a providential God – the God of Abraham, Isaac and Jacob; and claims that the law was neither literally given by God (to Moses) nor is any longer binding on Jews. Such opinions would have been troubling both to the rabbis and governors of the Portuguese community and to the Calvinist authorities within whose bailiwick the Jews resided.

To all appearances, Spinoza was content finally to have an excuse for departing from the community and leaving Judaism behind; his faith and religious commitment were, by this point, gone. Within a few years, he left Amsterdam altogether. By the time his extant correspondence begins, in 1661, he is living in Rijnsburg, not far from Leiden. While in Rijnsburg, he worked on the "Treatise on the Emendation of the Intellect", an essay on philosophical method, and the "Short Treatise on God, Man and His Well-Being", an initial but aborted effort to lay out his metaphysical, epistemological and moral views. His critical exposition of Descartes's *Principles of Philosophy*, the only work he published under his own name in his lifetime, was completed in 1663, after he had moved to Voorburg, outside The Hague. This work brought him a wide reputation as a proponent of the Cartesian philosophy, although he clearly rejected some important elements of Descartes's thought.

Spinoza, like many intellectuals of the time (including Descartes himself), was not a philosopher in the professional, academic sense of the term. In fact, he turned down the offer of a professorship at the University of Heidelberg because he was afraid that, with the conditions such a post imposed on him, it would compromise his freedom of thought. He was able to support himself by lens grinding, although he also benefited from the generosity of his close circle of devoted friends.

By the mid-1660s, Spinoza was working on what would eventually be called the *Ethics*, his philosophical masterpiece. However, when he saw the principles of toleration in the Netherlands being threatened by reactionary forces, he put it aside to complete his "scandalous" *Theological–Political Treatise*, published anonymously and to great alarm in 1670. When Spinoza died in 1677, in The Hague, he was still at work on his *Political Treatise*; this was soon published by his friends along with his other unpublished writings, including a *Compendium to Hebrew Grammar*.

The *Ethics*

Spinoza probably began working on the *Ethics* (the original Latin title is *Ethica*) in late 1663. Although he had a substantial draft by 1665, and probably a complete, nearly definitive version by 1675, he decided not to publish the work, in the light of the public outcry generated by the *Theological–Political Treatise*. Although a draft of the *Ethics* circulated among his friends, and its theses were discussed in a number of circles – Leibniz probably saw a copy of it when he was in Paris in the early 1670s – it did not appear in print until after his death.

The *Ethics* is one of the most difficult books in the history of philosophy, not the least because of its format. At first approach, the mere appearance of the work is daunting, even intimidating to the non-philosopher. With its Euclidean architecture of definitions, axioms, propositions, demonstrations, postulates, scholia and corollaries, it looks all but impenetrable. But this layout is not some superficial shell for material that could have been presented in a different, more accessible manner. Spinoza was looking to provide a more rigorous and persuasive presentation for his philosophical ideas about God, the human being and happiness than what they had received in the "Short Treatise". He decided that the best way to do this would be to adopt the method of the geometers, with its deductive procedure and absolutely certain conclusions. But besides being methodologically essential (and perhaps rhetorically and pedagogically useful) – the deductions constitute the argument for Spinoza's complex and often counterintuitive theses – the geometrical method bears an intimate relationship to the content of Spinoza's metaphysics and epistemology. The structure of the universe, with its causally necessary relations, is mirrored by the structure of ideas, with their logically necessary connections. Moreover, Spinoza's conception of what constitutes knowledge in its ideal form, the intuitive perception of the essences of things, initially involves a dynamic, rationally discursive apprehension, not unlike the way in which the propositions of the *Ethics* are related to each other. Despite the difficulty of the work, Spinoza clearly believed that anyone – and we are all endowed with the same cognitive faculties – with sufficient self-mastery and intellectual attentiveness can perceive the truth to the highest degree.

The *Ethics* is an ambitious and multifaceted work. It is also bold to the point of audacity, as one would expect of a systematic and unforgiving critique of the traditional philosophical conceptions of God, the human being and the universe, and, above all, of the religions and the theological and moral beliefs grounded thereupon. What Spinoza intends to demonstrate (in the strongest sense of that word) is the truth about God, nature and especially ourselves; and the highest principles of society, religion and the good life. Despite the great deal of metaphysics, physics, anthropology and psychology that take up Parts I–III,

Spinoza took the crucial message of the work to be ethical in nature. It consists in showing that our happiness and well-being lie not in a life enslaved to the passions and to the transitory goods we ordinarily pursue, nor in the related unreflective attachment to the organized superstitions that pass as religion, but rather in the life of reason. To clarify and support these broadly ethical conclusions, however, Spinoza must first demystify the universe and show it for what it really is. This requires laying out some metaphysical foundations, the project of Part I.

"On God"

"On God" begins with some deceptively simple definitions of terms that would be familiar to any seventeenth-century philosopher, especially one working in the Cartesian tradition. "By substance I understand what is in itself and is conceived through itself"; "By attribute I understand what the intellect perceives of a substance, as constituting its essence"; "By mode I understand the affections of a substance, or that which is in another through which it is also conceived"; "By God I understand a being absolutely infinite, i.e., a substance consisting of an infinity of attributes, of which each one expresses an eternal and infinite essence." A substance is basically that which has the highest degree of ontological independence and exists in its own right, without the need of anything else. An attribute is the general nature of a substance, what constitutes the *kind* of being it is in the broadest sense. A mode, because it inheres in a substance and is thus ontologically dependent upon it, is a particular expression or manifestation of that attribute or nature. If substances are things, then one traditional way to look at modes – although it may not accurately capture Spinoza's meaning – is as properties of things. If a human soul is a substance (as Descartes had thought, but Spinoza will deny), then its attribute is "thinking", and any particular thought or idea is a mode of it. If a human body is a substance, then its attribute is "body-ness" or "extension", and its particular shape, size and motion are modes of it (since human-body-shape is, like circularity or squareness, just one particular way of being extended).

The definitions of Part I are, in effect, simply clear concepts that ground the rest of his system. They are followed by a number of axioms that, he assumes, will be regarded as obvious and unproblematic by the philosophically informed, such as "Whatever is, is either in itself or in another", and "From a given determinate cause the effect follows necessarily". From these, the first proposition necessarily follows, and every subsequent proposition can be demonstrated using only what precedes it.[1]

In propositions 1–15 of Part I, Spinoza presents the basic elements of his picture of God. In the Cartesian framework that Spinoza adopts, the basic metaphysical category is substance. A substance is an ontologically independent, self-subsisting thing that itself depends on nothing else for its being. Whatever is, either is a substance or belongs to a substance as a modification (or, alternatively, a mode or affection or property) of it. According to Spinoza, God is the infinite, necessarily existing (that is, uncaused), unique substance of the universe. There is only one substance in the universe; it is God; and everything else that is, is in God.

- Proposition 1: A substance is prior in nature to its modifications.
- Proposition 2: Two substances having different attributes have nothing in common with one another. (In other words, if two substances differ in nature, then they have nothing in common.)
- Proposition 3: If things have nothing in common with one another, one of them cannot be the cause of the other.
- Proposition 4: Two or more distinct things are distinguished from one another, either by a difference in the attributes [i.e. the natures or essences] of the substances or by a difference in their affections [i.e. their accidental properties].
- Proposition 5: In nature, there cannot be two or more substances of the same nature or attribute.
- Proposition 6: One substance cannot be produced by another substance.
- Proposition 7: It pertains to the nature of a substance to exist.
- Proposition 8: Every substance is necessarily infinite.
- Proposition 9: The more reality or being each thing has, the more attributes belong to it.
- Proposition 10: Each attribute of a substance must be conceived through itself.
- Proposition 11: God, or a substance consisting of infinite attributes, each of which expresses eternal and infinite essence, necessarily exists. (The proof of this proposition consists simply in the classic "ontological proof for God's existence". Spinoza writes that "if you deny this, conceive, if you can, that God does not exist. Therefore, by axiom 7 ('If a thing can be conceived as not existing, its essence does not involve existence'), his essence does not involve existence. But this, by proposition 7, is absurd. Therefore, God necessarily exists, q.e.d.".)
- Proposition 12: No attribute of a substance can be truly conceived from which it follows that the substance can be divided.
- Proposition 13: A substance which is absolutely infinite is indivisible.
- Proposition 14: Except God, no substance can be or be conceived.

This proof that God – an infinite, necessary and uncaused, indivisible being – is the only substance of the universe proceeds in three simple steps. First, establish

41

that no two substances can share an attribute or essence (Ip5). Then, prove that there is a substance with infinite attributes (i.e. God) (Ip11). It follows, in conclusion, that the existence of that infinite substance precludes the existence of any other substance. For if there *were* to be a second substance, it would have to have *some* attribute or essence. But since God has *all* possible attributes, then the attribute to be possessed by this second substance would be one of the attributes already possessed by God. But it has already been established that no two substances can have the same attribute. Therefore, there can be, besides God, no such second substance.

If God is the only substance, and (by axiom 1) whatever is, is either a substance or *in* a substance, then everything else must be in God. "Whatever is, is in God, and nothing can be or be conceived without God" (Ip15).

As soon as this preliminary conclusion has been established, Spinoza immediately reveals the objective of his attack. His definition of God – condemned since his excommunication from the Jewish community as a "God existing in only a philosophical sense" – is meant to preclude any anthropomorphizing of the divine being. In the scholium to proposition 15, he writes against "those who feign a God, like man, consisting of a body and a mind, and subject to passions. But how far they wander from the true knowledge of God, is sufficiently established by what has already been demonstrated". Besides being false, such an anthropomorphic conception of God can have only deleterious effects on human freedom and activity because of the superstitious behaviour that it encourages.

Much of the technical language of Part I is, to all appearances, right out of Descartes. But even the most devoted Cartesian would have had a hard time understanding the full import of propositions 1–15. What does it mean to say that God is substance and that everything else is "in" God? Is Spinoza saying that rocks, tables, chairs, birds, mountains, rivers and human beings are all *properties* of God, and hence can be predicated of God (just as one would say that the table "is red")? It seems very odd to think that objects and individuals – what we ordinarily think of as independent "things" – are, in fact, merely properties of a thing. Spinoza was sensitive to the strangeness of this kind of talk, not to mention the philosophical problems to which it gives rise. When a person feels pain, does it follow that the pain is ultimately just a *property* of God, and thus that God feels pain? Conundrums such as this may explain why, as of proposition 16, there is a subtle but important shift in Spinoza's language. God is now described not so much as the underlying substance of all things, but as the universal, immanent and sustaining cause of all that exists: "From the necessity of the divine nature there must follow infinitely many things in infinitely many modes, (i.e., everything that can fall under an infinite intellect)".

According to the traditional Judeo-Christian conception of divinity, God is a transcendent creator, a being who causes a world distinct from himself to come into being by creating it out of nothing. God produces that world by a spontaneous act of free will, and could just as easily have not created anything outside himself. By contrast, Spinoza's God is the cause of all things because all things follow causally and necessarily from the divine nature. Or, as he puts it, from God's infinite power or nature "all things have necessarily flowed, or always followed, by the same necessity and in the same way as from the nature of a triangle it follows, from eternity and to eternity, that its three angles are equal to two right angles" (Ip17s1). The existence of the world is, thus, mathematically necessary. It is impossible that God should exist but not the world. This does not mean that God does not cause the world to come into being freely, since nothing *outside* God constrains him to bring it into existence. But Spinoza does deny that God creates the world by some arbitrary and undetermined act of free will. God could not have done otherwise. There are no possible alternatives to the actual world, and absolutely no contingency or spontaneity within that world. Everything is absolutely and necessarily determined.

> In nature there is nothing contingent, but all things have been determined from the necessity of the divine nature to exist and produce an effect in a certain way. (Ip29)

> Things could have been produced by God in no other way, and in no other order than they have been produced. (Ip33)

There are, however, differences in the way things depend on God. Some features of the universe follow necessarily from God – or, more precisely, from the absolute nature of one of God's attributes – in a direct and unmediated manner. These are the universal and eternal aspects of the world, and they do not come into or go out of being. They include the most general laws of the universe, together governing all things in all ways. From the attribute of extension there follow the principles governing all extended objects (the truths of geometry) and laws governing the motion and rest of bodies (the laws of physics); from the attribute of thought, there follow laws of thought (logic). These are what Spinoza calls the immediate infinite modes of God's attributes. Particular and individual things, by contrast, are causally more remote from God. They are nothing but "affections of God's attributes, or modes by which God's attributes are expressed in a certain and determinate way" (Ip25c). The familiar objects of the everyday world are but finite modes of the attributes of substance, although they belong to distinct infinite causal series that themselves follow mediately but eternally from God.

There are two causal orders or dimensions governing the production and actions of particular things. On the one hand, things are determined by the general laws of the universe that follow immediately from God's natures. On the other hand, each particular thing is determined to act and to be acted upon by other particular things. Thus, the actual behaviour of a body in motion is a function not just of the universal laws of motion, but also of the other bodies in motion and rest surrounding it and with which it comes into contact.

Spinoza's metaphysics of God is neatly summed up in a phrase that occurs in the Latin (but not the Dutch) edition of the *Ethics*: "God, or Nature", *Deus, sive Natura*: "That eternal and infinite being we call God, or Nature, acts from the same necessity from which he exists" (IV, Preface). It is an ambiguous phrase, since Spinoza could be read as trying either to divinize nature or to naturalize God. But for the careful reader there is no mistaking Spinoza's intention. The friends who, after his death, published his writings must have left out the "or Nature" clause from the more widely accessible Dutch version out of fear of the reaction that this identification would, predictably, arouse among a vernacular audience.

There are, Spinoza insists, two sides of Nature. First, there is the active, productive aspect of the universe: God and his attributes, from which all else follows. This is what Spinoza, employing the same terms he used in the "Short Treatise", calls *Natura naturans*, "naturing Nature". Strictly speaking, this is identical with God. The other aspect of the universe is that which is produced and sustained by the active aspect, *Natura naturata*, "natured Nature". "By *Natura naturata* I understand whatever follows from the necessity of God's nature, or from any of God's attributes, i.e., all the modes of God's attributes insofar as they are considered as things that are in God, and can neither be nor be conceived without God" (Ip29s).

Spinoza's fundamental insight in Part I is that Nature is an indivisible, uncaused, substantial whole; in fact, it is the *only* substantial whole. Outside Nature, there is nothing, and everything that exists is a part of Nature and is brought into being by Nature with a deterministic necessity. This unified, unique, productive, necessary being just *is* what is meant by "God". Because of the necessity inherent in Nature, there is no teleology in the universe. Nature does not act for any ends, and things do not exist for any set purposes. There are no "final causes" (to use the common Aristotelian phrase). God does not "do" things for the sake of anything else. The order of things just follows from God's essences with an inviolable determinism. All talk of God's purposes, intentions, goals, preferences or aims is just an anthropomorphizing fiction.

> All the prejudices I here undertake to expose depend on this one: that men commonly suppose that all natural things act, as men do, on

account of an end; indeed, they maintain as certain that God himself directs all things to some certain end, for they say that God has made all things for man, and man that he might worship God.

(I, Appendix)

God is not some goal-oriented planner who then judges things by how well they conform to his purposes. Things happen only because of Nature and its laws. "Nature has no end set before it ... All things proceed by a certain eternal necessity of nature" (*ibid*.) To believe otherwise is to fall prey to the same superstitions that lie at the heart of the organized religions.

> [People] find – both in themselves and outside themselves – many means that are very helpful in seeking their own advantage, e.g., eyes for seeing, teeth for chewing, plants and animals for food, the sun for light, the sea for supporting fish ... Hence, they consider all natural things as means to their own advantage. And knowing that they had found these means, not provided them for themselves, they had reason to believe that there was someone else who had prepared those means for their use. For after they considered things as means, they could not believe that the things had made themselves; but from the means they were accustomed to prepare for themselves, they had to infer that there was a ruler, or a number of rulers of nature, endowed with human freedom, who had taken care of all things for them, and made all things for their use.
>
> And since they had never heard anything about the temperament of these rulers, they had to judge it from their own. Hence, they maintained that the Gods direct all things for the use of men in order to bind men to them and be held by men in the highest honor. So it has happened that each of them has thought up from his own temperament different ways of worshipping God, so that God might love them above all the rest, and direct the whole of Nature according to the needs of their blind desire and insatiable greed. Thus this prejudice was changed into superstition, and struck deep roots in their minds. (I, Appendix)

A judging God who has plans and acts purposively is a God to be obeyed and placated. Opportunistic preachers are then able to play on our hopes and fears in the face of such a God. They prescribe ways of acting that are calculated to avoid being punished by that God and earn his rewards. But, Spinoza insists, to see God or Nature as acting for the sake of ends – to find purpose in Nature – is to misconstrue Nature and "turn it upside down" by putting the effect (the end result) before the true cause.

Nor does God perform miracles, since there are no departures whatsoever from the necessary course of nature. The belief in miracles is due only to ignorance of the true causes of phenomena.

> If a stone has fallen from a room onto someone's head and killed him, they will show, in the following way, that the stone fell in order to kill the man. For if it did not fall to that end, God willing it, how could so many circumstances have concurred by chance (for often many circumstances do concur at once)? Perhaps you will answer that it happened because the wind was blowing hard and the man was walking that way. But they will persist: why was the wind blowing hard at that time? why was the man walking that way at that time? If you answer again that the wind arose then because on the preceding day, while the weather was still calm, the sea began to toss, and that the man had been invited by a friend, they will press on – for there is no end to the questions which can be asked: but why was the sea tossing? why was the man invited at just that time? And so they will not stop asking for the causes of causes until you take refuge in the will of God, i.e., the sanctuary of ignorance. (I, Appendix)

This is strong language, and Spinoza is clearly not unaware of the risks of his position. The same preachers who take advantage of our credulity will fulminate against anyone who tries to pull aside the curtain and reveal the truths of Nature.

> One who seeks the true causes of miracles, and is eager, like an educated man, to understand natural things, not to wonder at them, like a fool, is generally considered and denounced as an impious heretic by those whom the people honor as interpreters of nature and the Gods. For they know that if ignorance is taken away, then foolish wonder, the only means they have of arguing and defending their authority, is also taken away. (*Ibid.*)

Spinoza is convinced that there is nothing in nature that is inexplicable by natural means. There are no brute facts, and there are no supernaturally caused events. Spinoza is deeply committed, perhaps more so than any other philosopher of the period, to the principle that there is an ultimate and rational explanation for anything and everything. As we shall see, it is the pursuit of such an understanding of nature and its ways – an understanding best captured by

Spinoza's own metaphysical system – that represents human virtue and, ultimately, our happiness.

The human mind

In Part II of the *Ethics*, Spinoza turns to the nature of the human being. The two attributes of God of which we have cognizance are extension and thought. This, in itself, involves what would have been an astounding thesis in the eyes of his contemporaries, one that was usually misunderstood and always attacked. When Spinoza claims in proposition 2 of Part II that "Extension is an attribute of God, or God is an extended thing", he was almost universally – but erroneously – interpreted as saying that God is literally corporeal. This goes some way towards explaining why "Spinozism" became, for his critics, synonymous with atheistic materialism.

What is in God is not matter itself, however, but extension as an essence. And extension and thought are two distinct essences that have absolutely nothing in common. The finite modes or expressions of extension are physical bodies; the finite modes of thought are ideas. Because extension and thought have nothing in common, the two realms of matter and mind are causally closed systems. Everything that is extended follows from the attribute of extension alone. Every bodily event is part of an infinite causal series of bodily events and is determined only by the nature of extension and its laws, in conjunction with its relations to other extended bodies. Similarly, every idea follows only from the attribute of thought. Any idea is an integral part of an infinite series of ideas and is determined by the nature of thought and its laws, along with its relations to other ideas. There is, in other words, no causal interaction between bodies and ideas, between the physical and the mental. There is, however, a thoroughgoing correlation and parallelism between the two series. For every mode in extension that is a relatively stable collection of matter, there is a corresponding mode in thought. In fact, he insists, "a mode of extension and the idea of that mode are one and the same thing, but expressed in two ways". Because of the fundamental and underlying unity of Nature, or of substance, thought and extension are just two different ways of "comprehending" one and the same Nature. Or, to put it another way, the series of ideas and the series of bodily events are two distinct ways in which one and the same underlying Nature manifests itself. Thus, every material thing has its own particular idea that expresses or represents it. Since that idea is just a mode of one of God's attributes – Thought – it is in God, and the infinite series of ideas constitutes God's mind. As he explains,

> A circle existing in nature and the idea of the existing circle, which is also in God, are one and the same thing, which is explained through different attributes. Therefore, whether we conceive nature under the attribute of Extension, or under the attribute of Thought, or under any other attribute, we shall find one and the same order, or one and the same connection of causes, i.e., that the same things follow one another. (IIp7s)

It follows from this, he argues, that the causal relations between bodies are mirrored in the logical relations between God's ideas. Or, as Spinoza notes in proposition 7, "the order and connection of ideas is the same as the order and connection of things".

One kind of extended body, however, is significantly more complex than any others in its composition and in its dispositions to act and be acted upon. That complexity is reflected in its corresponding idea. The body in question is the human body; and its corresponding idea is the human mind or soul. The mind, then, like any other idea, is simply one particular mode of God's attribute thought. Whatever happens in the body is reflected or expressed in the mind. In this way, the mind perceives, more or less obscurely, what is taking place in its body. And through its body's interactions with other bodies, the mind is aware of what is happening in the physical world around it. This is because the effects in the human body from its causal interaction with other bodies are, like any event in the body, necessarily expressed by corresponding events (or ideas) in the mind. But the human mind no more interacts with its body than any mode of thought interacts with a mode of extension.

One of the pressing questions in seventeenth-century philosophy, and perhaps the most celebrated legacy of Descartes's dualism, is the problem of how two radically different substances such as mind and body enter into a union in a human being and cause effects in each other. How can the extended body causally engage the unextended mind, which is incapable of contact or motion, and "move" it, that is, cause mental effects such as pains, sensations and perceptions? Spinoza, in effect, denies that the human being is a union of two *substances*. The human mind and the human body are two different expressions – under Thought and under Extension – of one and the same thing: the person. And because there is no causal interaction between the mind and the body, the so-called mind–body problem does not, technically speaking, arise. It would be a mistake, however, to believe that Spinoza adopted his monism simply as an *ad hoc* way to resolve the mind–body problem. He was motivated by more important considerations, including both the demands of his metaphysics of substance and, as we shall see, his moral concern to eliminate the belief in personal immortality, which in his opinion is supported by Cartesian soul–body dualism.

The human mind, like God, contains ideas. Some of these ideas – sensory images, qualitative "feels" (like pains and pleasures), perceptual data – are imprecise qualitative phenomena, being the expression in thought of states of the body as it is affected by the bodies surrounding it. Such ideas do not convey adequate and true knowledge of the world, but only a relative, partial and subjective picture of how things presently seem to be to the perceiver. There is no systematic order to these perceptions, nor any critical oversight by reason. "As long as the human Mind perceives things from the common order of nature, it does not have an adequate, but only a confused and mutilated knowledge of itself, of its own Body, and of external bodies" (IIp29c). Under such circumstances, we are simply determined in our ideas by our fortuitous and haphazard encounter with things in the external world. This superficial acquaintance will never provide us with knowledge of the essences of those things. In fact, it is an invariable source of falsehood and error. This "knowledge from random experience" is also the origin of great delusions, since we – thinking ourselves free – are, in our ignorance, unaware of just how we *are* determined by causes.

Adequate ideas, on the other hand, are formed in a rational and orderly manner, and are necessarily true and revelatory of the essences of things. "Reason", the second kind of knowledge (after "random experience"), is the apprehension of the essence of a thing through a discursive, inferential procedure, one that involves deduction. "A true idea means nothing other than knowing a thing perfectly, or in the best way (IIp43s)." It involves grasping a thing's causal connections not just to other objects but, more importantly, to the attributes of God and the infinite modes (the laws of nature) that follow immediately from them. The adequate idea of a thing clearly and distinctly situates its object in all of its causal nexuses and shows not just *that* it is, but *how* and *why* it necessarily is. The person who truly knows a thing sees the reasons why the thing was determined to be and could not have been otherwise. "It is of the nature of Reason to regard things as necessary, not as contingent" (IIp44). The belief that some thing is accidental or spontaneous can be based only on an inadequate grasp of the thing's causal explanation, on a partial and "mutilated" familiarity with it. To perceive by way of adequate ideas is to perceive the necessity inherent in Nature.

Sense-experience alone could never provide the information conveyed by an adequate idea. The senses present things only as they appear from a given perspective at a given moment in time. An adequate idea, on the other hand, by showing how a thing follows necessarily from one or another of God's attributes, presents it in its "eternal" aspects – *sub specie aeternitatis*, as Spinoza puts it – without any relation to time. "Reason perceives this necessity of things truly, i.e., as it is in itself. But this necessity of things is the very necessity of God's eternal nature. Therefore, it is of the nature of Reason to regard things under this species of eternity" (IIp44).

The third kind of knowledge, intuition or *scientia intuitiva*, takes what is known by reason and grasps it in a single act of the mind. With intuition, one proceeds immediately "from an adequate idea of the formal essence of certain attributes of God to the adequate knowledge of the essence of things" (IIp40s2). Spinoza compares knowing by the second and third kinds of knowledge, respectively, with knowing a mathematical theorem by going through its proof and seeing how its conclusion follows from the previous steps, and knowing it all at once through a single intuitive apprehension. There is no more certain or useful knowledge for a human being to pursue.

Spinoza's conception of adequate knowledge reveals an unrivalled optimism in the cognitive powers of the human being. Not even Descartes believed that we could know all of Nature and its innermost secrets with the degree of depth and certainty that Spinoza thought possible. Most remarkably, because Spinoza thought that the adequate knowledge of any object, and of Nature as a whole, involves a thorough knowledge of God and of how things related to God and his attributes, he also had no scruples about claiming that we can, at least in principle, know God perfectly and adequately. "The knowledge of God's eternal and infinite essence that each idea involves is adequate and perfect" (IIp46). "The human Mind has an adequate knowledge of God's eternal and infinite essence" (IIp47). No other philosopher in history has been willing to make this claim. But, then again, no other philosopher identified God with Nature.

Spinoza engages in such a detailed analysis of the composition of the human being because it is essential to his goal of showing how the human being is a part of Nature, existing within the same causal nexuses as other extended and mental beings. This has serious ethical implications. It implies that a human being is not endowed with freedom, at least in the ordinary sense of that term. Because our minds and the events in our minds are simply ideas that exist within the causal series of ideas that follows from God's attribute thought, our actions and volitions are as necessarily determined as any other natural events. "In the Mind there is no absolute, or free, will, but the Mind is determined to will this or that by a cause that is also determined by another, and this again by another, and so to infinity" (IIp48).

The affects

With his analysis of the human being and its place in nature, Spinoza hopes to dispel a great and very common mistake, that is, the belief that human beings occupy a realm of their own, separate from the rest of nature, in which they exercise free and absolute dominion. Indeed, what is true of the will (and, of course, of our bodies) is true of all the phenomena of our psychological lives. Spinoza believes that this is something that has not been sufficiently understood by previous thinkers, who seem to have wanted to place the human being on a pedestal outside (or above) nature.

> Most of those who have written about the Affects, and men's way of living, seem to treat, not of natural things, which follow the common laws of nature, but of things that are outside nature. Indeed they seem to conceive man in nature as a dominion within a dominion. For they believe that man disturbs, rather than follows, the order of nature, that he has absolute power over his actions, and that he is determined only by himself. (III, Preface)

Descartes, for example, believed that if the freedom of the human being is to be preserved, the soul must be exempt from the kind of deterministic laws that rule over the material universe.

Spinoza's aim in Parts III and IV is, as he says in his Preface to Part III, to restore the human being and his volitional and emotional life into their proper place in nature. For nothing stands outside nature, not even the human mind.

> Nature is always the same, and its virtue and power of acting are everywhere one and the same, i.e., the laws and rules of nature, according to which all things happen, and change from one form to another, are always and everywhere the same. So the way of understanding the nature of anything, of whatever kind, must also be the same, viz. through the universal laws and rules of nature. (*Ibid.*)

Our affects – our love, anger, hate, envy, pride, jealousy and so on – "follow from the same necessity and force of nature as the other singular things" (*ibid.*). Spinoza, therefore, explains these emotions – as determined in their occurrence as are a body in motion and the properties of a mathematical figure – just as he would explain any other things in nature.

> I shall treat the nature and power of the affects, and the power of the mind over them, by the same method by which, in the preceding parts, I treated God and the mind, and I shall consider human actions and appetites just as if it were a question of lines, planes, and bodies. (*Ibid.*)

51

Our affects are divided into actions and passions. When the cause of an event lies in our own nature – more particularly, our knowledge or adequate ideas – then it is a case of the mind acting. On the other hand, when something happens in us the cause of which lies outside of our nature, then we are passive and being acted upon. Usually what takes place, both when we are acting and when we are being acted upon, is some change in our mental or physical capacities, what Spinoza calls "an increase or decrease in our power of acting" or in our "power to persevere in being". All beings are naturally endowed with such a power or striving. This *conatus*, a kind of existential inertia, constitutes the "essence" of any being. "Each thing, as far as it can by its own power, strives to persevere in its being" (IIIp6). An affect just *is* any change in this power, for better or for worse. Affects that are actions are changes in this power that have their source (or "adequate cause") in our nature alone; affects that are passions are those changes in this power that originate outside us.

What we should strive for is to be free from the turmoil of the passions – or, since this is not absolutely possible, at least to learn how to moderate and restrain them – and become active, autonomous beings. If we can achieve this, then we shall be "free" to the extent that whatever happens to us will result not from our relations with things outside us, but from our own nature (as that follows from, and is ultimately and necessarily determined by the attributes of God of which our minds and bodies are modes). We shall, consequently, be truly liberated from the troublesome emotional ups and downs of this life. The way to bring this about is to increase our knowledge, our store of adequate ideas, and eliminate as far as possible our inadequate ideas, which follow not from the nature of the mind alone but from its being an expression of how our body is affected by other bodies. In other words, we need to free ourselves from a reliance on the senses and the imagination, since a life of the senses and images is a life being affected and led by the objects around us, and rely as much as we can only on our rational faculties, which deal with what is eternal and necessary.

Because of our innate striving to persevere – which, in the human being, is called "will" or "appetite" – we naturally pursue those things that we believe will benefit us by increasing our power of acting and shun or flee those things that we believe will harm us by decreasing our power of acting. This provides Spinoza with a foundation for cataloguing the human passions. For the passions are all functions of the ways in which external things affect our powers or capacities. Joy, for example, is simply the movement or passage to a greater capacity for action. "By Joy ... I shall understand that passion by which the Mind passes to a greater perfection" (IIIp11s). Being a passion, joy is always brought about by some external object. Sadness, on the other hand, is the passage to a lesser state of perfection, also occasioned by a thing outside us. Love is simply Joy accompanied by an awareness of the external cause that brings about the passage to a greater perfection. We love that object that benefits us and causes us joy. Hate is nothing but "Sadness with the accompanying idea of an external cause". Hope is simply "an inconstant Joy which has arisen from the image of a future or past thing whose outcome we doubt". We hope for a thing whose presence, as yet uncertain, will bring about joy. We fear, however, a thing whose presence, equally uncertain, will bring about sadness. When that whose outcome was doubtful becomes certain, hope is changed into confidence, while fear is changed into despair.

All of the human emotions, in so far as they are passions, are constantly directed outwards, towards things and their capacities to affect us one way or another. Aroused by our passions and desires, we seek or flee those things that we believe cause joy or sadness. "We strive to further the occurrence of whatever we imagine will lead to Joy, and to avert or destroy what we imagine is contrary to it, or will lead to Sadness" (IIIp28). Our hopes and fears fluctuate depending on whether we regard the objects of our desires or aversions as remote, near, necessary, possible or unlikely. But the objects of our passions, being external to us, are completely beyond our control. Thus, the more we allow ourselves to be controlled by *them*, the more we are subject to passions and the less active and free we are. The upshot is a fairly pathetic picture of a life mired in the passions and pursuing and fleeing the changeable and fleeting objects that occasion them: "We are driven about in many ways by external causes, and ... like waves on the sea, driven by contrary winds, we toss about, not knowing our outcome and fate" (IIIp59s). The title of Part IV of the *Ethics* reveals with perfect clarity Spinoza's evaluation of such a life for a human being: "On Human Bondage, or the Powers of the Affects". He explains that the human being's

> lack of power to moderate and restrain the affects I call Bondage. For the man who is subject to affects is under the control, not of himself, but of fortune, in whose power he so greatly is that often, though he sees the better for himself, he is still forced to follow the worse.
>
> (IV, Preface)

It is, he says, a kind of "sickness of the mind" to suffer too much love for a thing "that is liable to many variations and that we can never fully possess".

"On Human Bondage" and human freedom

The solution that Spinoza offers to the human predicament is an ancient one. Since we cannot control the objects that we tend to value and that we allow to influence our well-being, we ought instead to try to control our evaluations themselves and thereby minimize the sway that external objects and the passions have over us. We can never eliminate the passive affects entirely. We are essentially a part of nature, and can never fully remove ourselves from the causal series that link us to external things. "It is impossible that a man should not be a part of Nature, and that he should be able to undergo no changes except those which can be understood through his own nature alone, and of which he is the adequate cause" (IVp4). But we can, ultimately, counteract the passions, understand them, control them, and achieve a certain degree of relief from their turmoil.

The path to restraining and moderating the affects is through virtue. Spinoza is a psychological and ethical egoist. All beings naturally seek their own advantage – to preserve their own being – and it is right for them to do so. This is what virtue consists in. Since we are thinking beings, endowed with intelligence and reason, what is to our greatest advantage is knowledge. Our virtue, therefore, consists in the pursuit of knowledge and understanding of adequate ideas. The best kind of knowledge is a purely intellectual intuition of the essences of things. This "third kind of knowledge" – beyond both random experience and ratiocination – sees things not in their temporal dimension, not in their duration and in relation to other particular things, but under the aspect of eternity, that is, abstracted from all considerations of time and place and situated in their relationship to God and his attributes. They are apprehended, that is, in their conceptual and causal relationship to the universal essences (thought and extension) and the eternal laws of nature.

> We conceive things as actual in two ways: either insofar as we conceive them to exist in relation to a certain time and place, or insofar as we conceive them to be contained in God and to follow from the necessity of the divine nature. But the things we conceive in this second way as true, or real, we conceive under a species of eternity, and to that extent they involve the eternal and infinite essence of God. (Vp39s)

But this is just to say that, ultimately, we strive for a knowledge of God. The concept of any body involves the concept of extension; and the concept of any idea or mind involves the concept of thought. But thought and extension just are God's attributes. So the proper and adequate conception of any body or mind necessarily involves the concept or knowledge of God. "The third kind of knowledge proceeds from an adequate idea of certain attributes of God to an adequate knowledge of the essence of things, and the more we understand things in this way, the more we understand God" (Vp25s). Knowledge of God is, thus, the mind's greatest good and its greatest virtue.

What we see when we understand things through the second and third kinds of knowledge, under the aspect of eternity and in relation to God, is the deterministic necessity of all things. We see that all bodies and their states follow necessarily from the essence of matter and the universal laws of physics; and we see that all ideas, including all the properties of minds, follow necessarily from the essence of thought and its universal laws. This insight can only weaken the power that the passions have over us. We are no longer hopeful or fearful of what shall come to pass, and no longer anxious or despondent over our possessions. We regard all things with equanimity, and we are not inordinately and irrationally affected in different ways by past, present or future events. The result is self-control and a calmness of mind.

> The more this knowledge that things are necessary is concerned with singular things, which we imagine more distinctly and vividly, the greater is this power of the Mind over the affects, as experience itself also testifies. For we see that Sadness over some good which has perished is lessened as soon as the man who has lost it realizes that this good could not, in any way, have been kept. Similarly, we see that [because we regard infancy as a natural and necessary thing], no one pities infants because of their inability to speak, to walk, or to reason, or because they live so many years, as it were, unconscious of themselves. (Vp6s)

Our affects themselves can be understood in this way, which further diminishes their power over us. Through knowledge of the affects, reordering them epistemically and especially separating them from their external causes and joining them to other thoughts in the mind, they are transformed into adequate ideas. With this kind of self-knowledge, passions become actions. "An affect which is a passion ceases to be a passion as soon as we form a clear and distinct idea of it" (Vp3).

Spinoza's ethical theory is, to a certain degree, Stoic, and recalls the doctrines of thinkers such as Cicero and Seneca:

> We do not have an absolute power to adapt things outside us to our use. Nevertheless, we shall bear calmly those things that happen to us contrary to what the principle of our advantage demands, if we are conscious that we have done our duty, that the power we have could not have extended itself to the point where we could have avoided

those things, and that we are a part of the whole of nature, whose order we follow. If we understand this clearly and distinctly, that part of us which is defined by understanding, i.e., the better part of us, will be entirely satisfied with this, and will strive to persevere in that satisfaction. For insofar as we understand, we can want nothing except what is necessary, nor absolutely be satisfied with anything except what is true.
(IV, Appendix)

What, in the end, replaces the passionate love for ephemeral "goods" is an intellectual love for an eternal, immutable good that we can fully and stably possess, God. The third kind of knowledge generates a love for its object, and this love consists in not joy, a passion, but blessedness itself. Taking his cue from Maimonides's view of human *eudaimonia*, Spinoza argues that the mind's intellectual love of God *is* our understanding of the universe, our virtue, our happiness, our well-being and our "salvation". It is also our freedom and autonomy, as we approach the condition wherein what happens to us follows from our nature (as a determinate and determined mode of one of God's attributes) alone and not as a result of the ways external things affect us. Spinoza's "free person" is one who bears the gifts and losses of fortune with equanimity, does only those things that he believes to be "the most important in life", takes care for the well-being of others (doing what he can to ensure that they, too, achieve some relief from the disturbances of the passions through understanding), and is not anxious about death. The free person neither hopes for any eternal, otherworldly rewards nor fears any eternal punishments.

This is because the free person knows that the soul is not immortal in any personal sense, but is endowed only with a certain kind of eternity. One element of the eternity belonging to the mind derives from the fact that an important part of the human mind's constitution is simply the idea of the essence of the human body. Thus, at a person's death and the end of his durational existence, just as the eternal essence of his body remains in extension, so the idea of that essence remains (eternally) in thought. This is what Spinoza means when he says that "the human mind cannot be absolutely destroyed with the body, but something of it remains which is eternal" (Vp23). Additionally, to the extent that a person achieves real knowledge – knowledge of the third kind – he participates in eternity, since the adequate ideas making up that knowledge are essentially eternal truths that belong among the contents of his mind. When the person dies, there is a sense in which a "part" of him remains eternally, namely, the ideas. In fact, Spinoza says, in a passage that has long puzzled interpreters, the more the mind consists of true and adequate ideas, the more of it remains – within God's attribute of thought – after the death of the body and the disappearance of that part of the mind that corresponds to the body's duration. "The mind's essence consists in knowledge; therefore, the more the mind knows things by the second and third kind of knowledge, the greater the part of it that remains" (Vp38d). Spinoza's intent is to show that while there is certainly a part of the mind that is eternal, this is merely an impersonal collection of ideas and there is no such thing as a true and robust immortality of the soul. This understanding of his place in the natural scheme of things brings to the free individual true peace of mind.

There are a number of social and political ramifications that follow from Spinoza's ethical doctrines of human action and well-being. Because disagreement and discord between human beings is always the result of our different and changeable passions, "free" individuals – who all share the same nature and act on the same principles – will naturally and effortlessly form a harmonious society.

> Insofar as men are torn by affects that are passions, they can be contrary to one another ... [But] insofar as men live according to the guidance of reason, they must do only those things that are good for human nature, and hence, for each man, i.e., those things that agree with the nature of each man. Hence, insofar as men live according to the guidance of reason, they must always agree among themselves.
>
> (IVp34–5)

Free human beings will be mutually beneficial and useful, and will be tolerant of the opinions and even the errors of others. However, human beings do not generally live under the guidance of reason. The state or sovereign, therefore, is required in order to ensure – not by reason, but by the threat of force – that individuals are protected from the unrestrained pursuit of self-interest on the part of other individuals. The transition from a state of nature, where each seeks his own advantage without limitation, to a civil state involves the universal renunciation of certain natural rights – such as "the right everyone has of avenging himself, and of judging good and evil" – and the investment of those prerogatives in a central authority. As long as human beings are guided by their passions, the state is necessary to bring it about that they "live harmoniously and be of assistance to one another" (IVp37s2).

Spinoza was a profoundly political individual. He was moved, in both an intellectual and personal way, by the political and religious turmoil raging in the Netherlands as it sought its national identity. He watched as the young republic's ideals of toleration and liberalism came under attack by the more conservative religious elements in seventeenth-century Dutch society. And despite its high abstraction and difficult metaphysical themes, the *Ethics* is an intensely political work. It bears an intimate relationship to the democratic and secular political project that Spinoza pursues in the *Theological–Political Treatise*. By offering a profoundly reductive and naturalistic conception of God – a God who does not perform miracles, establish covenants with select groups of people, issue laws or stand in judgement over us – and eliminating the pernicious and superstitious belief in personal immortality – a belief that can only strengthen the passions of hope and fear – he hoped to undermine the influence that ecclesiastics waged in contemporary state politics. At heart an atheist, he realized that our happiness must come from our own internal, natural resources. The *Ethics* represents the most sustained and eloquent argument we have for this intellectualist view of human flourishing.

Notes

1. References to the *Ethics* are by part (I–V), proposition (p), definition (d), scholium (s) and corollary (c), and quoted text is taken from *Ethics*, in *The Collected Writings of Spinoza*, vol. 1, E. Curley (trans.) (Princeton, NJ: Princeton University Press, 1985).

Bibliography

Works by Spinoza

Spinoza 1925, 1972. *Spinoza Opera*, 5 vols, C. Gebhardt (ed.). Heidelberg: Carl Winters [volume 5, 1987].
Spinoza 1985. *Ethics*, in *The Collected Writings of Spinoza*, vol. 1, E. Curley (trans.). Princeton, NJ: Princeton University Press.
Spinoza 1989. *Theological–Political Treatise*, S. Shirley (trans.). Leiden: Brill.
Spinoza 1995. *The Letters*, S. Shirley (trans.). Indianapolis, IN: Hackett.

Further reading

Allison, H. 1987. *Benedict de Spinoza: An Introduction*. New Haven, CT: Yale University Press.
Bennett, J. 1984. *A Study of Spinoza's Ethics*. Indianapolis, IN: Hackett.
Curley, E. 1969. *Spinoza's Metaphysics: An Essay in Interpretation*. Cambridge, MA: Harvard University Press.
Curley, E. 1988. *Behind the Geometric Method*. Princeton, NJ: Princeton University Press.
Delahunty, R. J. 1985. *Spinoza*. London: Routledge & Kegan Paul.

Della Rocca, M. 1996. *Representation and the Mind–Body Problem in Spinoza*. Oxford: Oxford University Press.

Donagan, A. 1988. *Spinoza*. Chicago, IL: University of Chicago Press.

Garrett, D. (ed.) 1996. *The Cambridge Companion to Spinoza*. Cambridge: Cambridge University Press.

Hampshire, S. 1987. *Spinoza*. Harmondsworth: Penguin.

Mason, R. 1997. *The God of Spinoza*. Cambridge: Cambridge University Press.

Nadler, S. 1999. *Spinoza: A Life*. Cambridge: Cambridge University Press.

Nadler, S. 2002. *Spinoza's Heresy: Immortality and the Jewish Mind*. Oxford: Oxford University Press.

Scruton, R. 1986. *Spinoza*. Oxford: Oxford University Press.

Smith, S. B. 1997. *Spinoza, Liberalism and the Question of Jewish Identity*. New Haven, CT: Yale University Press.

Wolfson, H. 1934. *The Philosophy of Spinoza*, 2 vols. Cambridge, MA: Harvard University Press.

Woolhouse, R. 1993. *Descartes, Spinoza, Leibniz: The Concept of Substance in Seventeenth Century Metaphysics*. London: Routledge.

Yovel, Y. 1989. *Spinoza and Other Heretics*, 2 vols. Princeton, NJ: Princeton University Press.

3

G. W. Leibniz
Monadology

Douglas Burnham

Introduction

Gottfried Wilhelm Leibniz wrote the *Monadology* in 1714, near the end of his life. It was a life of considerable accomplishment. He was born in Leipzig in 1646 and although the son of a professor of moral philosophy, and educated in the law, Leibniz chose neither of these as a career. Instead, he became an intellectual all-rounder at the court of the Duke of Hanover, working as librarian, official historian, legal advisor and, frequently enough, international diplomat. In these capacities he travelled often and widely in Europe, giving him ample opportunity to meet the foremost intellectuals of the day, including the philosopher Spinoza. Leibniz was a polymath, who made significant contributions in many areas of physics, logic, history, librarianship and, of course, philosophy and theology, while also working on ideal languages, mechanical clocks, mining machinery, and a host of other projects. Among other achievements in mathematics, he invented the mathematical technique of calculus independently of, but at around the same time as, Newton, setting off a long-running, nationalistic controversy.

It is little wonder, then, that he published relatively little. What he often called his philosophical "system" was more or less completed by the 1680s when he wrote the "Discourse on Metaphysics" (1686). Like many others of his works, this was not published in his lifetime, and only appeared in print more than 250 years later. After the "Discourse", over the next 30 years or so, Leibniz worked out additional details and implications of this system, changed the emphasis here and there, and invented new terms to describe and arguments to defend his position, but many key points of the "system" remained substantially the same. Leibniz wrote a great deal of philosophy in various forms, but with the exception of a relatively small handful of brief works (and one longer work), none appeared in print, that is, produced for public consumption by a press. In fact, though, many of Leibniz's unpublished works were circulated among his friends and acquaintances throughout Europe, and he also wrote many hundreds of philosophically oriented letters back and forth to these friends. Leibniz's friends and acquaintances were among the greatest and most influential intellectuals of the day. So his work and its implications were by no means unknown. Leibniz's significance clearly cannot be judged from his list of publications.

Four years before the *Monadology*, Leibniz finally wrote and published a "big" book: the *Theodicy*. The chief concern of this book was to pursue the theological implications of his philosophy, and to defend at least a limited rationality for an enquiry into God and His creation. Leibniz also hoped, as he had all his life, to demonstrate a philosophical mediation between the Catholic Church and the various Protestant churches. The *Theodicy* is not quite a comprehensive statement of Leibniz's philosophy (it leaves out much of his work on the metaphysics of nature, on logic, and on epistemology); nevertheless it was clearly an important text for its author. You will note that accompanying many of the short paragraphs of the *Monadology* are references to parallel passages in the *Theodicy*. Thus, we should at least in part think of the *Monadology* as a "companion" piece to the earlier and more extensive book. With the *Monadology*, he hoped to introduce his work to a much wider audience, and to encourage that audience to turn for further information to the *Theodicy*. (The same can be said of another brief "overview" of his philosophy, written in the same year (1714): *The Principles of Nature and Grace*.)

All this explains Leibniz's intentions with the *Monadology*, and it also helps us to understand it style. For the *Monadology* (it was not Leibniz's own title) has all the appearance of an overview, and quick and self-assured summation. It is brief, perhaps the briefest of any great work in the history of philosophy. This brevity, combined with the clarity of language, the staggering range of topics, the dizzying boldness and confidence of its ideas, and the sense of completeness and interconnectedness that comes from being the overview of a system, makes it also among the most truly beautiful of philosophical texts. Anyone who is not delighted or even moved by the *Monadology* (while perhaps rejecting the truth of every proposition) lacks philosophical spirit.

However, despite the appearance of completeness, the *Monadology* would be misleading if it were the only philosophical work of Leibniz one read. Many claims are simply not argued for, or the arguments are highly abbreviated; many important topics and implications are only indicated and not pursued. Part of the extraordinary nature of the *Monadology* is the way that brief statements or fragments of argumentation can be decompressed into positions rich with consequences. The aim of the following is to move patiently through the text, idea by idea, supplementing it where necessary from Leibniz's philosophical output.[1] We shall not follow Leibniz's order exactly, however, in order better to show the manner in which the system "hangs together".

Substance (*Monadology* §§1–18)

Leibniz takes us straight into the thick of things. The word "monad" is Leibniz's own invention; it means that which is one. A monad, then, is an existing entity that is *essentially* one, an individual. Such an entity is not, then, a part of something else, or a random collection of other things; nor is it nominally one thing (that is, treated as one for some purpose, as we might treat 30 sheep as one flock, or the elements of a machine as one thing). (See the discussion in "Correspondence with Arnauld", PE 88–9.) Rather, the monad's oneness is built into it, as a metaphysical feature. As essentially one, it can have no parts (because then it would be at best nominally one), and thus it cannot be divided. Accordingly, Leibniz calls it "simple". Monads, however, can be a part of composites. Most, if not all, of the things we encounter day to day are composites. They can be divided up: I can smash a window, give blood, and so on. Leibniz then says an odd thing: "there must be simple substances, because there are composites" (§2). What is the argument here? Why do there have to be basic units of substance at all, rather than all composites only being made up of continuous matter?

One answer might be that Leibniz was an atomist; and §3 raises just this. The word "atom" comes from the Greek, meaning something that cannot be cut or divided. Atomism was certainly a prominent enough theory from the seventeenth century on. According to atomism, matter is not infinitely divisible. Rather, all of nature is composed of aggregates of tiny, indivisible units of matter, each with a tiny but not infinitely small mass and extension, and which come in a limited number of basic types (elements). Such atomism was, of course, highly important for the development of modern science. But the modern scientific account of an atom is not the metaphysical notion of earlier atomists. The modern atom is certainly not "unsplittable", for example.

Leibniz, in a sense, anticipated the splitting of the atom. The fact that a material atom is an *extended* entity means that its being one thing, rather than two or more, is an accidental and not essential feature. It must in principle be possible to divide anything extended. The bonds that hold it together may be strong, they may even be infinitely strong, but are not different in their essence to a bit of glue that holds two things together ("A New System of Nature", PE 142). Leibniz accordingly argues that strict material atomism is incoherent because it requires what could only be a miraculous indivisibility. And, if atoms are not truly indivisible, then there is no difference between an atomic theory and a theory of a material continuum, which is divisibility "all the way down".

But there is a more important reason why Leibniz is not an atomist in this sense, which also explains why composites must be understood as made up of simple substances. Try re-reading the above quoted sentence as if it read: "... there must be simples, because composites ARE". The issue is: how can even a composite exist as a real unity or individual? An aggregate of material atoms, Leibniz argues, could only ever be nominally one thing. There would be no reason why it was complete and whole as it was, rather than, for example, larger or smaller, a different shape or colour, a different density, or even a different composition altogether. Again, there would be no essential difference between me, as a real individual, and a mound of earth or a flock of sheep (nominal unities).

The same objection applies to a "composite" made up of continuous matter. Indeed, given the infinite divisibility of what, in nature, is called matter, then the shape or mass of a material body "is never exact and strictly determinate" ("Correspondence with Arnauld", PT 131). Leibniz therefore argues that in no strict sense does a mere mass of matter have properties at all. I can, to some extent, impose a useful nominal unity on it: "this is *my* mound of dirt; and it is different from *yours* in this way ...". But this unity, and the properties of it (size, shape, mass, etc.), do not *belong originally* to the mound, and moreover could never be rigorously defined.

Regardless, then, of how we conceive of matter (whether as atomically discrete, or continuous), it becomes impossible to understand how a material composite could exist as something in its own right. This is a problem because some composite entities clearly do exist as real individuals, for example, me. We can understand this, Leibniz argues, only if we stop thinking in terms of continuous matter and material bodies, and start thinking in terms of simple substances. Composites are possible only because they are composites *of* genuine simple substances. Such an entity, then, is not a substance, but substances. In that way it is possible for such an entity to have definite properties, and to exist as a real thing. However, this "composite" cannot be in the sense of a whole made up of *parts*, because we would then be back to the problem of divisibility and extension. That is, the substances would be acting just like atoms, and the problem of the independent existence of some composites would not have been solved.

Leibniz often draws an elaborate analogy with the relation between a line and points (which are indivisible unities). First of all, a line cannot be meaningfully said to have points as its "parts"; rather, a point is a *different type of entity*. Analogously, composites do not have monads as parts. Secondly, the division of the line into parts (called "segments") is a *possible* mathematical operation. That is, the division of any given line is only ideal. Real things, if they are composites in any sense, on the other hand, are *already actually divided*. The division is real. Mathematical objects, then, are infinitely divisible and have only "ideal" or "indeterminate" parts.

Leibniz's solution is a combination of the above features of "mathematical" and "real" division. A real composite substance is actually divided into simple substances. However, simple monads are not "parts" of the *material* composite body; rather, it has individual monads as its "foundation", just as the line has points. Actually existing and in-themselves unified monads are the "foundation" of the phenomena of material body, rather than its parts.[2] (Leibniz tries to explain this notion of foundation with another analogy: a rainbow is a mere phenomenon that has its foundation in real things – light and the optics of water droplets.) So Leibniz's theory of composite substances requires that we think of matter and material things as effects of underlying substances. Indeed, he will argue that the whole problem of composites and divisibility is, like the rainbow, a type of illusion. We will have much more to say below about this distinction between the phenomena studied by physics and their metaphysical foundation in substance. However, that a body is founded upon a multitude of unities is only *one* condition of organic bodies being real unities. We will examine the other key condition below under the headings "entelechy" and "soul".

So monads are simple substances. This has several important consequences. First, in order to not fall to the same objection Leibniz made to material atoms, monads cannot be extended in space (§3). This claim, and related observations concerning time relations, have enormous consequences for how we must understand space and time (see below). Secondly, Leibniz argues that all *natural* "dissolution" (coming to an end, ceasing to be) is part by part (like a sugar cube dissolving in water, or a log burning in a fireplace). A natural force could not affect the whole of a composite simultaneously. This means that composites can cease to be, but simple substances (not having parts) cannot (§4). Thirdly, the same argument applies to coming-into-being. Natural creation builds composites up, part by part (like the growth of a foetus, or a crystal). A monad could not come into existence naturally (§5). Accordingly, monads exist because of a non-natural act of creation, and cease to exist through non-natural annihilation (§6). The distinction between natural and non-natural creation will turn out to have theological implications, and we shall pursue these below. Notice, for the moment, that a monad is a necessary being within the domain of the forces of creation and destruction of nature, but (contra Spinoza's scandalous pantheism) is a contingent being within the domain of non-natural creation and destruction. Fourthly, there is no way in which a monad could be altered by something outside it. Any natural force, Leibniz argues, works by changing the motions internal to a thing, or by adding to, removing from, rearranging, splitting or fusing its parts. In this way catching a heavy ball transmits motion from the ball to the skin of the hand, from the skin to muscle, from muscle to bone, and from the bones of the hand to those of the wrist, arm and so on. A *very* heavy ball might tear apart two parts of the hand, resulting in a bruise or sprain. But a monad has no parts, and there is nothing for a natural force to act upon. Nor could anything be added or subtracted from it. Monads, therefore, must be immune from all natural causation. Leibniz expresses this in a typically clear but striking metaphor: monads have no "windows". Moreover, all properties of a monad are dependent upon the substance. If (in general) there is the property of having mass, or being brittle, or in love, there must be some *thing*, a substance, that has (or exists as) the mass, is brittle or in love. A property is not the kind of thing that could "stroll around" independently of a substance, and thus could not be passed directly from one substance to another.

For Leibniz, all four of these consequences follow directly from the initial conception of a monad. Starting in §8, Leibniz turns to the question of what qualities monads do have. A substance without any qualities could not be said to exist (as in the analysis of mere matter above). Monads must have at least one property each. Further, monads must have differing properties from each other, otherwise they would all be the same, and nothing would change. Leibniz argues that change is an event for which there must be a reason. (This follows from the principle of sufficient reason, which we shall discuss below.) This reason will either be the internal properties of monads, or their relations. If all monads had the same properties, then even their relations would be the same; and thus change would be impossible (would have no "reason"). Leibniz here assumes, without argument, a "plenum". This is a traditional notion in physics describing a space that is filled with *matter* at every point. The notion of plenum was commonplace in the seventeenth and eighteenth centuries; philosophers in the tradition of Descartes (and many others) argued against the possibility of a true void.[3] If there were a void, then substances that were in themselves unchanging could at least change their relative position within surrounding void. But given a plenum of substances, all with identical and unchanging properties, what could possibly change?

Clearly, though, there is change in nature; so monads must not have merely one, identical, constant quality or set thereof. Leibniz argues that all monads are not the same, and that this is clear from the variety of things in the world and the possibility of change and movement. (But he also must argue that no two monads could have the same set of properties. That is, no two could be "indiscernible". The reasons, however, are more metaphysical than physical. We shall return to this famous argument below.)

Indeed, Leibniz goes so far as to assert that change is continual even within all "created" substances (§10); certainly, there is no evidence of absolute permanence in nature. Moreover, that change can not be from one property to the next, but rather from a rich set of simultaneous properties (he calls these "details in the changes") to another set that partly overlaps (§§12, 13). This set is described as a "multiplicity" within the unity of the monad. The reasoning is that, again, natural changes happen by degrees or part by part, so if a monad had only one property at a time, it could not change (this is the "law of continuity"; see "A Specimen of Dynamics", PE 133). Any new property would be a *complete* and *all at once* change. But the subsequent sets partly overlap; thus the changes to the set can be "part by part".

Since these changes cannot come from outside the monad, they must come from an "internal principle". Monads change according to causes or reasons that lie within them. The whole sequence of the sets of properties exhibited by a monad, from its creation to its annihilation, is arrived at because of this internal principle alone. Monads are "incorporal automata" (§18). The monad has no parts, but its complex set of properties acts "as if" they are parts. The "parts" of the set of exhibited properties interact. This interaction provides explanations of the changes. This explanation is analogous, but *only* analogous, to the way that the interacting movements of the parts of a machine explain the machine's changes. The machine and its parts, however, are both of the same ontological order; a monad and its properties are not. Leibniz has a preferred analogy: consider a mathematical curve. It follows a single law; but at every point on the line, the tangent (which is a representation of what the curve is "doing" at that point) is different. So there is one inner law, but a spontaneous diversity of properties ("Explanation of Bayle's Difficulties", PT 206 and cf. 235, 246). Since everything needed to account for future changes in the monad is already within the monad, Leibniz famously says the monad bears "traces" of its past and is "pregnant" with its own future (§22).

If it appears, in nature, as though one thing has an effect upon another (the ball hits my hand) this is, at a fundamental level, because the sequence of properties exhibited by monads are "harmonized" in advance. It is as if, to use one of Leibniz's favourite analogies, we set two well-made clocks going at the same time. The clocks would always appear coordinated, just as if they were actually influencing one another. But, in fact, there is no such influence. The clocks are quite independently following their own course. And so, according to Leibniz's reasoning, we must posit a universe containing an infinite number of monads, each following its own course, that course having been harmonized in advance such that the properties exhibited by each are coordinated.

In fact, when it comes to the study of nature, this coordination is so perfect and so regular that scientists *should* for the most part ignore the above metaphysical claims, and instead talk about causes and effects as the interaction of masses, elasticities, forces and velocities. Thus, Leibniz talks about two points of view on reality: the phenomenal (concerned with natural appearances) and the metaphysical. We have already encountered this distinction above in saying, for example, that Leibniz is happy to concede to the Cartesians the continuity and infinite divisibility of matter, but not of substance. This required that we distinguish between the phenomena of material bodies, as studied by physics, and the substantial entities that are the foundation of the phenomena. The metaphysics may contain the ultimate truth of things, but despite this, and with only a few exceptions, metaphysics just gets in the way of physics. See, for example, the "Discourse on Metaphysics" (PE 42–3). There are important exceptions to this restriction (and perhaps Leibniz is not fully consistent here). Above all, principles such as sufficient reason have universal validity, and using such principles Leibniz shows where he believes many contemporary physicists go wrong. Also, Leibniz himself employs metaphysical arguments in analysing the relationship between momentum and kinetic energy (*ibid*. 49–53). Nevertheless, physics should generally be understood as an autonomous discipline.

If, for example, in doing physics we start speaking about substances, souls and so on, then we end up with a nonsensical theory of atoms, or may even begin to speak of miracles or occult qualities (such as gravity; see "Against Barbaric Physics", PE 312ff.). Once the physicist abandons the phenomenally sensible, then anything goes. There is, however, a barrier the other way too. The legitimacy of physics is confined to the sphere of natural explanation, and should not take itself too seriously and start to pursue metaphysics. That is to say, within the sphere of composite, extended bodies, this law-governed mechanical cause and effect account (which is typical of eighteenth-century physics after Newton) is perfectly legitimate (indeed, Leibniz thought, more legitimate than Newtonians with their occult qualities, gave it credit for). But if we import these notions into metaphysics, or consider them as "primitive and inexplicable" ("Against Barbaric Physics", PE 317) – that is to say, as forming the basis of metaphysical reality – then again we are speaking nonsense.

The action of the internal principle of change in a monad is termed "appetition" (§15). Although appetite does not always, perhaps ever, fully attain its goal, nevertheless it brings about changes. The notion of "appetite" is suggestive: my appetite is the "force" that *draws* me to make up for what I lack (as with food). A monad, considered as having one or a set of properties, is lacking something in the sense that it has not brought to completion its internal principle of change. The monad is essentially on-the-way, and has not fulfilled itself. This general, metaphysical notion of "appetition" appears to be based on an analogy with human and animal appetite (e.g. hunger). But perhaps we should think the other way round; humans and other animals must have appetites (in the narrow sense) because they are substantial entities and all substances have "appetition". "Hunger" is one of the actions of the principle of change characteristic of the dominant monad of an organic body.

We have been speaking of "sets" of properties, as if the monad existed through a series of "snapshots" of time. This way of speaking is convenient, certainly. It also ties in with a very traditional and compelling way of thinking about determinism: that any one "snapshot" of all the material states in the universe would allow one to discover the whole of the past, and anticipate the whole of the future (see Laplace, "Philosophical Essay on Probability" in Cottingham (1996), for example). But this cannot be precisely Leibniz's meaning, since it is clearly modelled on efficient causes (causation in the sense of one thing or event "bringing about" a subsequent thing or event), rather than final causes (causation in the reverse sense of having an end or purpose: why buy a ticket on Monday? So as to get into the game on Tuesday). Leibniz is happy to admit that the study of physics is primarily concerned with efficient causes. But efficient causes never operate discontinuously in time, or work in reverse; however, the *metaphysical* web of sufficient reasons is not necessarily organized linearly or continuously in time. Furthermore, the simple determinist model misses the sense of striving of a monad; such language Leibniz uses precisely to distinguish spontaneous change in the monad from phenomenal cause and effect.

Accordingly, Leibniz borrows again from Aristotle (and from medieval philosophers influenced by him) the notion of *entelechy* (a move that no doubt earned Leibniz hoots of derision from the dominant anti-Aristotelianism of his time). We need to investigate this notion briefly.

Of souls, entelechies and bodies (*Monadology* §§19–28, 49–50, 61–82)

For Aristotle, the soul is the form of a body such that it is alive. Regarding souls, Aristotle distinguishes between a "faculty"/"capacity" (*hexis*) and the activity of that faculty (*energeia*). We are living bodies, and have the faculty for thinking, perceiving or obtaining nourishment. We have these faculties (*hexis*) even when

69

we are asleep and not employing (*energeia*) any of them (cf. *Monadology* §20).[4] An ambiguity arises: having these faculties even in an inactive way is potential with respect to the activity. However, even having them inactively is actuality as opposed to being not alive at all (and thus not even having the faculty). The notion of *entelechy* (often translated as "actuality") is an attempt to clear this up by distinguishing between these two senses of the actual. The "first entelechy" is the soul as *hexis* (a faculty, even if currently inactive), the "second entelechy" is the soul as *energeia* (a faculty in use).[5]

What Leibniz picks up on, however, is that "entelechy" in Greek means more than "actuality", but also "fulfilment" or "having reached perfection or completion". This has two consequences. First, Leibniz thinks of the first entelechy as not merely a faculty or capacity, but also what he calls "appetition", which is the monad striving towards the complete fulfilment of its internal principle. Secondly, the perfection of the monad even as first entelechy is that its principle of change is internal; it has a "sufficiency" to itself (§18). The monad exists as a being that (in one sense) strives to attain to that which (in another sense) it already is. So "entelechy" gathers together these ideas from Aristotle: (i) the soul as the form of (the dominant and organizing substance of) the phenomenally appearing body and thus also the body's capacity for various functions (we shall return to this below in talking about organic bodies and substantial forms); (ii) the soul existing in such a way as to be characterized by appetition; (iii) the perfection of this appetition in so far as it is an internal or autonomous principle of striving for completion.

All entelechies exist in a pre-established harmony with each other. Because of this, monads do have *ideal* relations with each other. Each monad "mirrors" or "expresses" (without being actually affected by) what happens to all other monads, from its own point of view, and this mirroring Leibniz calls "perception" (§14). So, metaphysically, monads express every aspect of their universe; so, equivalently, within the physics of a plenum of material bodies, there could be no movement of one body that does not register in some way on every other body (§61). However, since metaphysically all properties of monads arrive through the internal principle rather than external causation, the monad would continue to change in its orderly way *even were no other monad actually in existence* ("Discourse on Metaphysics" §14, PE 47). Leibniz certainly does not believe this infamous claim to be true, merely that it is in principle possible.

Leibniz makes a number of brief but important points concerning perception:

(i) Perceptions or thoughts can be clear or obscure, distinct or confused. "Clarity" means that we can pick out the object of the perception from others. "Distinct" means that we are able to give an explanation of, and a definition of the content of the object, that could even serve as a replacement for the clear perception (NECHU 254ff.; "Meditations on Knowledge, Truth and Ideas", PE 23ff.). Leibniz, for example, argues that we can easily enough have a clear perception of a red thing, but not a distinct perception: red cannot be defined, it is ultimately merely ostensive, requiring examples. The language of clarity and distinctness is Descartes's; the definitions are slightly different.

(ii) There are no real causal relations, but in so far as a monad has a relatively distinct (as opposed to confused) perception of its relation to another, and thus also contains in its perceptions the explanation for the change of state, we can say that it "acts" and the other is "passive" or "acted upon" (§§49, 52). That is the metaphysical meaning of phenomenal causation.

(iii) Relatedly, those monads capable of distinct perceptions are capable of spontaneity (although, of course, metaphysically, all monads have to be considered as active, striving entities). Because imperfection is defined as a limitation (a relation of dependence or passivity to something else), an active monad with distinct perceptions is more "perfect" (§50). Indeed, it is also more "real", since its properties and identity are not a mere shadow cast by entities outside it (§41).

(iv) Because perception is a relation to all monads, it is always vastly (indeed, infinitely) complex, and always more or less confused. It is essential to the type of being of a finite monad that it contains infinite perceptual relationality; Leibniz calls this its being "sensible". We shall return to this ontological issue later.

(v) Think about our quite ordinary perceptual relations: I am presented with simultaneous and complex sets of sensory data, some of which I may not even be aware of at the time (§16). Equally, perception does not cease with sleep (§21). Leibniz calls the multitude of unnoticed perceptions "*petites perceptions*". He uses this notion to make important points about psychology, memory and free will (cf. especially NEHU). Leibniz also argues that if perception were not in some areas stronger or more distinct than others, there would be nothing to notice, nothing to become conscious of, and we would always be "bare monads". Human bodies, then, if they are to have relatively distinct perceptions must have senses that concentrate perceptions – eyes, noses, ears, that gather sense information – and of course also motive powers that allow eyes to turn, hands to reach out and so on (§§24–5). This echoes Aristotle: we do not see because we have eyes, but have eyes because we are seeing beings.

(vi) Many philosophers in Leibniz's day (as now) have tried to account for perception by means of natural causes. This is an example, for Leibniz, of physics taking itself too seriously. The discussion of the hypothetical thinking machine in §17 is intended to prove that the type of phenomena called "perceiving" or "thinking" is just not analysable in terms of mechanical cause and effect relations. Physics is out of its proper sphere when it tries to understand what happens within a monad (see also §79).

(vii) Memory plays a key role for Leibniz in animal and rational souls. It allows unconscious habits to form (§§26–7), as well as conscious judgements concerning what will happen in the future based merely upon what did happen in the past. Leibniz's point in §28 is that, most of the time, even we rational beings do not think about the reasons why something is likely to happen in the future, we just rely upon habitual expectations. Memory thus "imitates" reason.

(viii) An observation should be made here similar to that made about "appetition" above. All monads are said to "perceive". This looks like a metaphysical term based on an analogy with "literal" human perception, but there is reason to believe the opposite: all substances perceive (broadly speaking); in human beings, this takes the specific form of perception (in the narrow sense).

While all monads are perceptive and appetitive, not all have memory, the possibility of distinct perception, and apperception (consciousness). These three characteristics distinguish what Leibniz calls "souls" from all other monads (§19) (the other types Leibniz often calls "bare" monads). For Leibniz, all animal bodies have a "soul". In turn, soul is distinguished into merely animal and rational, by the presence in the latter of "knowledge of eternal and necessary truths" (§29). The principle of internal change in a soul is properly understood according to "final causes"; that is, what happens to the monad is best accounted for by thinking in terms of purposes or goals, or more generally in terms of its striving to complete itself (§79). On the other hand, phenomenal bodies, the objects of study in physics, are best understood according to efficient causes. The distinction here, as so often, comes from Aristotle.

Where there is talk of a soul, though, talk of an organic body cannot be far away. For Leibniz, the notion of pre-established harmony also solves the problem of the relation of mind and body. We have already seen both that real causation between substances is impossible on principle, and that in particular a causal explanation (in terms of body properties) of perception or thought (mind properties) is absurd. In §80, Leibniz insists not only that the incorporeal soul cannot add "force" to the system of material bodies, but also (unlike for Descartes) it cannot even change the direction of the motion in a body. The argument concerns Leibniz's discovery of the distinction between (in modern terminology) kinetic energy (the quantity of which is independent of direction) and momentum (which is not). Accordingly, to cause a diversion in the direction of motion of a body would require the application of real force – and the mind–body problem remains unsolved (See "Discourse on Metaphysics", PE 49–52 and "A Specimen of Dynamics", PE 177ff.).[6]

The solution is simple, Leibniz believes. The body, as a composite substance, will be in a pre-established harmony with the soul or mind, and both will be in harmony with all other monads too. What happens in the nervous system will have a corresponding change in the soul; and when the soul exerts itself (as will), there will be corresponding changes in the body. Again, this is like the two clocks, except now one is corporeal and the other incorporeal (§§18, 64).

My body is not merely *any* composite, however; it is *mine*. This property of being mine is moreover not a natural property (like being tanned or balding, for example). Rather, it is an effect of the soul. Organic bodies are organized around one monad, the soul. Leibniz sums all this up in the notion of "substantial form". Perhaps because of its vivid scholastic associations, Leibniz does not employ this expression in the *Monadology*, preferring to speak of "constituting" or "dominant" entelechies (§62–3, 70); but the idea is the same (see "On Nature Itself", PE 162; "Discourse on Metaphysics", PE 42–4). The soul, as substantial form, is that single monad that makes a composite body *one thing*; it serves as the principle of the organization and continuing identity of the body. Indeed, that which composes the body changes (as a composite, remember, it has no fixed and determinate natural properties), but the identity does not (§71). On the other hand, the body serves as an explanation of why the mind does not mirror or express everything equally. The soul's perception of the universe is pre-harmonized to agree with the body's organs of sense, which, as we saw above, gather and concentrate perceptions. The soul's ideal mirroring of its world is organized in a manner parallel to the body's real causal relations to other bodies (§63). As such, we have the possibility of relatively distinct perceptions and thoughts of the universe. To this extent, we understand the current state of our being, and something of the concatenation of reasons that produced it (normally those things nearest and most influential in time or space), and also something of the real destination of our internal principle (again, normally the nearest in time) (§60–1).

Now, rational souls are more perfect, and more capable of distinct thought, than other souls, but even they are not god-like. Not all thoughts of a rational soul are absolutely distinct, and as soon as there are "confused thoughts, there is sense, there is matter" (T §124). Matter exists in order to be the object (and the explanation for) confused thoughts. In turn, confused thoughts are by their nature *sensible*; and exist because rational minds are finite ("limited" (§60)) in nature. Therefore rational souls are always connected with a body, and only a God would be "completely detached from bodies" (§72). (Also, as we know, given that there is confused thought, the body is a mechanism for accounting for why, within that confusion, at least some degree of clarity and distinctness can be had in perception.)

Monads, as we know, cannot be naturally created or destroyed. (Here, the order of *nature* is distinguished from the order of the *supernatural*, which includes such events as creation or other miracles. We can make this distinction, although we may have as yet no reason to admit the existence of the latter.) Therefore, as long as there have naturally been bodies, there must also have been souls. This means that *what will become* rational souls are already existent and connected to an "undeveloped" but "preformed" body *before the conception or birth* of the organism as we know it (§73–5); and that *what had been* the rational soul will still remain with some "enfolded" or "diminished" version of its body *after the organism* (as we know it) *dies* (§76–7). When the body dies, neither body nor soul simply cease to exist (this cannot happen as a natural event), but the soul ceases to have ownership over the bulk of the body, and this leaves the body a mere composite of matter. This also solves a puzzle (which remains a puzzle in biology today) of how to account for the transition from inorganic to organic bodies. Leibniz argues that this transformation never happens naturally, but that organic bodies rather grow and diminish (§74–5). What we normally call "life" is simply a period of enhanced activity.

Since composite bodies are actually divisible without end, a body does not have to be of a certain size in order for a certain level of complexity and organization to be possible. (As we shall see, size not only doesn't matter, but it is not even a real property.) Leibniz was impressed by the results Leeuwenhoek had with early versions of the microscope, discovering countless apparently complex animals in a drop of pond water. Thus, there is no reason for any particular level of compositeness to be a more legitimate "place" for souls and bodies to exist than any other. (See the discussion of "sufficient reason" below.) All composite bodies contain multitudes of other bodies and substantial forms, and they, in turn, still others (§66–8). And likewise in the reverse direction; our bodies must be contained within the bodies of inconceivably large animals, and so on. Thus, Leibniz writes grandly, "There is nothing fallow, sterile or dead in the universe, no chaos and no confusion except in appearance ..." (§69). This is a metaphysics entirely consummate with moral and aesthetic principles.

Rationality and the problem of freedom (§§29–36)

Whereas perception and memory together can "imitate" reason by leading us to unthinking expectations concerning the future, human souls have the additional capacity of reason. Leibniz defines reason, simply enough, as the "linking together of truths" according to basic rules. The truths in question are either experiential or *a priori* (T §1). Reason in turn is made possible by the knowledge of eternal and necessary truths (§29), which characterize the most essential of these rules. Only through reason turning inwards in "reflective acts" do we raise ourselves to knowledge of ourselves. This will involve knowledge of immaterial substances, and leads (by the conceiving as unlimited that which is, in us, limited) to the idea of a God (§30).

The eternal and necessary truths upon which all reasoning is based are the *principle of contradiction* (of two propositions that contradict one another, at least one must be false) and the *principle of sufficient reason* (§§31–2). According to the latter, for everything that is the case, there will be an adequate set of reasons for it being the case rather than otherwise. Although, as Leibniz notes, given the finite nature of our comprehension of things, the full set of reasons is probably unknown to us, nevertheless this principle can be productively used in a *reductio ad absurdum*. That is, Leibniz frequently argues that if some X were true, it would follow that there could be no sufficient reason (even for an infinite mind) why some other fact Y is true; therefore, X cannot be true.

For example, above we noted in passing that no two monads could be "indiscernible" (§9). Leibniz calls this the principle of the identity of indiscernibles, and he argues that it follows from the principle of sufficient reason. The argument goes something like this: let us suppose two monads or bodies (A and B) that are in fact different, although they exhibit precisely the same set of properties. It is true, then, that A is where A is, and B is where B is. But, because all properties are identical, there is and could be no sufficient reason why that state of affairs is true, and not the other way around (A happens to be where B is, etc.). From that it follows that the supposition is false. Either, then, there are not two things, only one; or the two things are not really identical in all respects (PE 32). Leibniz uses a slight variation on this argument to demonstrate that space and time are ideal. Space and time are, for Leibniz, means of describing the order and relations of substances; they are not independent "containers" or "substances" *in which* monads exist (PE 32–5). The order and relations, that is, are not independently existing things, but are merely ways of expressing the immanent properties of substances. Although the ideality of space and time is not a major theme in the *Monadology*, it clearly lies behind Leibniz's confidence in key claims above, such as the non-extensive nature of monads, the plenum of matter and the inadequacy of a notion of change modelled upon phenomenal causation. Thus, again, Leibniz can argue that indiscernible substances (purportedly two substances with exactly the same properties) must be identical (that is, must in fact be one thing not two). The difference between any two substances that are otherwise the same would be their location in space or in time; but space and time are in fact nothing but *properties of* substances, and therefore the substances could never have been "the same" in the first place.[7]

Leibniz admits that truths of fact (all truths learned from our experience) are different from truths of reasoning; the key difference is that the former are contingent (they could have been otherwise) and the latter are necessary (their opposite entails a contradiction). The necessity of truths of reasoning follows from the fact that they can be analysed back to "primitive" truths, just as theorems of Euclidean geometry can be analysed back to "definitions, axioms and postulates" (§34). Examples of primitive definitions, such as "possibility" and "necessity" are given in the *Theodicy* (T §282). These primitive truths cannot be proven beyond the fact that, employing the principle of contradiction, their opposites entail a contradiction (§33, 35).

Truths of fact are contingent, but not without reason. The *complete* web of reasons that make something be in a certain way are, unquestionably, beyond our human capacities of knowing and perceiving.[8] However, although not explicitly stated in §36, Leibniz must also be arguing that truths of fact are different from mere observations or passively formed generalizations about the world. Otherwise, there would be no difference from the "Empiric" physicians who merely follow tradition, which Leibniz mentioned in §28. In "Against Barbaric Physics", written around the time of the *Monadology*, Leibniz makes related comments on scientific method (PE 312ff.). Physics, then, is a rational enterprise, in so far as it is an activity of a "rational soul", and could never achieve any understanding were it entirely empirical (in any sense of that word). However, physics is not "rational" if by that we mean physics in the rationalist tradition of Descartes, since we have already seen Leibniz distinguish between the study of physical phenomena and metaphysics.

Because the principle of sufficient reason applies even to contingent truths about substances, this allows us to say something more about the internal principle of change in every monad. It cannot be that this principle of change merely details and brings about the various successive sets of properties exhibited by the monad. Rather, as we have already hinted, these sets must be comprehensively linked so that the whole accounts for each element within it. Indeed, this is why Leibniz calls it a "principle". Although the *content* of the internal principle may be contingent, nevertheless it is *organized* according to necessary laws, and ultimately the principle of sufficient reason. The principle of change therefore functions like a concept of the identity of the monad; that is to say, of the definition of the monad as a whole and (from out of that) at every moment of time.

Leibniz accordingly employs the concept of a "complete notion". This would be a conceptual equivalent of the internal principle, expressing with perfect clarity and distinctness the identity of the individual substance, which must include not only what properties are in fact exhibited, but also an account of the reasons for those properties (see especially "Discourse on Metaphysics", PE 40ff., §8ff.). Such a complete notion must be possible (were there a god-like mind capable of perfect distinctness in its understanding). It would appear to follow that truths about a monad could, in principle, be derived *analytically* from the complete notion, in the same way as "unmarried man" is derived from "bachelor". Does this mean that such truths are not, after all, contingent, but are rather necessary?

Leibniz distinguishes between hypothetical necessity and absolute necessity ("Letters to Arnauld", PE 69–70). Something is absolutely necessary if its opposite entails a contradiction. On the other hand, something X is hypothetically necessary if, *given that* X *actually exists*, then whatever is entailed by the concept of X must also exist. For example, if a unicorn exists, then there must exist a horse-like animal with one horn; but there is no contradiction in unicorns not existing at all. Such a hypothetical "necessity" is, Leibniz argues, just what we mean by the notion of "contingency". Contingency cannot mean arbitrary or random, not least because of the principle of sufficient reason. Contingent truths about substances are hypothetical necessities: they are true and can be analytically derived from the complete notion provided only that the object of that notion actually exists. This allows Leibniz to answer ingeniously any number of objections, which normally centre on the problem of human freedom. If (to use the example discussed at length in his correspondence with Arnauld) it is analytically true of Adam that he was to sin, then was his sin free? And if not, was it even a sin?

Leibniz answers that Adam was who he was. And the man that he was, was a man who, under certain circumstances, would *choose freely* to sin. It was certainly possible that a man *a bit like* Adam not sin under those conditions, although in that case he would have been a slightly different Adam, inhabiting a slightly different universe ("Letters to Arnauld", PE 71–4). What is just nonsense, though, is to demand that Adam exist as the actual Adam and *also* that he not do the things Adam does. My human freedom consists of the unfettered ability to *be who I am*. Indeed, my freedom would be compromised entirely were, by some miraculous interference, I were not allowed to *be myself*.

The complete notion of me includes all of my decisions. Again, that seems to entail that the decision is analytically true of me. But Leibniz also argues that this analysis is infinite in extent – it would involve working out from an act to all the past (and future) events that make the act hypothetically necessary for my total being. Leibniz often gives an analogy. Take a square that has sides precisely a round number of units in length (say, 1 metre). The diagonal of that square will have a definite length, *but one that cannot be analysed into those units*. Now, if there were a perfect intelligence, capable of seeing all notions distinctly, that intelligence could see the whole infinite web of reasons that amount to the sufficient reason of my action, and its relation to my total identity as a substance. But even that perfect intelligence could not *complete* the analysis, reducing it to a simple equation or primitive truths ("On Freedom", LE 96), any more than a perfect intelligence could analyse the diagonal of a square into the units of its sides. Since a contingent truth is one the opposite of which does not analyse back to a contradiction, truths contained in my complete concept are contingent. Thus, there is this all-important caveat to talking about the "analytically true".

Moreover, we should also divide contingent truths into (at least) two classes.[9] It will be noticed that the above argument about infinite analysis applies as much to events in the merely material world as to the actions of rational beings. In both cases, on Leibniz's principles, the reasons extend throughout the universe and time. Nevertheless, there are available certain "subordinate universal laws" that are capable of describing the motions of physical bodies (e.g. Newton's laws of motion or gravity) ("Necessary and Contingent Truths", PW 100–101). The principles according to which physical bodies must act are not infinite in variety, nor are the physical variables that feed into those actions. For this reason, although contingent, the exact position of the planet Venus on a given night can be calculated to the nth decimal place. But this is not the case with human actions, which, as we have seen, are not part of the order of nature. We can generalize *statistically* about human psychology, but these are not laws. The suspension of the force of natural causation would be a miracle; but freedom partly consists of the ability to suspend even the most forceful final cause by a kind of "private miracle" (*ibid*.).

Human agents are not, of course, entirely free. "I am not free to fly like an eagle", Leibniz writes ("Dialogue on Human Freedom", PE 112). Just as my body is constrained by its physical properties, so is my mind by the multitude of perceptions that continually "bombard" me. For every action, there is always a reason. Accordingly, Leibniz argues against the notion of "freedom of indifference": that I can be free only when there is no reason for choosing X above Y or Y above X. Others – Aristotle and, more famously, the medieval philosopher Buridan – objected that in such as case no choice or action could happen at all. Leibniz argues that this dispute is pointless, since such absolute indifference is impossible. The infinite complexity of my perceptions of the world ensures that my reasons for acting on that world could never be perfectly balanced. The argument is similar to the identity of indiscernibles. (See "Letter to Coste", PE 194–5.)

In a being capable of thought, the reason for acting will be the appearance of the best ("Discourse on Metaphysics", §29). I always act in this way, broadly speaking; I act according to what I take to be the best for me, even though it sometimes appears best only "through a whim, or contrariness" (see "Letter to Coste", PE 193–4). Moreover, by my self-discipline I can "accustom" myself to see what is the best more distinctly, consistently and morally (*ibid*. 195). That is, I can train my rational ability to see the best, such that my actions follow from distinctly thought final causes concerning the best, rather than from confused thoughts, or even from efficient causes. My ability to make bad judgements, however, is not itself a contingent defect. The type of being that I am (limited and thus encountering my world through perception) is such that my "vision" of the best must always be more or less confused.

This discussion of freedom has, apparently, taken us far from the *Monadology*. But this is only apparent, since that text ends with a consideration of the moral nature of the universe described, and of the human place in it. Freedom and related topics, although not explicitly mentioned there, are required to understand Leibniz's vision.

Creation and pre-established harmony (§§37–48, 51–60)

Of course, in analysing the web of reasons for some contingent fact – "why are you late today?" – the set of results will always (individually or as a whole) be other contingent facts, such as "because my alarm clock didn't ring". As such, they are reasons but not in themselves a "sufficient reason". No matter how far this analysis is carried, the result will always be just another contingent (and thus not sufficient) reason.

From this observation philosophical theology follows. Something that is outside the series of contingent reasons for things must exist that serves as sufficient reason (§37). This something cannot itself be diverse, because then there would still be needed a sufficient reason of why this diversity functions together; thus this something must be one (§39). The something is a necessary being and "this is what we call *God*" (§38). God contains the series of contingent things not as such – that is, God is not "made up" of or identical with contingent things – but rather contains them "eminently".

This is a scholastic notion that describes degrees of being or perfection. Some X is said to contain Y "eminently" if X contains to a superior degree all the qualities and perfections of Y, together with the capacity to bring about Y ("Principles of Nature and Grace" §9, PE 210). (Analogously, and loosely, a cookie cutter contains the shape of the cookies eminently, since it has the perfect form of that shape and is the mechanism by which they are shaped.) The X can then serve as a sufficient reason of Y, in the way that Y on its own, as a series of contingent things and reasons for things, could not (§39). This is clearly a version of the cosmological argument. (Leibniz also develops a variation on the ontological argument in §45.)

The argument passes very quickly. Arguments that prove the existence of God do not have pride of place in his major works, in the way, for example, that Descartes devotes the best part of two of six *Meditations*. Leibniz is much more interested in how the notion of God functions within metaphysics, morals and theology. In the *Monadology*, there are three key topics: the nature of divine being, the nature of the act of creation, and the "city of God". We shall look at the first two below, and turn to the third of these in the last section of this essay.

We already know that the divine being contains all the positive properties of creation eminently. Imperfection, Leibniz argues, is not a positive property, but a limitation, which is only possible through something outside the being that limits it. This must mean that the divine being has these positive properties in a not only superior but infinitely perfect form (§40, 41). In the case of a monad, limitation consists first of all of the relation of dependence upon that which provides a sufficient reason for its nature and existence. Moreover, the monad is limited through its sensible relation to all other monads. These relations are not contingent, however, in the sense that the monad would be infinite and perfect were they removed. Rather, they are essential to the nature of the monad, which is pre-adapted to the existence of other monads (even should no other monads *actually* exist). The monad is thus "incapable of being without limits" (§42).

The divine being, however, is not merely a first cause, but rather an intelligence that chooses creation. God chooses creation from an infinite number of other possible creations. This is why Leibniz makes so much of the concept of possibility in §§43–5. Above, we distinguished between necessary and contingent truths. Necessary truths concern the structure of *any possible* creation, relating to the nature of the mind of God, rather than to any object outside that mind (§46). Most contingent truths are true only in *this creation* (e.g. the essence of a particular monad, and thus of every other monad reciprocally pre-adapted to it). Other contingent truths are, at most, only true for a fraction of possible creations (e.g. that gravity is a force operating according to an inverse square law, as opposed to, say, an inverse cube law). Leibniz argues that one reason why his notion of "contingency" is valid is because truths incompatible with contingent truths were *really* possible, as options for creation rejected by God. Analogously, my having a tuna sandwich for lunch was really possible, since one was there to be purchased, I had the money and I even thought about it, although I eventually chose to eat a bowl of soup, because that seemed the best action. The tuna sandwich possibility was within the range of my intellect, will and power.

Moral and theological consequences (§§83–90)

However, since God's intellect presented possibilities, there must be a sufficient reason for the particular possibility chosen. This is the principle of the best of all possible worlds. God has three aspects: knowledge, which is the contemplation of possibility; will, which chooses among the possibilities those that are to be made actual; and power, which equates to eminent being, and is thus the source of all that exists (§48). We can also distinguish between "antecedent" and "consequent" will (§90). The former concerns general principles that are to be enacted; the latter concerns the whole of creation. For example, a general repugnance to evil, and the desire to save *every* soul, must be part of the antecedent will of God. But evil does exist (at least, "exists" in the sense of a limitation), and not every soul is saved. The *complete* satisfaction of *all* of these antecedent principles need not be part of the consequent will, since there may be wider reasons why some evil and even consequent damnation is to be permitted in the chosen creation. That creation is chosen that satisfies to the maximum degree all of the objects of antecedent will in order of their significance. This world, the actual world, must be the best of all possible worlds. A more perfect world is not possible, because it would involve a contradiction.

This claim was subject to no small amount of ridicule (famously by Voltaire, in *Candide*). This is a world of sin, Leibniz's opponents variously argued, in which the number of the damned far outnumbers the number of the saved; and in which moreover human beings are afflicted by disease, natural disasters, and the nasty consequences (intended or not) of the actions of others. To claim no better world to be within the reach of an infinitely wise and powerful being is just fatuous. Leibniz's claim just exacerbates the issues in the traditional problem of evil. In the *Theodicy*, Leibniz spends hundreds of pages defending his position, and related issues. The defence takes a number of forms; here are a few of the key ones:

(i) The distinction between antecedent and consequent will already solves certain problems. For example, we can say no longer that God *wills* sin; rather, that God *permits* sin as ultimately contributing to the wider good of creation.

(ii) We see and know only a tiny fraction of the universe; to judge the goodness or orderliness of the whole from this small sample is very poor reasoning indeed. There is also something monstrous in each individual monad believing the universe was created just for it, and judging from its own point of view. In §57, Leibniz compares this to one person's view on a city, instead of thinking of the real city as the combination of all possible points of view upon it. Since the essence of a monad consists in large part of its pre-established harmony with all others, only the whole can be judged.

(iii) It is not merely that what appears to us as disorder *might be* ordered according to a "general will", but that absolute or real disorder itself is an impossible concept. Leibniz the mathematician offers an analogy: there is no line or curve so complex or broken up that a single equation cannot be found for it (cf. T 277). Disorder is an appearance, not a reality.

(iv) Human beings tend to notice occasional evils rather than more constant goods, both in ourselves and in others, precisely because the former are a disturbance of the general order. This leads us to exaggerate the amount of evil. In fact, most people's lives are well worth living. (Which is not to deny that at least a few are not. This creates a slightly different problem: why should some be chosen to make particular sacrifices?)

(v) This universe maximizes complexity and variety, together with order and the least number of basic principles, all to the glory of God (§58). Each existent monad limits and (virtually) affects all the others. To ask that the interaction between monads never be destructive or damaging is to severely limit the possibilities of such a universe.

(vi) That such a rich universe should have no moral evil in it is rigorously impossible. Human and other created beings are free but ontologically limited beings, and thus intrinsically susceptible to the commission of sinful acts. Thus, a world without evil would also be a world without freedom and the good.

Leibniz was forced to defend the principle of the best in these (and other) ways, but, as should be obvious by now, he did not see the problem as a terribly serious one. True insight into the nature of creation does not need to worry about the problem of evil since the magnificence and justice of God are all too evident. The intellectual and moral society of God with created, rational beings, forms the final topic as the *Monadology* reaches its fervent conclusion.

This "society" makes up a "moral world within the natural world" (§86). The mere existence of this "within" is, for Leibniz, the finest testimony to God's greatness. Just as there must be a pre-established harmony between the phenomenal world of efficient causes and the metaphysical world of final causes, so there is a harmony between the natural and moral worlds. The grace of God, by which our sins are forgiven and our good deeds rewarded, coordinates even with events in the natural world (§§87–9). Acts of grace, reward and punishment are not miracles with which God intervenes in creation in order to "correct" it; instead, by virtue of the awesome act of creation, they are pre-harmonized with the rules of, and events within, the material world.

Not least among the gifts of God is the faculty of reason by means of which the splendour and wisdom of the giver can be appreciated, and the sublime joy that accompanies this can be felt. This Leibniz calls "pure love" (§90). This same faculty allows us to distinguish between antecedent and consequent will. This distinction permits us to participate freely in the maximization of the former (the maximization, that is, of moral actions). This participation consists of our striving to carry out these duties, and to gradually recreate ourselves into beings whose life-direction is concordant with antecedent will, and to encourage others to do the same, while admiring and being contented with the consequent will, knowing it is for the best.

Conclusions

What are we to make of this remarkable little book? The *Monadology* is a summary overview of a system of philosophy. What significance does this system have for us? The influence of Leibniz takes several paths; let us consider just five of these.

First, German philosophy in the eighteenth century was Leibnizian in flavour throughout. Only at the end of that century, in the writings of Kant, is a new direction taken. However, even that new direction still bears the stamp of several of Leibniz's key preoccupations. Four examples will suffice to show this. First, Kant also stresses the far-reaching significance of characterizing the finitude of human minds in terms of "sensibility". As we saw above, Leibniz finds in this notion the key to the problem of the limitation of created beings. Secondly, like Leibniz, Kant's philosophy centrally involves a meditation on the notion of possibility. Thirdly, the problem of relationality is vital. In Leibniz, the analyses of space and time, cause and effect, activity and passivity and so forth all depend on the way he thinks about relations. Fourthly, and finally, Kant too requires a version of the phenomenal/metaphysical distinction so essential to understanding Leibniz.

The second path of influence is that, partly through pioneering work by Bertrand Russell, Leibniz came to have an important influence over the course of twentieth-century philosophy, at least in the English-speaking world. Russell's debate with F. H. Bradley on the very Leibnizian subject of relations is sometimes said to be the beginning of "analytic" philosophy. The issues of predication, truth, possibility and formalized accounts of the sciences, all carried a Leibnizian stamp. Indeed, reading the first few pages of Wittgenstein's *Tractatus* will recall the *Monadology* not only in terms of style, but also in terms of the arguments concerning unity, atomism and the possibility of meaning.

Thirdly, Leibniz's arguments concerning morality and freedom have become classics of their kind. His analysis of the compatibility between some type of determinism and a properly understood notion of freedom have stimulated enormous, and productive, controversies. Similarly with his accounts of the identity of the soul, and the solution to the problem of evil.

Fourthly, the concepts of expression, relation and the monad had an avowed significance for Edmund Husserl and his phenomenology. Phenomenology began in the early years of the twentieth century, and has a continuing influence over much of what is often called "continental" philosophy. Accordingly, Leibnizian themes show up frequently thereafter: for example, the account of the striving of consciousness to make up its essential lack and become being, which is so central to Sartre's phenomenological existentialism.

Fifthly, let us look at things more broadly. Putting aside particular ideas Leibniz had, or particular arguments he developed, which were picked up by later philosophers, there is another type of influence. Leibniz was among the most important contributors to how philosophy for the past century or so has been written and conducted. Descartes, Spinoza and Hume, in their different ways, are also influential in this regard, but none of them feel so "modern" to the reader today as many of Leibniz's essays or letters. Although partly a result of his busy and varied life, Leibniz work consists largely of short, carefully demarcated discussions of particular problems (Leibniz's *Theodicy*, though, rather wanders and repeats itself), these short essays are invariably scholarly in the sense that Leibniz locates his position with respect to the writings of his contemporaries. This way of "doing business" was perfectly suited to the growing professionalization of the discipline of philosophy, its increasing location (indeed, confinement) in universities, and its relation to the relatively new phenomena of the academic journal. Consider another, related, example: as a first-class logician, his arguments and formulations always have the clarity, neatness and orderliness that we have come to expect in philosophical writing. This is true to such an extent that a figure like Nietzsche is often (and probably unfairly) excluded from the ranks of philosophers mainly because he doesn't write like Leibniz or, say, Spinoza. One only has to think about the model answers of examination boards, or the standard forms (and their criteria) of assessment at universities, to see the prevalence of this mode of doing philosophy.

However, Leibniz's bold and dizzyingly creative philosophy also provides a model, but one that recent philosophy has by and large elected to ignore. The *Monadology* is a remarkable text. I am of the opinion that its remarkableness is in part its own justification. Borges, the great Argentinean poet and writer of fictions, provided a reason for this. If you wish to find the finest achievements of the human imagination, he argued, do not look to fantastic tales, dramas or epics; instead look to philosophical systems. The world would be a much poorer place if we did not have the *Monadology* to astound us. Perhaps it is time that philosophers again took the risk of imagination.

Notes

1. References to the *Monadology* are simply given as paragraph numbers in parentheses: e.g. (§12). References to other texts by Leibniz are given by title, together with an abbreviated version of the book title and either a section or page number: ("A New System of Nature", PE 142). The abbreviations are as follows: *New Essays Concerning Human Understanding*, NECHU; *Philosophical Essays*, PE; *Philosophical Texts*, PT; *Theodicy*, T.
2. Dividing the problem of infinite divisibility into ideal and real, Leibniz believes, solves the "labyrinth of the continuum". Those troubled by this "labyrinth" are so because they confuse the real and the ideal. So, the real intellectual background to this work lies in the mathematics of the continuum problem. However, for brief discussions see "Comments on Fardella" (PE 103ff.), "Note on Foucher"(PE 145–7) and "Letters to de Volder" (PE 178–86). Note that Leibniz's vocabulary changes through these texts, but the underlying idea seems constant enough.
3. See Descartes, *Principles of Philosophy*, part II, R. Ariew (ed.) (Indianapolis, IN: Hackett, 2000), 255–60, and Leibniz (PE 328ff.).
4. This is analogous but not identical to the more general distinction between a non-living thing's potentiality for movement (*dunamis*) and movement itself (*kinesis*). Aristotle needs two distinctions here because a ball's potential for movement is different from a soul's potential for thought; the ball cannot move itself, for one thing.
5. The relevant passages in Aristotle include "On the Soul" (Ch. II) and "Metaphysics" (Chs VII–IX).
6. Leibniz also felt that energy was a better description of the fundamental, conserved quantity of phenomenal motion. This is because he thought it was non-relational in nature, and thus fits much better with the ideality of space and time.
7. Leibniz's famous correspondence with Samuel Clarke is the primary source for these arguments. This correspondence is published on its own, and substantial selections are also found in most anthologies.
8. This "beyond" is not quantitative in nature; rather, it follows from the ontological characterization of monads in terms of perception. Nevertheless, the human mind is an imitation of the mind of God in so far as it can recognize and work with distinctly thought objects of pure reason (necessary truths) through the "natural light".
9. For a more thorough discussion, please see my entry on Leibniz in the Internet Encyclopedia of Philosophy www.utm.edu/research/iep/.

Bibliography

Works by Leibniz in English

Leibniz, G. W. 1956. *Correspondence with Clarke*, N. Alexander (ed.). Manchester: Manchester University Press.
Leibniz, G. W. 1966. *Logical Papers*, G. H. R. Parkinson (ed. and trans.). Oxford: Oxford University Press.
Leibniz, G. W. 1967. *Leibniz–Arnauld Correspondence*, H. T. Mason (ed. and trans.).

Manchester: Manchester University Press.

Leibniz, G. W. 1972. *Political Writings of Leibniz*, P. Riley (ed. and trans.). Cambridge: Cambridge University Press.

Leibniz, G. W. 1973. *Philosophical Writings*, G. H. R. Parkinson (ed.), M. Morris & G. H. R. Parkinson (trans.). London: Everyman.

Leibniz, G. W. 1985. *Theodicy* (T), A. Farrer (ed.), E. M. Huggard (trans.). Chicago, IL: Open Court.

Leibniz, G. W. 1989. *Philosophical Essays* (PE), R. Ariew & D. Graber (eds and trans.). Indianapolis, IN: Hackett.

Leibniz, G. W. 1996. *New Essays Concerning Human Understanding* (NECHU), P. Remnant & J. Bennett (eds and trans.). Cambridge: Cambridge University Press.

Leibniz, G. W. 1998. *Philosophical Texts* (PT), R. Francks & R. S. Woolhouse (eds and trans.). Oxford: Oxford University Press.

Leibniz, G. W. 2001. *Labyrinth of the Continuum*, R. T. W. Arthur (ed. and trans.). New Haven, CT: Yale University Press.

Other works

Brown, S. 1984. *Leibniz*. Minneapolis, MN: University of Minnesota Press.

Cottingham, J. 1996. *Western Philosophy*. Oxford: Blackwell.

Descartes, R. 2000. *Principles of Philosophy*, part II, R. Ariew (ed.). Indianapolis, IN: Hackett.

Hooker, M. (ed.) 1982. *Leibniz: Critical and Interpretative Essays*. Minneapolis, MN: University of Minnesota Press.

Jolley, N. (ed.) 1995. *The Cambridge Companion to Leibniz*. Cambridge: Cambridge University Press.

Jolley, N. 1998. *The Light of the Soul: Theories of Ideas in Leibniz, Malbranche, and Descartes*. Oxford: Clarendon Press.

Mercer, C. 2001. *Leibniz Metaphysics*. Cambridge: Cambridge University Press.

Rescher, N. 1979. *Leibniz*. Oxford: Blackwell.

Rescher, N. 2003. *On Leibniz*. Pittsburgh, PA: University of Pittsburgh Press.

Russell, B. 1992. *A Critical Exposition of the Philosophy of Leibniz*. London: Routledge.

Wilson, C. 1989. *Leibniz's Metaphysics: A Historical and Comparative Study*. Manchester: Manchester University Press.

Wilson, C. (ed.) 2001. *Leibniz*. Dartmouth: Ashgate.

Woolhouse, R. S. 1993. *Descartes, Spinoza, Leibniz: The Concept of Substance in Seventeenth Century Metaphysics*. London: Routledge.

Woolhouse, R. S. (ed.) 1993. *Gottfried Wilhelm Leibniz: Critical Assessments*, 4 vols. London: Routledge.

Further reading

The Hackett (1989) and Oxford (1998) anthologies are both excellent and both contain the *Monadology*. Anyone wishing to pursue Leibniz's thought further would also need the *New Essays* (1996), the *Correspondence with Clarke* (1956) and probably also the *Theodicy* (1985).

Of secondary books, Brown (1984), Mercer (2001) and Rescher (2003) are all good, but I would recommend the *Cambridge Companion to Leibniz* (Jolley 1995) and other anthologies of essays as better places to start for most readers. It may be large and intimidating, but don't overlook the four volumes of Woolhouse's *Gottfried Wilhelm Leibniz: Critical Assessments* (1993) either. Russell's *Critical Exposition of the Philosophy of Leibniz* (1992) is a classic, but is of largely historical interest now.

4

Thomas Hobbes
Leviathan

G. A. J. Rogers

Introduction

Hobbes's most important philosophical work in English was undoubtedly *Leviathan*, which was published right in the middle of the seventeenth century, in 1651. It is too often regarded as a work of political philosophy only, when any serious attention to its texts shows it to be much more than that, containing as it does elements drawn from Hobbes's wider account of human beings and the world, which is his whole philosophical system. In that sense it can be argued that *Leviathan* is part of a complete philosophy, which stands in marked contrast with the then still most influential philosophy in Europe, that of the ancient Greek Aristotle. In the thirteenth century Thomas Aquinas had combined Aristotle's philosophy with Christian theology into a synthesis that came to dominate the universities, then just being created across Europe, for the next four hundred years. It was Hobbes's objective to supply an alternative and superior system to that of Aristotle and his Christian followers that would combine an atomistic materialism with an account of knowledge and society that would identify an intelligible and practical system of government where peace and prosperity would flourish. The name "Leviathan" derives from the Bible. It is described as a large and powerful sea creature, impossible to defeat, with whom it is not even possible to enter a contract (see especially Job 42). In its fearful aspect it perhaps detracts from Hobbes's intention to reveal the state – "that mortal God" – which Leviathan represents, as a necessary force for human good, second only in power and importance for humanity to God himself.

That Hobbes chose a biblical source for the image and title of his *magnum opus* is significant. The place of religion within his philosophy is central. To give some indication of that we might note that the Bible is cited over seven hundred times in the text and more than half the book is devoted to discussing politics and religion. Nor should this surprise us. Hobbes was quite sure that religious belief was very much part of human nature and differences in religious views were perhaps the single greatest cause of civil and international conflict. When he wrote *Leviathan*, the English Civil War, in substantial part fuelled by religious differences, had scarcely finished and in continental Europe the Thirty Years War between Protestant and Catholic countries had raged for three decades with terrible destruction and loss of life.

Although Hobbes never actually says it in so many words, he clearly believed that *Leviathan* was a work of science. In the seventeenth century "science" was a term taken over from the Latin "*scientia*", meaning knowledge. To talk of anything being a science was to claim that it was knowledge, and stood in contrast with conjecture or hypothesis or even natural histories, which were not causal explanations but simply a catalogue of facts. Science for Hobbes also had another crucial property. It was not just any kind of knowledge, it was knowledge of causes. He explained what he meant by this. Science is true philosophy and true philosophy is knowledge of causes. As an example he asks us to consider a circle. A circle is a figure that is generated by the rotation of a point at an equal distance from another point (e.g. by using a compass). When we understand this we know what a circle is through an understanding of how such a figure can be produced.[1]

Science in this sense, the sense that it is certain knowledge of causes, was very limited, and Hobbes made a famous statement, which, if not modest, nevertheless has much truth in it. He wrote in the Introduction to his Latin work *De Corpore* [*Of Body*] that the science of astronomy was created by the Greeks, that the science of motion was created by Galileo, the science of the human body by William Harvey and the science of politics was no older than his own work *De Cive* [*The Citizen*]. Of course Aristotle had written a very famous work on politics but what Hobbes was claiming was that *De Cive* was the first to demonstrate its conclusions by showing the causes of human social behaviour and therefore the origins and nature of civil society and the state in the conclusive way that marks Euclidean geometrical method. *Leviathan*, published nine years later, covers more comprehensively much the same territory as *De Cive* and employs the same method.

It was especially the example of geometry that provided a standard of proof and knowledge for many philosophers, Hobbes included, in the seventeenth century. The story is that while on his travels as a tutor Hobbes found himself in a library where a copy of Euclid's geometry lay on the table. Hobbes began to read it and, it is said, it happened to be open at the proof of Pythagoras's theorem, that the three angles of a triangle are equal to two right angles. Hobbes was doubtful of the claim but worked backwards through the proof and was at last convinced of its truth. This, it was said by Aubrey, "made him in love with Geometry".[2] What he liked about it was the way in which it was possible to demonstrate unlikely claims, clearly and beyond any reasonable doubt, by the power of reason alone. The truth of the theorem flowed from the truth of the axioms, which were themselves self-evident. It supplied him with a paradigm, which can be found in all his major works, for what counted as demonstrating something to be true from premises that could not be denied. It is a method well employed throughout *Leviathan*.

In a famous fragment of his autobiography Hobbes tells us that "fear and I were born twins. My mother hearing of the Spanish Armada sailing up the English Channel gave premature birth to me". Hobbes often showed courage in his life, not least in fearlessly speaking out for what he saw as the truth, but it cannot be denied that fear plays an important part in his political theory, as we shall see.

The main argument of *Leviathan* can be briefly and easily stated and I shall begin by outlining it in a few words. It is that human beings are by nature self-centred and their most important drive is that for security. Fear of insecurity is the most powerful motivating force in political behaviour. Without government men will compete ceaselessly for the limited goods naturally available and the result will be conflict and the likelihood of an early death. There is no natural basis for any mutual trust as I can see that you want the goods as much as I do and will be as willing as I am to attempt to obtain them by whatever means we may. The only sure way in which this competition can be avoided is by people agreeing to recognize one person as the sovereign power and agreeing to obey that sovereign, whose job it will be to provide stability and peace. With a stable government peace and prosperity can flourish and individuals can live together in harmony. Such is Hobbes's argument. But any brief statement of this kind fails to do justice to the subtlety of Hobbes's philosophy, which has an internal coherence unrivalled by the works of most other major philosophers.

Leviathan Part One

The famous frontispiece of *Leviathan* depicts a huge figure holding a sword and a mace, the symbols of civic power and authority. But the body and limbs of the figure are composed of many smaller figures. The giant figure represents the state and the smaller figures the citizens of which it is composed. The work is divided into four parts, titled "Of Man", "Of Commonwealth", "Of A Christian Commonwealth" and "Of the Kingdom of Darkness". There is a brief Introduction in which Hobbes makes some important points. Part One, "Of Man", by which of course he means "man" in a generic sense, itself divides into two parts. The first of these provides an account of human psychology from his materialist and atomist point of view, which offers an analysis of human motivation, the unique role that speech plays in human interaction, a mechanical account of the passions and the place of power in human action. In the later chapters of Part One, Hobbes examines the implications of his account so far for the behaviour of human beings independently of their living in civil society; this prior state has come to be called "the state of nature".

The account of pre-social human beings as offered is both original and powerful. That Hobbes begins from consideration of the nature of human beings and not with a description of the state is significant. He is going to claim, as the frontispiece already does, that the state is made up of atoms, and these atoms, like the atoms in elements, are to be treated as identical. The individual is, therefore, at the heart of his account, but it is the common characteristics of those individuals, their shared nature, that he wishes first to highlight. Any science must identify universal characteristics of its subject matter. If politics is indeed to be made a science then it is from these characteristics that Hobbes must begin. In Part One of *Leviathan* he begins to set out the major conceptual points that he is going to deploy in his account of the nature and origins of civil society.

In his Introduction, Hobbes shows his deep commitment to the mechanical conception of human beings and nature that is a feature of his general philosophy. Central to this is his ontology: that is, what he takes as the fundamental entities or existing things. According to Hobbes the only things (or perhaps the only finite existing things) are material objects. He says that something is either body or it is nothing, and he really means it. Our human bodies are really mechanical systems, rather like a clock. But it is not only our bodies that are such a system. All our mental life is also the product, and even identical with, matter in motion. There is, according to the implications of Hobbes's analysis, an identity between my experiences, thoughts and memories and the motions of particles in the brain. Hobbes never attempts a thorough examination of this philosophical position, which in recent years has come to be called the mind–brain identity theory. But he was the first to present and argue for it in modern times and it is undoubtedly the case that he thought it was true. In propounding it at all he was well aware that he was putting forward a view that would be condemned by most philosophers and theologians but, with the exception of a few scattered remarks by ancient Greek atomist thinkers, which scarcely amount to an account, its originality can scarcely be doubted.

To appreciate that originality it is worth saying something about the alternative accounts of human beings and the world then widely accepted, with which Hobbes's system stands in marked contrast. According to Aristotle, and later medieval philosophy generally, man was naturally a social animal. If something is natural then it arises from within the object – in this case human beings themselves – entirely spontaneously, without the need for external causes. If human beings are naturally social then no explanation is required for the fact that they live in groups governed by rules and interact socially with others in the familiar way. As such, human beings are responding to their natural inclinations and no further explanation is required. Hobbes, however, has a different picture of human behaviour, which might be characterized as much more individualist. According to this, the primary drives in human beings are self-centred rather than socially orientated. The natural state of man is an isolated one, probably within a small social group – the family – but not in a wider society. The existence of society, then, is not natural but stands in need of explanation.

Hobbes's account goes well beyond any claims known to have been made by any previous philosopher and for this reason alone he deserves full acknowledgement. When he advocated it he well knew it was inconsistent with much traditional Christian teaching and not easily squared with the doctrines of the Church of England. However, he always claimed his views were entirely consistent with the doctrines of the Anglican Church and strove hard to demonstrate this. He returns to such matters in greater detail in his account of the nature of spirit and in his analysis of particular psychological concepts central to persons, such as the emotions, or, as they were usually called in the seventeenth century, the passions.

Hobbes identifies the emotions or passions as the driving forces that generate our behaviour. He also claims that these forces are to be found universally in human beings and it is their universality that enables him to reach a knowledge of general truths about us. Such universal truths are vital if he is to offer a science of human nature and of human society, which of course is his goal. People, he says, have in common a variety of passions – desire, fear and hope, for example – which are the driving forces of our behaviour. Hobbes is careful to say that the objects of these passions, what we individually desire, fear or hope for, may and usually do vary from one person to another, but the underlying passion that leads to those specific wants and fears are common to all. The foundation of this understanding of the common nature in human beings is to be discovered by a careful analysis of our own motivations. When we do so we shall discover, Hobbes says, that the motives for the actions of others are the same as we find in ourselves. It is understanding this common human nature that is vital for anybody who aspires to lead a nation and that he believes his own work, *Leviathan*, will help to reveal.

What then, according to Hobbes, are human beings and how do they acquire knowledge and understanding? Hobbes begins by revealing that he is an empiricist in his account of how we come by knowledge. That is, he believes that all our thoughts derive ultimately from sense-experience. The cause of sense-experience, he says, is always the mechanical action of motion on the five sense-organs – the eyes, ears, nose and so on – which are conveyed to the brain and heart. Hobbes was well aware that the account he was offering of sense-experience and its cause was quite at odds with the Aristotelian account offered in the universities, which Hobbes aspired to replace.

A crucial faculty in Hobbes's account is the imagination, which, like memory he treats as decaying sense. To understand Hobbes's argument we have to see how he employs the new understanding of motion that Galileo had developed, and applies it to the mind, or, for Hobbes, its equivalent, the brain. Just as Hobbes challenged the understanding of natural behaviour so Galileo had earlier abandoned the Aristotelian talk of "natural place" and its accompanying teleological explanation of change – meaning explanation in terms of a final end or goal – and instead offered mathematical descriptions of motion combined with the adoption of the principle of inertia. That principle states that, once in motion, objects will move in straight lines at constant velocity (that is to say in an unchanging way) unless some external factor causes a deviation in that motion. Galileo's account of motion, especially his principle of inertia, was to be very important for Hobbes's account of the imagination and thus to his philosophy of motivation.

According to Hobbes the imagination is crucial in our nature for it is the imagination that leads us to action. Hobbes appeals to the truth of Galileo's principle of inertia to explain how it works. Motions in the brain, caused by sense, continue to move after their cause has disappeared. These motions provide us with images of things that are no longer present or that no longer exist, but that can still motivate us. Our dreams are the product of such motions and so are all our imaginings. It is these imaginings that lead to actions. We imagine something desirable or fearful and, accordingly, move towards it or away from it. Thus, when I want an ice cream I have in my brain motions of atoms, which is my imagining the ice cream in the freezer and what it would taste like. This causes me to move towards the freezer to obtain it. Or, seeing the oncoming bus, I have an image of my body being struck by it and the subsequent pain, and as a result I remain on the pavement.

Whether Hobbes's materialism is a coherent account of the mental remains a matter of contemporary dispute. To be plausible it has to overcome a set of objections that are by no means easily set aside. One of these is the so-called problem of intentionality. It is often taken to be a feature of the mental that it is always directed at an object Thus a desire is always a desire *for* something, a belief is always a belief *about* something, a hope a hope *for* something. This intentional object does not appear to be reducible to any physical property of the brain in the materialist terms that Hobbes's account would appear to require.

Another area of considerable originality and dispute in Hobbes's philosophy relates to his understanding of freedom, or liberty with regard to the will. The nature and existence of free will was a considerable problem not only within philosophy but for theology as well. If we did not act freely how could we be held responsible for our actions, and, therefore, how could we deserve either reward or punishment in this life or the afterlife? The problem of free will seems to take on a particular urgency with the introduction of the mechanical account of human behaviour that we find in Hobbes, but also in an importantly different form in Descartes's philosophy. If Hobbes is right that all there is are bodies in motion and that every new motion is the product of impact of one body on another then there seems little room for free choice on our part. All our decisions being motions in our brains and themselves the product of previous motions, then how can there be free human action? In contrast to Hobbes, for Descartes the answer is that the mind is not a body but a spiritual substance, not subject to physical laws, but capable of causing changes of motion in parts of our bodies to produce our differing, free, actions. But obviously Hobbes cannot appeal to such a spiritual realm within his system. His own answer has come to be known as compatibilism. Although it is usually attributed to David Hume, writing a century after Hobbes, it is Hobbes who deserves the credit for its introduction into modern discussion. Hobbes begins from the premise that all human beings believe that every event has a cause. If this is true then it applies to all human thoughts and actions as well as to any movements in the inanimate world. But being free, Hobbes says, is nothing to do with being uncaused, but with being unhindered. Hobbes's own words on the subject are as clear as anything we might wish: "Liberty or Freedom", he writes,

> signifieth (properly) the absence of opposition; (by opposition, I mean external impediments of motion) and may be applied no less to irrational and inanimate creatures than to rational. For whatsoever is so tied or environed, as it cannot move, but within a certain space, which space is determined by the opposition of some external body, we say it hath not liberty to go further.[3]   (L: 166–67; EW III: 196)

95

So human beings have liberty just in so far as nothing (or nobody) prevents their action. Lack of liberty is always a matter of external constraint. Hobbes sees no conflict between talking of human behaviour as always being caused by previous events internal to the person and it being free, that is, not prevented by any external circumstance. The water is free to flow down hill, if there is no dam preventing it, and the person is free if nothing physically prevents that person from acting. Hobbes is quite happy to accept that this means that we can still be said to be free to do something, even though we are under threat if we do or do not so act. We can still choose to do the action even if it has unpleasant consequences; it becomes a factor in our reaching our decision but not a determining one.

So far human behaviour is identical with that of animals. But in one respect we differ from them. For human beings have the capacity to use words and communicate with others by speech. This is the attribute that distinguishes us from all other animals and provides us with all those other goals and fears that animals cannot have. It enables us to communicate with others about things that do or do not yet exist and also to develop methods of both communication and deception (lying) in characteristically human ways. Words are used "to transfer our mental discourse into verbal" (L: 27; EW III: 19).[4] They are essentially names. As such they are always names of particular things, for all that exists, Hobbes says, is particular: *Peter, John, this tree*. We do, however, have universal terms as well, such as *man, horse* and *tree*. But, says Hobbes, these do not denote any particular thing. They just recall "any one of those many" (L: 28; EW III: 21). This is Hobbes's nominalism: that only particulars can be said to exist and that all universal terms must be explicable in terms of particulars if they are to have meaning. Successful communication and also correct reasoning, Hobbes says, depends on clear and precise definitions of our terms. It is lack of clarity and confusion in our language that too often mislead us and lead us to absurd beliefs. Words, he says, "are wise mens counters, they do but reckon by them: but they are the money of fools" (L: 31; EW III: 25) and by this he means that one should not rely on the authority of famous people for the implications of words but work them out for oneself.

Hobbes was one of the first people in modern times to see the importance of language to our thinking and it was central to his account of reason. The paradigm of reasoning, Hobbes says, is arithmetic, adding or subtracting, which, when it is done in words, is "conceiving of the consequence of the names of all the parts, to the name of the whole" (L: 35; EW III: 29). Good reasoning, then, is always going to depend on good definition. In contrast, absurdity is substantially the product of confusions in our language. These can be avoided not just by experience but only when aided by "industry": the careful imposition of names combined with the adoption of an orderly method to move from names to sentences and then on to the deductions made from them. Hobbes sums up his account by saying that the proper use of language depends on exact definitions, which will help to increase our knowledge and thus benefit mankind.

Human behaviour is governed, Hobbes says, by our emotions. Our actions are voluntary motions triggered by the internal promptings of our desires and aversions. Things we desire, for the most part, we call "good", and things to which we are averse we call "evil". Hobbes offers us definitions of many of the words used for our emotions, such as for hope, which he defines as an "appetite with an opinion of attaining" it (L: 46; EW III: 43), and curiosity, which Hobbes sees as a uniquely human emotion, as "desire to know why and how" (L: 47; EW III: 44).

Hobbes's account of good and evil in terms of desire and aversion has often been taken to imply that he is a subjectivist about morality but nothing could be more wrong. It is a kind of psychological truth for Hobbes that we call things to which we are averse, "evil" and things we desire "good". But for him, through the use of our reason, we have the ability to see, for example that certain actions are just and others unjust. Thus it is plain obvious that punishing the innocent is wrong and punishing the guilty is just. We can also see that actions that conflict with the laws of nature, themselves understood as moral injunctions that we can discover by reason and that are certainly true (see below) are wrong and ones that follow from those laws are right. Hobbes is thus never a mere subjectivist about morality and any reading of him that implies that he is, is mistaken. However, he was often taken to be a subjectivist who was committed to the claim that whatever we decide is right is right and that there could be no independent criterion that might be employed.

When he turns to knowledge Hobbes give us two kinds, which he calls "knowledge of fact" or absolute knowledge and "knowledge of the consequence of one affirmation to another" which is conditional (L: 67; EW III: 71). As an example of the latter he gives, "If the figure be a circle, then any straight line through the centre shall divide it into two equal parts" (L: 67; EW III: 71). (Given what we have already seen, it is no surprise that Hobbes's examples of certain knowledge are often taken from geometry.) It is the latter kind of knowledge that is required in a philosopher. The former kind is called "history" (as in natural history). Hobbes then offers us a table of the branches of this kind of knowledge, which includes as two major sub-divisions "Consequences from the Accidents [or properties] of bodies natural; which is called Natural Philosophy" and "Consequences from the Accidents of *Politique* Bodies; which is called Politics and Civil Philosophy" (L: 68; EW III: 72). The latter is the science he claims to have invented, which he is now offering us in *Leviathan*.

Pursuing his account of the nature of human beings, Hobbes turns to the nature and place of power. Power is our ability to get what we want. Obviously we always want to get what we want so power is central to our lives. Hobbes stresses that there are many sources of power, but they include riches, reputation, success and nobility. The sciences, however, and therefore Hobbes's own writings, are but small power as only a small band of initiated can appreciate intellectual achievement. But the power of one individual is as nothing compared to the power of a group united under one leader. Power is so important that Hobbes sees obtaining it as a driving force in our lives. He writes:

> I put it for a general inclination of all mankind, a perpetual and restless desire of power after power, that ceaseth only in death. And the cause of this, is not always that a man hopes for a more intensive delight, than he has already attained to; or that he cannot be content with a moderate power: but because he cannot assure the power and means to live well, which he hath present, without the acquisition of more. (L: 80; EW III: 86)

So we all seek power so that we can continue to enjoy security, protect what is already ours, increase our holdings and obtain other benefits that power brings. Nor is there any natural upper limit to the amount of power we might seek. Even the millionaire seeks to make another million and the emperor seeks to expand his empire. Left to itself, then, this restless desire for more is certain to lead to conflicts unless it is controlled in some way.

We find a significant change of direction in Hobbes's presentation in Chapter 12, "Of Religion". Religion, although in part a feature of isolated human beings, is also for Hobbes a very important social phenomenon and therefore relates strongly to man in society. Hobbes offers a variety of insights into the nature of religious belief, including its corruption by superstition and by clergy who take advantage of the ignorance of many ordinary people to advance their own causes.

Although we have already noted it, it is worth stressing here that even before Hobbes published *Leviathan* he was well known as subscribing to a form of materialism. But it is important to realize that Hobbes did not see this as implying any kind of atheism. It was, however, taken by Hobbes to imply mortalism, a not uncommon belief in mid-seventeenth-century England. Mortalism was the view that we really did cease to exist when our body parts were dispersed following death, but that at the resurrection God would reassemble them again into our original bodies, and therefore with our original minds and memories, for the Last Judgement. Once again, Hobbes saw mortalism as entirely consistent with the Scriptures. Although throughout his long adult life he was regarded by many as an atheist, he was always quick to deny it. Even if this might be regarded as the prudent thing to do, he also gave ample testimony to the effect that he was a loyal member of the Church of England until his dying day. In *Leviathan* he early gave it as his view that God's infinite attributes made it impossible to say anything coherent about God's nature because our finite minds cannot make sense of infinities. All we can know is that he does exist, and that all that human beings can do is honour him.

In Chapter 12 Hobbes begins by offering what we might see as an explanation for the strong inclination human beings have for believing in a deity. He begins by pointing out that of all living creatures in our experience, only human beings believe in God. This belief has a variety of causes. Thus human beings are inquisitive about the causes of events. When we can discover no apparent or rational cause then it is tempting to invent explanations. It is also natural to look for the causes of our own good luck or misfortune in life. Secondly, when something comes into existence it is natural for us to want to know why it did so and why at that particular time. We suppose that some agent is responsible for our state and are fearful of its power over us. This might lead us to a belief in many gods, as did the ancient gentiles, which itself in time led to religious toleration within the Roman Empire, where the worship of different gods was permitted. It might also lead to a recognition that the causal chain of events must lead endlessly back in time unless there is just one first cause of them all. It was this alternative that Hobbes seems to have accepted. There was, he thought, a single all powerful first cause, which can be identified with what we can call God.

The first important monotheists were the Jews. Hobbes points out that their belief in just one God had important social consequences. They believed that God had by revelation given to them a commandment to worship him alone and had given them rules of behaviour set out in the Ten Commandments and other rules of conduct. As a result the Jews

> thought it unlawful to acknowledge subjection to any mortal king or state … where God himself, by supernatural revelation, planted religion; there he also made to himself a peculiar kingdom and gave laws, not only of behaviour towards himself but also towards one another. (L: 95; EW III: 105–6)

It was this that put them at odds with the Roman Empire and led to their persecution, which spread also into the condemnation of Christianity, which shared Jewish positions about the relationship between religion and the state.

Other important facets of religion were its promises to foretell the future and to correct perceived injustices with the promise of eternal rewards and punishments. The failures of the ancient gentile religions and the success of

Christianity are in part explained by the corruption of the ancient gentile priests; similar causes account for the rejection of the authority of the Pope in the Protestant countries at the Reformation.

Hobbes's almost sociological treatment of religion was unlikely to endear him to his detractors but we can be impressed with its very modern causal account of the phenomenon of religious belief without Hobbes at any point indicating that he was not himself a committed Christian. Indeed, he can be said to face up to difficult questions about the authority of religion in people's lives in a way that remains a powerful account to this day.

The state of nature

In the remaining chapters of Part One, Hobbes offers us an analysis of key concepts that he is to use in the account of civil society that is to come in Part Two. In the first of these he gives us his most famous picture of the nature of the human condition, which is central to his whole argument and which has captured the imagination of many who know nothing else about him. The chapter is entitled "Of the Natural condition of Mankind, as concerning their Felicity and Misery", although in truth it is much more about "misery" than "felicity". In his account Hobbes is going to ask us to imagine how human beings would behave towards one another in a situation in which there was no independent authority overseeing them. This picture has come to be called Hobbes's account of "the state of nature". His answer, if true, is frightening. Whether it is altogether plausible is often doubted but it may not be as far from the truth as many have hoped.

The starting-point of Hobbes's account is his belief that individuals are primarily concerned with their own survival. Our most basic desire is to continue to live beyond the present. This is Hobbes's psychological egotism, the view that our most driving urge is for our individual self-survival, manifest no doubt at its most basic when we seek to run away from a perceived imminent danger, perhaps with little consideration for others in a similar condition. Of course we know that not everybody acts so selfishly. Some human beings do very brave things. But bravery, Hobbes would say, is a social virtue that comes into play in any major way only within the framework of society and plays little role in the pre-social condition.

Granted the egotism, then, the next factor in Hobbes's account is our natural belief that, with regards to the goods that naturally exist, our rights to them are at least equal to those of anybody else. This claim, about the equality of human beings, which is not unconnected to their egotism, is crucial to the whole of Hobbes's positive system. When Hobbes says that everybody is naturally equal he does not mean that everybody is the same as everybody else either in strength or intelligence. Manifestly they are not. But they are not so different in natural qualities that it is obvious that one person ought to be preferred or give way to another. As Hobbes puts it,

> From this equality of ability ariseth equality of hope in the attaining of our ends. And therefore if any two men desire the same thing, which nevertheless they cannot both enjoy, they become enemies; and in the way to their end ... endeavour to destroy or subdue one another. (L: 100; EW III: 111)

Without an external authority to settle our disputes we soon resort to force. Perceived equality, then, leaves no natural way in which to settle disputes as there is no natural hierarchy among human beings. In such a condition, mankind "without a common power to keep them all in awe" (*ibid.*) is in a state of war. This does not necessarily entail actual conflict but only the real possibility that a resort to violence may arise to settle a dispute. Hobbes, in his probably most often quoted words, says that in this state of nature,

> there is no place for industry, because the fruit thereof is uncertain, and consequently no culture of the earth, no navigation, nor use of the commodities that may be imported by sea ... no account of time, no arts, no letters, no society, and which is worst of all, continual fear and danger of violent death, and the life of man, solitary, poor, nasty, brutish and short. (L: 102; EW III: 113)

Hobbes is aware that many people believe that there was never such a time as this but he reminds us that some societies, as described by travellers from Africa and the Americas, appeared in the seventeenth century as still being very close to that condition. Further, the relationship between state and state was too often also a state of war, at least analogous to the relationship between human beings in the state of nature. No doubt, too, Hobbes was well aware of the atrocities committed in both the English Civil War, of very recent memory, and the Thirty Years War in continental Europe, with enormous loss of life. The implication of Hobbes's vision of inter-state conflict would seem to imply that the only rational move is to seek a world government, but that in its turn would require a sovereign power the likes of which has never yet been even a remote possibility.

But there is perhaps a more fruitful way to regard Hobbes's account of the state of nature. We can think of it not as an attempt to reconstruct our early history but as a kind of thought experiment. Thought experiments were very common in the new physics of Galileo and others. Thus Galileo asks us to imagine a variety of simple experiments in order to grasp more clearly what a particular concept entails. Consider an object in free fall, he suggests. Falling, it accelerates according to a precise law. Now think of an object rising, say a stone thrown vertically in the air. It de-accelerates at precisely the same rate. Now consider an object falling or rising vertically and then changing direction to the horizontal. In this plane it would not have a tendency to accelerate nor to de-accelerate and would in principle move on a horizontal plane at constant velocity for ever. It was just such thought experiments that helped Galileo reach the principle of inertial motion. That the experiment is impossible actually to do in practice was no impediment to its illumination. Hobbes, with his picture of the state of nature, may equally be inviting us to participate in a thought experiment. To consider how human beings would behave if the restrictions imposed by a civil power were removed we do not have to understand Hobbes as saying that there was ever such an historical state, even though some human conditions seem to approach very close to the one that he envisages. All that is needed is that, if Hobbes's psychology of human beings is correct, it gives an accurate picture of how human beings would behave in this hypothetical state.

The laws of nature

In the condition of the state of nature, Hobbes goes on to claim, there is no justice or injustice: "Where there is no common power, there is no law, where no law, no injustice. Force and fraud are in war the two cardinal virtues" (L: 103; EW III: 115). Obviously life in such conditions is intolerable. Human beings long for peace, and reason suggests "convenient articles of peace, upon which men may be drawn to agreement" (*Ibid.*). These articles are, Hobbes says, what are called the laws of nature. The use of this phrase should not mislead us into thinking that Hobbes's laws of nature are of the same kind as the laws of nature as understood in the natural sciences. In the natural sciences the laws of nature are descriptive of how objects actually behave. Thus Newton's law of gravitation says that any object attracts another with a force proportional to their masses and inversely proportional to the square of the distance between them. This is a description of how massy objects behave in relation to one another, and Boyle's law of gases and Hooke's law of springs are also descriptive. In contrast, laws of nature, understood as Hobbes was using the term, are prescriptive, not descriptive. They say how rational human beings should behave, not necessarily how actually we do. Unfortunately for us not everybody does keep to these kinds of law, hence the need for a sovereign power.

The laws of nature play a crucial role in Hobbes's account of the foundation of the state and thus of political science and society. What a law of nature is Hobbes makes very clear: it is "a precept or general rule found out by reason" whereby a person is forbidden to do that which threatens his life. In the state of nature everybody has a right to everything, even another's body, and it is the lack of security to which this leads that is contrary to the interest of everyone. Consequently it is, says Hobbes, a general rule of reason "That every man ought to endeavour peace, as far as he has hope of attaining it, and wherein he cannot obtain it, that he may seek and use all helps and advantages of war" (L: 105; EW III: 117). This law is binding on everybody without exception and is known to us all through our natural rational faculty. As we have already noted, that the law is so binding gives the lie to the claim that Hobbes is a moral subjectivist.

From the first law of nature, Hobbes says, there logically follows a second: "That a man be willing, when others are so too, as far-forth as for peace and defence of himself he shall think it necessary, to lay down his right to all things, and be contented with so much liberty against other men as he would allow other men against himself" (L: 105; EW III: 118). Hobbes immediately associates this with the law of the Gospel, which Hobbes glosses as "whatsoever you require that others should do to you, that do yet to them" (*ibid.*), thereby directly linking his own account with Christian doctrine.

When a right is transferred voluntarily, as is the force of the second law, then there is somebody to whom that right is transferred. Furthermore, when a transfer is made it can only be understood as done for the sake of some benefit for the person giving up the right, otherwise it would be absurd or unintelligible. Such mutual transfers are, says Hobbes, contracts. It is these contracts that establish civil society. Contracts can only be made between language users, as they are essentially verbal. Further, the persons who enter a contract must be in a position to keep the contract; they must be able to deliver on the contract. If they are not then the contract is null and void. However, a contract does not fail to be binding if it is entered into because of fear or intimidation. Such contracts are as binding as ones entered into without any threat because it is still a free agreement, even under threat, says Hobbes. We could refuse to enter into such an agreement, even if the alternative is unpleasant, even death. However, the only sure way by which we can guarantee people keeping their contracts is fear. If they break them then they must know that they are likely to suffer for it. Good will is not enough. The keeping of contracts requires that the person with whom one contracts is powerful enough to make non-compliance the irrational choice.

From this second law of nature a substantial number of further laws follow logically, Hobbes says. The first of these is that we should keep our covenants because not to do so, even when it appears to our advantage, is almost always imprudent, although whether that counts as a moral reason for keeping them is somewhat problematic. Other laws require us to show gratitude for benefits bestowed gratuitously by others, and to try to accommodate others, pardon offences and not seek revenge if it will have bad consequences, and there are a further dozen others, although no doubt Hobbes could have offered many more if he wished. They are all summed up, he says, by the injunction: "do not that to another, which thou wouldest not have done to thy self" (L: 126; EW III: 145).

The status of Hobbes's laws of nature is far from clear. Some of them appear to be truths of reason, the denial of which appear to be contradictions. Others seem to be rules of prudence. Others hover in between. Hobbes himself sometimes treats them as theorems and at other times as edicts of the deity. There is probably no single answer to the question of their status. But it is probably true that to ignore them is, in some wide sense of rationality, always an irrational act, and perhaps that is all that Hobbes requires of them. But it is important to see that for Hobbes any law implies a lawgiver, because laws are commands issued by an authority. Hobbes would no doubt have been keen to point out that the lawgiver is of course God, who embodies reason, for Hobbes perhaps literally. In other words, to identify them as laws entails a commitment to the existence of a commanding deity. But he also acknowledges that the laws could be construed as rules of prudence, binding on us as rational beings. So understood they would not have to be seen as commands from a higher authority but simply as rules of practical reason, binding on any finite rational creature who could come to understand them, including, of course, any person who came to occupy the position of sovereign within a state. Either way, whether understood as commands of a deity or self-imposed rational behaviour they have a strong sanction to support them: the wrath of God in the next life and/or the horrors of the state of nature in this.

Hobbes's account of the state of nature and the introduction of the contract to escape its awful consequences is often attacked for the following reason. How could any rational person in the state of nature enter into a contract of the kind required? Without a power already in place to enforce it we would have no reason to suppose it would be kept by the other parties. Without a guarantee how can it be rational, therefore, to make any such agreement? Hobbes has various possible answers to this challenge, of which perhaps the most convincing is that the hope that people will keep the contract long enough to establish the state and its power of enforcement is more rational than to continue in the uncertainty of the state of nature. It is, in other words, our only rational hope. As it is also to the advantage of the others to recognize the contract and for it to work there is more chance of its success than not. Against this it is often argued that if human beings are as self-centred as Hobbes claims then they would never trust each other enough to take the risk. To which Hobbes would no doubt reply that fear of remaining in the state of nature would be sufficient to produce the result he predicts. We might also note that even if Hobbes is over-pessimistic about human nature it may well be that his model of explaining society in terms of a contract is fruitful enough to be a very useful hypothesis to explain much about the moral basis of society. Certainly he was neither the first nor the last to make use of the notion to explain and justify the institution of a sovereign. Hobbes recognized that somebody might reason as follows: I shall enter the contract, that is agree to observe it, but then renege whenever it appears to be in my interest. Hobbes's answer is that only a fool would take such a risk, for he would soon discover that reneging brought swift retribution, leaving the cheat back in the state of nature or worse.

The commonwealth

Having given his picture of life in the state of nature and the injunctions that hold there, in Book II, "Of Commonwealth", Hobbes considers the conditions required for the creation of a state and their implications. Unlike animals that naturally live in groups, such as bees and ants, naturally egotistical human beings will only obey the laws of nature if they see that as to their advantage. Hobbes says that this requires a contract that is sanctioned by a power sufficient to keep the group in awe of it and enforce compliance. So the creation of that common power becomes a priority and can be achieved only through a contract of the parties who wish to enter into such an agreement. It is, Hobbes says, "as if every man should say to every man, I authorise and give up my right of governing myself to this man, or to this assembly of men, on this condition, that thou give up thy right to him, and authorise his actions in like manner" (L: 136–7; EW III: 158). It is this contract that establishes the commonwealth, "that great Leviathan ... that mortal God, to which we owe under the immortal God, our peace and defence" (L: 137; EW III: 158).

Hobbes's view that the state is founded on a contract and is therefore artificial and not natural was linked by him to two other crucial doctrines: the equality of all the citizens within the state to be bound by the contract and the obligation on the person identified as the sovereign to act with the aid of his citizens to provide the conditions of peace and common defence that the Leviathan had been created to provide.

Thus created, the power of the sovereign, according to Hobbes, is necessarily considerable. The physical power of the sovereign is a sum of the power of each of the individuals who agree to become citizens. In a very straightforward sense the sovereign has at his disposal all those individuals who have agreed to obey his command by entering into the contract. Although he is bound by the law of nature in his actions, as is everybody both within and outside the state, it is the sovereign who must decide on, formulate, propagate and enforce the laws that he enacts. He alone must decide what needs to be done to protect the state and its individual members and to provide the conditions for peace and prosperity. Of course, the sovereign has a duty to obey the laws of nature, but within that framework he can decide to take whatever actions he believes are needed, including making appropriate laws within the state, enforcing them and going to war with other states, to protect the Leviathan's interest, that is, the interests of the covenanted citizens. Further, since the sovereign is the one person who must decide on all legislation and state actions there can be no appeal against his decision; nor can he ever be accused by any of his citizens of acting unjustly because the law is his decision alone. He thus has complete power to determine the distribution of goods within the state and to make whatever laws he believes are necessary for peace and security. It is not surprising, then, that Hobbes has been seen as authorizing a form of dictatorship, or even tyranny. He, however, and with some good reason, would deny this. First of all, in any society there has to be some final arbiter of what is legal action on the part of the government and, whoever that arbiter is, the decision is necessarily one against which there cannot be appeal. Further, the sovereign must always act within the framework of the law of nature, even though he must himself decide which action might be held to violate that law. Furthermore, if the citizens were to decide that a supposed sovereign was not providing them with peace and security they would not in fact obey those laws that they saw as threatening them, a state of affairs that could soon lead to civil war.

It is worth adding something here about Hobbes's account of law. We have seen that laws are commands and so require a commander who has the authority to issue them. This requires the recognition of that authority by those who are commanded. But anybody who fails to recognize that authority places themselves in a state of war with the power who purports to be that authority and is thereby entitled to use whatever power lies at his disposal to enforce his will. Normally this will be the full power of the state. But might not some person refuse to obey a given law because he or she regarded it as unjust? For Hobbes such a view of any particular law – the view that I am excused from breaking a law because I take it to be unjust – rests on a confusion. For any command of the sovereign is by its very nature just. There is no further appeal possible, for whoever could decide on the appeal would, by that authority, be the sovereign power. What the law is and what the just law is are, for Hobbes, identical. In entering into civil society I have thereby agreed to accept the command of the sovereign power. Of course, I may claim that the law as promulgated conflicts with the law of nature. But who is to decide if this is true or not? The only possible person to make that judgement is, once again, the sovereign. For Hobbes the law is always and simply the edicts, suitably promulgated, of the sovereign. There are or can be no others and there can be no appeal against them to any higher authority.

This said, there was, for Hobbes, an important exception to our requirement to obey the sovereign, which goes right to the heart of Hobbes's political philosophy. The reason why anybody enters the social contract and becomes a member of civil society is to protect himself against the threats of the state of nature. It would therefore be quite irrational to allow that I should accept without protest any harms done to me by the state. I would retain a residual right to protect myself against punishment and injury. It is, then, for Hobbes, quite right for the condemned man to try to escape from jail to avoid capital punishment. So Hobbes would not have agreed with Socrates, who chose to accept the punishment of death imposed by the Athenians, out of respect for the laws of Athens, when he could have escaped. For Hobbes, Socrates's action was irrational, induced by his love of Athens.

Hobbes was, of course, well aware that there were a variety of possible constitutions that a state could adopt. Of these there were three basic kinds – monarchy, democracy or aristocracy – according to the number of people who exercise sovereignty. But Hobbes seems always to have favoured one-person rule. A major advantage was that in a monarchy the public and private interest of the sovereign coincide. And there cannot be a conflict of interest if there is only one ruler, whereas a democracy or aristocracy can develop internal conflicts, which lead to civil war. There are other major disadvantages to democratic or aristocratic forms of government that, in a variety of ways, lead to weak government, a major fault for Hobbes, which he always saw as leading to a risk of civil war or economic decline. A major weakness in a monarchy concerns the right of succession and how it may be determined. But although Hobbes saw problems here he was inclined to favour the right of the nearest male relative to be given inheritance. He favoured a male line for the reason that "men are naturally fitter than women for actions of labour and danger" (L: 157; EW III: 183), reasons that, whatever their merit in the seventeenth century, hardly apply today. He never seems to have considered the possibility of presidential rule, where a leader is elected by the citizens, but if he had it would have counted as a kind of monarchy.

There is much in Book 2 of *Leviathan* that relates to quite specific matters of state government and the laws that need to be enacted for a civilized society to flourish. Further, it is always precisely expressed and well argued, but not always likely to hold the attention of a reader in the early twenty-first century. But some matters raise important questions for Hobbes's whole programme. He is aware of many of these and takes care to try to meet possible objections. One relates to punishment. A punishment, he says, is an evil inflicted by public authority on somebody who has broken the law. Its point is to discourage further breaking of the law by either the person being punished or by others. Hobbes recognized that the institution of punishment raises an important question about its legality, given his claim that people only join the commonwealth voluntarily for their own benefit, yet punishment is, by definition, something unpleasant, normally inflicted on such a voluntary member of society. Hobbes's answer is that when the contract was entered the only person who is not a party to it is the sovereign; recall that it is the citizens who agree one with another to accept some person or group as sovereign, and the sovereign himself makes no such contract. So the sovereign retains the right he had in the state of nature to take action against transgressors (except that he must not in so doing infringe the law of nature). As Hobbes puts it, "For the subjects did not give the sovereign that right [the right to punish] but only in laying down theirs, strengthened him to use his own [right to inflict harm through punishment]" (L: 245; EW III: 298). Of course, it follows from this that, within the state, private individuals can never, as a matter of logic, punish; punishment must always be something inflicted by public authority. For the private individual never has a right to impose on another citizen something that is a harm (e.g. deprivation of goods, incarceration, physical beating or death) whereas the sovereign, through the state, is entitled to impose such harms, for example, fines, imprisonment or even capital punishment.

Another very important matter relates to civil liberty. Hobbes claims that within the state and apart from the laws of nature, which are universally binding, citizens are only required to obey those laws that have been properly promulgated. With regard to all other behaviour the liberty of the citizen is "the silence of the law. In cases where the sovereign has prescribed no rule, there the subject has the liberty to do or forbear, according to his own discretion" (L: 175; EW III: 206).

The last chapter in Book 2 is titled "Of the Kingdom of God by Nature", and in it Hobbes makes some important remarks about religion and the state. Hobbes's words often imply a commitment to religion that is quite at odds with those who wished to saddle him with the label "atheist". Thus he writes, "Whether men will or not, they must be subject always to the divine power. By denying the existence or providence of God men may shake off their ease but not their yoke" (L: 280; EW III: 344). God, Hobbes says, can only be said to reign if he governs by his word and by promise of rewards and punishments. To rule by words requires that we can come to know what God's word is. There are two ways in which we can do this, Hobbes says. The first of these is by natural reason, as with the laws of nature, which all men can be said to comprehend and see by reason to be true. The second is by revelation: God speaking to individuals directly or through a prophet. God's right to reign is guaranteed by his infinite and irresistible power. It would always be irrational not to obey him. But disputes can easily arise among men about how best to honour God, and here Hobbes is very clear that the head of the state, the sovereign, must also be head of the church and decide about matters of dispute and interpretation of religious practice. He thus confirmed the English practice, since Henry VIII declared himself head of the Church of England, that the monarch was sovereign of both state and church. Any other solution, Hobbes claimed, would only lead to civil strive and weaken the authority of the sovereign, with dangerous consequences for civil peace.

Hobbes ends Book 2 of *Leviathan* with an appeal: that a sovereign (perhaps Cromwell or Charles II) will read it carefully and adopt as policy the understanding of justice within the state that it contains. He concludes with the thought that the sovereign "in protecting the public teaching of it, convert this truth of speculation into the utility of practice" (L: 290; EW III: 358). It is interesting to know that Hobbes gave Charles II, still in exile in Paris, a beautifully prepared manuscript copy of *Leviathan* (now in the British Library). Whether he ever read it we shall probably never know.

The Christian commonwealth

With Book 3 of *Leviathan* we have a substantial change in methodology. In the first two books, Hobbes tells us, he has derived his argument from the resources of natural reason and definitions universally agreed. But in the book titled "Of a Christian Commonwealth" he will now draw not only on reason but also on revelation to argue his case. The latter is the second way in which God communicates with us, the prophetical method of informing us of his intentions for the world, and here, of course, it is the Bible that is the great source of knowledge for Protestant Christians. It is not, therefore, surprising that citation of the Bible plays a large part in both remaining books of Hobbes's masterpiece. In many ways Book 3 of *Leviathan* is a Protestant Christian commentary on the Bible in which the great message that Hobbes wishes to convey is that his philosophy, as expounded in Books 1 and 2 is compatible with the truth of Christianity and in particular supports the understanding of Christian teaching advanced by the Church of England. This can be illustrated in a variety of ways from Hobbes's text. There is, first of all, Hobbes's account of the Bible as containing God's prophetic word. It is through the Bible that God passes to us knowledge of those truths that cannot be reached by reason unaided. It therefore becomes very important to be able to tell which are true and which are false prophets, which books of the Bible can be trusted and which are of doubtful authenticity. Thus, for example, Hobbes argues that Moses could not have been the author of all the books of the *Pentateuch* as some of it refers to events that occurred after Moses's death.

In his account of the Christian religion Hobbes offers powerful accounts of key religious concepts, often with an eye to their compatibility with his own philosophy. We are thus given a sustained analysis of the ambiguous concept "spirit", which in some Biblical contexts has no ontological implications (for example, the word "spirit" in the phrase "the spirit of God" often means nothing but God himself) but at other times implies a subtle body, such as air. But, Hobbes is clear that nowhere in the Bible does it have to be read as implying a non-material substance. So Hobbes's commitment to the view that if something is not body then it is nothing, that is, his uncompromising materialism, is, he claims, entirely consistent with Christian doctrine. Similarly Hobbes's definition of a miracle as "a work of God (besides his operation by the way of nature, ordained by the creation) done for the making manifest to his elect the mission of an extraordinary minister for their salvation" (L: 347; EW III: 432) is quite compatible with his philosophy.

Hobbes is well aware that the most intractable problems in religion are often disputes over correct religious interpretation of scripture and therefore disagreement about correct religious practice. As with the Church of England, he believed that the age of miracles was past and that there were no contemporary prophets sent from God. As a result it was a central claim of his account of religion and the state that the two institutions had to be united under one authority. This is neatly captured in his definition of a Church, which is: "A Company of men professing Christian religion, united in the person of one sovereign, at whose command they ought to assemble and without whose authority they ought not to assemble" (L: 369; EW III: 459). This powerful commitment to an Erastian philosophy was central to the whole of Hobbes's account of church and state and for him provided a major bulwark against civil disorder. Because no one can know what the correct interpretation of many disputed texts in the Bible is it was impossible for there to be a universal church that all would be bound to obey. The only safe alternative was a national church with the head of state and church the very same person.

The kingdom of darkness

The fourth part of *Leviathan*, "Of the Kingdom of Darkness", is by far the shortest. Its subject is those forces that, by propagating false doctrines, attempt to extinguish both the light of nature and of the Bible and thereby destroy the possibility of the people gaining salvation. The methods used to achieve this dark end, Hobbes says, are: first of all, the practice of misinterpretation of the Scriptures; secondly, the introduction of the demonology of the heathen poets, the belief in ghosts and fairies and "other old wives tales"; thirdly, the corruption of Christian teaching by mixing it with the erroneous philosophy of the Greeks, especially that of Aristotle. In general, what he argues in this book is aimed primarily at the churches, both Catholic and others, which he sees as constituting a threat to peace and good government. Thus the Pope is seen as threatening stability with the claim that only he, as vicar general of the Kingdom of God on earth, or his representative, can lawfully crown a monarch. Similarly, Hobbes rejects the claim of a distinction between civil and canon law and the further claim to the supremacy of the latter. Hobbes gives many other examples of what he says are misinterpretations of biblical texts that are designed to increase the influence and power of the Church, by which he almost always means the power of the Pope and the Roman Church in matters that should be left entirely to individual sovereigns to resolve.

In the following chapters Hobbes attacks, in full theological flow, the claims that there are non-corporeal spirits, belief in which leads to various idolatrous practices and the myths that have their origin in the acceptance of philosophically false claims, especially from the philosophy of Aristotle. These are then used to support false theological doctrines, such as the existence of non-material spirits or the doctrine of purgatory, which are all designed to give the Pope authority outside his papal kingdoms and thus threaten the stability of other states.

Finale

The final section in *Leviathan*, "A Review and a Conclusion", allows Hobbes to make some suggestions for emendation of his argument, for example by suggesting an addition to the laws of nature to the effect that men have a duty to obey the sovereign in times of war as well as in times of peace, implying that they might have a duty to fight for their country. It also allows Hobbes to offer a justification to the royalists of England for their willingness to accept the rule of Cromwell after their defeat in the civil war. Thus he makes clear that he never thought that the right to rule of English kings depended on the rightness of the cause of William the Conqueror but simply on the fact that they were in power and could enforce their will, as Cromwell evidently was in 1651. If moral rightness of the former kind was required, "there is scarce a commonwealth in the world whose beginnings can in conscience be justified" (L: 561; EW III: 706). Finally, he claims that in his book there is nothing that is contrary to the word of God or of good manners, or that in any way tends to civil unrest, and nothing to militate against it being profitably taught in the universities. Although that was not *Leviathan*'s immediate fate, because it aroused so much hostility, it certainly has been read widely in the three and a half centuries since its publication and today features on the syllabus of many, perhaps most, universities throughout the world, a position occupied by few other texts of political philosophy or anything else.

Notes

1. On this see especially the opening chapters of *Elements of Philosophy. The First Section, Concerning Body (De Corpore)*, *The English Works of Thomas Hobbes*, 11 vols, W. Molesworth (ed.), (London: Longman, Brown and Longmans, 1839–45). This edition is hereafter cited as EW. The Molesworth edition was reprinted with the same pagination as *The Collected Works of Thomas Hobbes* (London: Routledge/Thoemmes Press, 1992).
2. "Thomas Hobbes" in *Aubrey's Brief Lives*, Oliver Lawson Dick (ed.) (Harmondsworth: Penguin, 1962), 230.
3. Quotations, although modernized, are taken from the critical edition of *Leviathan* in two volumes edited by G. A. J. Rogers and Karl Schuhmann (Bristol: Thoemmes Continuum, 2003). This edition is hereafter cited as L. References are given by page number to this edition but also by reference to the volume and page numbers of EW.
4. *Leviathan*, Book I, Chapter 4, but see note 3 for explanation of citations.

Bibliography

Works by Hobbes

Hobbes, T. 2003. *Leviathan*, 2 vols, G. A. J. Rogers & K. Schuhmann (eds). Bristol: Thoemmes Continuum.
Hobbes, T. 1994. *Leviathan*, E. Curley (ed.). Indianapolis, IN: Hackett.
Hobbes, T. 1839–45. *The English Works of Thomas Hobbes*, 11 vols. London: Longman, Brown and Longmans. Reprinted as *The Collected Works of Thomas Hobbes* (London: Routledge/Thoemmes Press, 1992).
Hobbes, T. 1994. *The Corespondence of Thomas Hobbes*, 2 vols, N. Malcolm (ed.). Oxford: Clarendon Press.
Hobbes, T. 1998. *On the Citizen*, R. Tuck & M. Silverthorne (ed. and trans.). Cambridge: Cambridge University Press.

Other works

Aubrey, J. 1994. "Life of Hobbes", in *Leviathan*, E. Curley (ed.), lxv–lxxi. Indianapolis, IN: Hackett.
Bowle, J. 1951. *Hobbes and His Critics*. London: Jonathan Cape.

Croom Robertson, G. 1886. *Hobbes*. Edinburgh: Blackwood and Sons.

Ewin, R. E. 1991. *Virtues and Rights: The Moral Philosophy of Thomas Hobbes*. Boulder, CO: Westview Press.

Gauthier, D. 1978. *The Logic of Leviathan: The Moral and Political Theory of Thomas Hobbes*. Oxford: Clarendon Press.

Goldsmith, M. 1966. *Hobbes's Science of Politics*. Irvington, NY: Columbia University Press.

Hampton, J. 1986. *Hobbes and the Social Contract Tradition*. Cambridge: Cambridge University Press.

Johnson, D. 1986. *The Rhetoric of* Leviathan. Princeton, NJ: Princeton University Press.

Kavka, G. 1986. *Hobbesian Moral and Political Theory*. Princeton, NJ: Princeton University Press.

Kraynak, R. P. 1990. *History and Modernity in the Thought of Thomas Hobbes*. Ithaca, NY: Cornell University Press.

Macpherson, C. B. 1962. *The Political Theory of Possessive Individualism*. Oxford: Clarendon Press.

Malcolm, N. 2002. *Aspects of Hobbes*. Oxford: Clarendon Press.

Martinich, A. P. 1992. *The Two Gods of Leviathan*. Cambridge: Cambridge University Press.

Martinich, A. P. 1995. *A Hobbes Dictionary*. Oxford: Blackwell.

Mintz, S. 1962. *The Hunting of* Leviathan. Cambridge: Cambridge University Press.

Oakeshott, M. 1975. *Hobbes on Civil Association*. Oxford: Blackwell.

Peters, R. S. 1956. *Hobbes*. Harmondsworth: Penguin.

Rogers, G. A. J. & A. Ryan (eds) 1988. *Perspectives on Thomas Hobbes*. Oxford: Clarendon Press.

Rogers, G. A. J. & T. Sorell 2000. *Hobbes and History*. London: Routledge.

Rogow, A. 1986. *Thomas Hobbes: Radical in the Service of Reaction*. New York: Norton.

Shapin, S. & S. Schaffer 1985. *Leviathan and the Air Pump: Hobbes, Boyle and the Experimental Life*. Princeton, NJ: Princeton University Press.

Skinner, Q. 1996. *Reason and Rhetoric in the Philosophy of Thomas Hobbes*. Cambridge: Cambridge University Press.

Sommerville, J. P. 1992. *Thomas Hobbes: Political Ideas in Historical Context*. London: Macmillan.

Sorell, T. 1986. *Hobbes*. London: Routledge & Kegan Paul.

Sorell, T. (ed.) 1996. *The Cambridge Companion to Thomas Hobbes*. Cambridge: Cambridge University Press.

Straus, L. 1988. *The Political Philosophy of Thomas Hobbes*. Chicago, IL: University of Chicago Press.

Tuck, R. 1989. *Hobbes*. Oxford: Clarendon Press.

Warrender, H. 1957. *The Political Philosophy of Thomas Hobbes*. Oxford: Clarendon Press.

Watkins, J. 1965. *Hobbes's System of Ideas*. London: Hutchinson.

Further reading

The edition of *Leviathan* edited by Edwin Curley (1994) is the best one for students. The following books are recommended as good introductions to central aspects of Hobbes's thought: Croom Robertson (1886), Goldsmith (1966), Martinich (1995), Peters (1956), Tuck (1989) and Sorell (1986, 1996).

5

John Locke

An Essay concerning Human Understanding

J. R. Milton

John Locke (1632–1704) was a man of wide intellectual interests. During the last 15 years of his life he published a series of books on a range of subjects that included politics, religion, economics and education, but in general philosophy all his energy was devoted to a single project. The *Essay concerning Human Understanding*, first published in 1690, is by far the most important of Locke's philosophical works. Four editions appeared during his lifetime and a fifth shortly after his death; all the later editions introduce significant changes, and both the second (1694) and the fourth (1700) contain wholly new chapters. The only other philosophical writings that Locke himself published (in 1697 and 1699) were a set of three very long letters defending the *Essay* against the criticisms of Edward Stillingfleet, Bishop of Worcester. After his death his literary executors published two shorter works that had originally been planned as chapters of the *Essay* but had grown too long for that purpose: the *Conduct of the Understanding* and the *Examination of Malebranche*.

The composition and purpose of the *Essay*

In the Epistle to the Reader that served as a preface to the *Essay*, Locke described how the work had arisen out of discussions with five or six of his friends on a quite different topic, and "having been thus begun by Chance, was continued by Intreaty; written by incoherent parcels; and, after long intervals of neglect,

115

resum'd again, as my Humour or Occasions permitted". The survival of material among Locke's own papers confirms the general accuracy of this story, and allows a few dates to be added. Two unfinished drafts (now known as Draft A and Draft B) date from 1671; neither corresponds in structure to the final *Essay*, although Draft B is considerably closer, but both address some of the same problems and both contain passages that were incorporated into the final work with only minor modifications. During the next 12 years Locke seems to have worked intermittently on his project during the intervals allowed by his other business, although not much can now be discerned of what he wrote. Entries in his journal show that during his visit to France (1675–79) he was in contact with followers of both Descartes and Gassendi, and was stimulated to reflection on a range of philosophical topics. Once back in England Locke seems to been occupied largely with political matters – it was during this period that he wrote the *Two Treatises of Government* – and it was not until he was forced into exile in the Netherlands in the autumn of 1683 that he finally had the leisure to turn his various drafts into a single coherent work. A copy of a draft of Books I and II (Draft C) dates from 1685, and by the end of 1686 a version in four books had been completed; this was probably quite close to the published version, although there can be little doubt that Locke continued to make alterations even after he returned to England in February 1689.

The process of composition just described explains many of the characteristics of the *Essay*. Locke tells us in the Epistle to the Reader that when he began writing he thought that all he would have to say could be contained on one sheet of paper; it must very quickly have become apparent that this was a wild underestimate, and as the work grew in bulk so Locke's control over its individual parts inevitably slackened. The overall structure of the *Essay* is quite clear, but the discussion of particular topics is often rambling and sometimes (as Locke himself acknowledged) repetitious. Locke was as parsimonious in his writing as he was in his financial affairs, and he clearly disliked having to discard material unless he had decided on later reflection that it was in some way mistaken. The greater part of the *Essay* is a patchwork of material written over a period of nearly 20 years, and some parts of the work that might appear at first sight to be afterthoughts are in fact very early.

The purpose of the *Essay* is announced in the first chapter: "to enquire into the Original, Certainty, and Extent of humane Knowledge; together, with the Grounds and Degrees of Belief, Opinion, and Assent" (I. i. 2). Locke disclaimed any intention of pursuing metaphysical enquiries into the essence of the mind and its relation to the body. Instead he proposed to pursue a "Historical, plain Method" and provide an account of how the mind (or more strictly, the understanding) works. This enquiry falls into three parts: into the origin of the ideas or notions that are present in our minds; into the extent of the knowledge that we can have by those ideas; and into the nature and grounds of faith or opinion. This duality of focus, on belief as well as on knowledge, is central to Locke's project. There is no evidence that he was ever attracted by any of the more radical forms of philosophical scepticism, and on the few occasions that he mentioned the kind of metaphysical doubts entertained by Descartes in the first Meditation, for example the possibility that we may be dreaming when we suppose ourselves awake, he treats the possibility with unconcealed derision (IV. ii. 14; IV. xi. 8). In the end, however, he was much less optimistic than Descartes about the possible extent of human knowledge, especially in natural philosophy. For Locke there were large areas of human concern where knowledge is not to be obtained but about which evidence of some kind is available, and the regulation by reason of our beliefs in these matters was of the highest importance. This was especially true in religion, where irrational beliefs could do immense harm.

Locke's project was therefore to discover the boundaries between those areas where knowledge is possible to human beings, those where knowledge is not available but the rational exercise of judgement can give us some guidance in the formation of our beliefs, and those that, for whatever reason, lie beyond the scope of the human intellect. In its ultimate goal the project was very similar to that subsequently undertaken by Kant in the *Critique of Pure Reason*, but the methods of the two philosophers were entirely different. Kant proposed a strictly *a priori* enquiry into the nature of reasoning as such; Locke hoped to achieve his goal by undertaking an empirical, wholly *a posteriori* enquiry into the workings of the human mind. He also wished to encourage his readers to think for themselves, and not to accept propositions simply because they were taught by approved authority:

> For, I think, we may as rationally hope to see with other Mens Eyes, as to know by other Mens Understandings. So much as we our selves consider and comprehend of Truth and Reason, so much we possess of real and true Knowledge. The floating of other Mens Opinions in our brains makes us not one jot the more knowing, though they happen to be true. (I. iv. 23)

The *Essay* is arranged in four books. Book I, "Of Innate Principles", and Book II, "Of Ideas", are devoted to the first part of Locke's project, the provision of an account of how the ideas that we use in thinking come to be in our minds. Book III, "Of Words", was described by Locke as an afterthought (II. xxxiii. 19; III. ix. 21) although some parts of it were already present in the 1671 drafts. The final two parts of the project are undertaken in Book IV, "Of Knowledge and Opinion".

Innate ideas and innate knowledge

Book I contains only four chapters and is by some way the shortest book in the *Essay*. The first chapter provides a general introduction to the *Essay* as a whole; the remaining three chapters consist of an elaborate onslaught on two varieties of what has since come to be called "nativism": the doctrine that all members of the human race come into the world with a knowledge of a certain set of basic speculative or practical (ethical) principles, or at least in possession of a variety of innate ideas. The aim is to clear the ground for an exposition of Locke's own rival account of how the understanding comes to possess its ideas.

The target – or targets – of Locke's polemic was not explicitly indicated in the *Essay*, and has been the subject of some controversy ever since. The only person mentioned by name was Lord Herbert of Cherbury, whose *De Veritate* had been published in 1624, and who had died in 1648. Herbert's views are discussed and confuted at some length, but no one has ever supposed that he was the main target: he simply wasn't important enough. Descartes was, and for that reason is a more plausible candidate; hostility to Cartesianism is one of the running themes of the *Essay*, even though Descartes himself was only occasionally mentioned by name. Nevertheless, it is unlikely that Locke had Descartes primarily in mind. There is a theory of innate ideas in Descartes, but it is not very conspicuous, and it hardly provides a very natural starting-point for anyone setting out to undermine his account of knowledge. Moreover, the earliest extended version of the polemic, in Draft B, concentrates primarily on the ethical uses of the doctrine, and Descartes said nothing about these. Modern scholarship has shown just how widely diffused innatist doctrines were in post-Restoration England, especially – although not exclusively – among the clergy. Locke was seen by his critics as undermining the foundations of morality and religion, and his rejection of these doctrines caused more outrage among his early readers than any other element in the *Essay*.

Innate knowledge presupposes innate ideas, but the converse is clearly not the case. Locke chose therefore to proceed gradually, first undermining the various theories of innate knowledge in Chapters ii and iii, before moving on to innate ideas in Chapter iv. The main argument used is very simple: if knowledge is innate (literally, in-born) then it must be possessed by everyone, at all times and in places. In fact this kind of universal assent is not observed, especially in ethical matters. Even in some of the most civilized societies unwanted children had been exposed and left to die, and among more barbarous peoples they were sometimes buried alive or else castrated and fattened so that they could be eaten (I. iii. 9). The perpetrators of these and similar actions were apparently untroubled by what they did, and were presumably therefore devoid of the innate moral knowledge that the advocates of innatism supposed to be universal.

Abstract speculative principles, such as "Whatever is, is", also appear not to receive universal assent – neither idiots nor young children think of them at all – and they cannot therefore be imprinted on the soul at its creation. If they were, then the soul on which they had been imprinted would be aware of them: "imprinting, if it signify any thing, being nothing else, but the making certain Truths to be perceived. For to imprint any thing on the Mind without the Mind's perceiving it, seems to me hardly intelligible" (I. ii. 5). That the children may be very young and the idiots intellectually very feeble makes no difference: "If therefore Children and *Ideots* have Souls, have Minds, with those Impressions upon them, they must unavoidably perceive them, and necessarily know and assent to these Truths" (I. ii. 5). This principle that anything in the mind must be consciously present to that mind seemed much less obvious to many of Locke's critics – notably Leibniz – than it did to Locke himself. Many of Locke's contemporaries held that innate knowledge is initially merely potential and only becomes actual as the soul in which it has been imprinted acquires the use of reason. Locke's response to this was that it made the thesis of innate knowledge entirely trivial. On this criterion of innateness any truth that we can come to know by the exercise of our reason will count as innate, and the advocate of this kind of innatism differs only from his opponents by his use of improper and misleading language.

A further objection to the view that we are all born with innate knowledge of general maxims such as "It is impossible for the same thing to both be and not be" is that no one can have any thought if they do not have the ideas it involves, and highly abstract ideas such as impossibility are acquired late. The first ideas that a child has are particular, and so therefore is its first knowledge: the child knows that the nurse that feeds it is not the same as the cat that it plays with long before it comes to grasp general principles of logic and metaphysics (I. ii. 25).

The final chapter of Book I is concerned specifically with the doctrine of innate ideas, as distinct from innate knowledge, and in particular with the idea of God. Locke did not deny that we have an idea of God, and indeed held (like many of his opponents) that without such an idea we cannot give an adequate account of morality (I. iii. 5). What he did deny is that any idea of God is innate. A battery of ethnographical material culled from Locke's very wide reading in travel literature is deployed to this end. Nations without any idea of God include not only peoples living "without help of Letters, and Discipline" in Africa and America, but also old and highly literate civilizations such as the

Chinese (I. iv. 8). Even if the idea of God had been universal, as opposed merely to being very widespread, this would not prove the idea to be innate, any more than it would show that the idea of the sun is innate. The variations in the ideas of God that can be observed in different societies, and even in our own, do not suggest that God has given all men an idea of himself. As Locke sardonically commented, universality of consent "if it prove any native impressions, 'twill be only this: That God imprinted on the minds of all Men, speaking the same Language, a Name for Himself, but not any *Idea*" (I. iv. 15).

An empiricist theory of the mind

In Book II Locke began the constructive part of his project. At birth the mind is "as we say, white Paper, void of all Characters, without any *Ideas*" (II. i. 2). This raises an obvious question: how does it obtain the material necessary for knowledge, or indeed for thought of any kind? Locke's answer is clear: from experience. "Our Observation employ'd either about *external, sensible Objects; or about the internal Operations of our Minds, perceived and reflected on by our selves, is that, which supplies our Understandings with all the materials of thinking.* These two are the Fountains of Knowledge, from whence all the Ideas we have, or can naturally have, do spring" (II. i. 2). Sensation provides us with ideas of sensible qualities such as "*Yellow, White, Heat, Cold, Soft, Hard, Bitter, Sweet*" (II. i. 3). Reflection, which might be called inner sense, gives the mind an awareness of its own operations, including "*Perception, Thinking, Doubting, Believing, Reasoning, Knowing, Willing*" (II. i. 4).

All ideas are either simple or complex, and all complex ideas can be broken down into combinations of simple ones. The examples Locke gives of simple ideas are ideas of individual sensible qualities: the coldness and hardness of a piece of ice, the smell and whiteness of a lily, the taste of sugar (II. ii. 1). Most simple ideas of sensation, including all those just mentioned, come from one sense only, but a few come from both sight and touch: these include "*Space*, or *Extension*, *Figure*, *Rest*, and *Motion*" (II. v). Simple ideas of reflection are treated much more briefly: they are derived from the two "great and principal Actions of the Mind ... *Perception*, or *Thinking*, and *Volition*, or *Willing*" (II. vi. 2).

If this account of the sources of our knowledge is to persuade a critical reader, Locke needs to give a reasonably perspicuous account of what an idea is, what makes any idea a simple idea, and how complex ideas are compounded out of simple ones. It is not clear that he succeeded in any of these tasks. At the end of the first chapter of the *Essay* he apologized to the reader for the frequent use of the (relatively) unfamiliar word "Idea":

It being that Term, which, I think, serves best to stand for whatsoever is the Object of the Understanding when a Man thinks, I have
used it to express whatever is meant by *Phantasm, Notion, Species*, or
whatever it is, which the Mind can be employ'd about in thinking.

(I. i. 8)

Locke was writing for his contemporaries, not for readers three centuries or
more later, and he can hardly be blamed if the terms he used to elucidate the
word now seem more obscure than the word itself. His explanation does
however make very clear the inclusive nature of the concept: phantasms were
sense-images in the imagination, notions were concepts, and in scholastic philosophy species could be either sensible species, similar to phantasms, or intelligible species in the intellect; for Aristotelians like Aquinas, intelligible species
were formed by abstraction from sensible species, but were entirely distinct
from them. Descartes made a sharp distinction between images derived from the
senses and purely intellectual ideas. Locke did not: he quite deliberately used the
word "idea" in a very broad sense, to include entities as apparently diverse as the
pain I feel if I stand too close to a fire and the concept of a million (II. viii. 16;
II. xvi. 2, 6).

Simple ideas count as simple because they contain "nothing but *one uniform
Appearance*, or Conception in the mind" (II. ii. 1). The former part of this characterization seems appropriate for a simple idea such as *white*, understood as the
sense-impression caused by a uniformly coloured surface, or a fainter copy of
this in the imagination, but it hardly seems applicable to an idea such as "*Unity*,
or One" (II. xvi. 1). According to Locke there is no idea that is "more simple"
than this – it has "no shadow of Variety or Composition in it" – but it is clear
that it is a simple, un-analysable concept, not a uniform sensory appearance.

The account of simple ideas finishes with one of the most widely discussed
chapters in the whole *Essay* (II. viii). The simple ideas that we receive by sensation are caused by bodies outside us, but although some of them accurately
represent what those bodies are like, others do not. The term "quality" had long
been used in Aristotelian physics and metaphysics, and for that reason had been
abandoned by many of the advocates of the new philosophy in the seventeenth
century, notably Descartes. Locke revived it, but with a change of meaning. A
quality was now defined as "the Power to produce any Idea in our mind" (II. viii.
8), so that "*White, Cold*, and *Round*" are all qualities of a snowball. Qualities, so
defined, fall into two groups. Some, which Locke called "primary qualities", are
characteristics of the bodies themselves: these include solidity, extension, figure
(i.e. shape) and mobility. (By solidity Locke did not mean hardness or rigidity but
impenetrability (II. iv. 4); in his sense a liquid has solidity.) The other group of

qualities are "secondary qualities". These are merely powers to produce ideas in us: they include colours such as whiteness, tangible qualities such as coldness, smells, tastes and the qualities of sounds. The ideas of primary qualities resemble the qualities in the bodies that cause them. The ideas of secondary qualities do not; the warmth that we feel when we touch a moderately hot body no more exists in that body than the pain we feel when we touch a very hot one (II. viii. 16).

This distinction between primary and secondary qualities has two aspects, one epistemological, the other scientific. Locke was attempting to draw a general distinction between those features of our perceptions of the world that we have only because we have the kind of sense-organs that we do, and those that we have because that is the way the world is. The question of whether such a distinction can be drawn at all – as Berkeley and a succession of later idealists denied – is quite separate from the question of which qualities fall into the two classes. In answering the second of these Locke was powerfully influenced by the mechanical or corpuscularian philosophy that was becoming increasingly dominant among the scientists working in the Royal Society (a body of which Locke himself was a rather inactive member). According to this account of nature the secondary qualities of bodies that are large enough to be perceived are caused by the shapes and arrangements of the sub-microscopic corpuscles from which they are composed. These corpuscles have certain qualities such as shape, position and motion, but they do not have colours or smells or tastes. To give an example that Locke used and clearly took very seriously, but did not firmly endorse, the warmth that we feel in our hand when we place it in a bowl of warm water is not caused by anything in the water that resembles that sensation, but rather by an increase in the speed of movement of the corpuscles in our hands caused by a transfer of motion from the faster-moving corpuscles in the water (II. viii. 21).

Complex ideas fall into three kinds: modes, relations and ideas of substances. Modes, in turn, can be divided into simple modes, formed by the repetition or combination of a single idea, and complex modes, formed by the combination of several different ideas. The terminology is reminiscent of Descartes, but the thought is quite different. For Descartes a mode is quite literally a modification of an attribute, so that a mode of extension is a way of being extended, such as being round or being square. Locke's modes are not modifications of anything; all complex ideas other than those of substances and relations are grouped together as modes, and the class inevitably has little internal unity.

Among the simple modes the most important are the modifications of the simple ideas of space, duration and number. Locke had little to say about the formation of simple modes from other ideas of sensation, and in the case of ideas of reflection the distinction between simple and mixed modes, present in Draft C of 1685, was dropped from the published *Essay*.

The account of the idea of space is thoroughly anti-Cartesian. For Descartes extension is the principal attribute of matter (or body), and no attribute can exist without a substance to which it belongs: empty space void of matter is a metaphysical impossibility. For Locke the ideas of body and extension are entirely distinct. By "body" we mean something that is both solid and extended, and has parts that are separable and movable: "Solidity is so inseparable an *Idea* from Body, that upon that depends its filling of Space, its Contact, Impulse, and Communication of Motion upon Impulse" (II. xiii. 11). Pure space is devoid of solidity, and its parts are inseparable and immovable. A vacuum is therefore something that certainly could exist in nature, and Locke was strongly inclined to think that one did: "the motion of Bodies, that are in our view and neighbourhood, seem to me plainly to evince it" (II. xiii. 22, xvii. 4). In any case the issue is one that can only be decided by reasoning from phenomena, not by *a priori* metaphysical demonstration.

Mixed modes are "such Combinations of simple *Ideas*, as are not looked upon to be the characteristical Marks of any real Beings that have a steady existence, but scattered and independent *Ideas*, put together by the Mind" (II. xxii. 1). Such modes can be found in the natural world, for example, a rainbow (II. xviii. 4; III. iv. 13), but nearly all Locke's examples come from human life: obligation, drunkenness, a lie, hypocrisy, sacrilege, murder, parricide and so on. The unity of such ideas does not come from anything in nature, but from a human decision to put the ideas together.

The account of the formation of our complex ideas that fills the central chapters of Book II is for the most part constructive rather than destructive. Locke's aim was to show that his theory could give a plausible account of how we acquire the ideas that his contemporaries generally claimed to possess, not to argue that their claims are in fact mistaken. The one partial exception to this generalization is the account of the idea of substance. For Descartes and his rationalist successors this was a fundamental metaphysical notion, given to us *a priori*. For Locke all our ideas are put together from ideas given in experience, and the ideas we get in this way cannot provide us with a clear idea of substance. Our senses give us evidence of qualities occurring together, and this accustoms us to suppose the existence of some substratum "wherein they do subsist, and from which they do result" (II. xxiii. 1), but when anyone enquires into the kind of notion he has of this substratum, "he will find he has no other *Idea* of it at all, but only a Supposition of he knows not what support of such Qualities, which are capable of producing simple *Ideas* in us" (II. xxiii. 2). The only idea of substance that we have is therefore a purely relative one; we have no idea of what substance is, and only a confused and obscure one of what it does (II. xiii. 19). Our ideas of particular substances, or kinds of substances, such as "a Man,

Horse, Gold, Water *etc.*" (II. xxiii. 3) each consist of a collection of perceptible qualities combined with the obscure idea of a support that binds them together.

The final class of complex ideas comprises ideas of relations, discussed in Chapters xxv–xxviii. (In the fourth edition of 1700 these ideas are no longer classed as complex ideas (II. xii. 1), but this late change of mind, which would badly undermine Locke's overall project, will be ignored here.) Most of the discussion is concerned with the nature of the relations themselves, and not how we come to have ideas of them, something that causes very few problems. This is particularly apparent in the longest and philosophically most interesting of these chapters, "Of Identity and Diversity", which first appeared in the second edition of 1694. The account of the origin of the idea – that "when considering any thing as existing at any determin'd time and place, we compare it with it self existing at another time, and thereon form the *Ideas* of *Identity* and *Diversity*" (II. xxvii. 1) – is obviously circular: no one could make the comparison unless they already possessed the idea. These matters are dealt with very quickly, and the remainder of the chapter consists of an elaborate and sophisticated discussion of trans-temporal identity, concentrating primarily on the identity of persons. Being the same *person* as someone who existed in the past is not the same as being the same *man*. For the latter, bodily continuity is a necessary and sufficient condition, for the former continuity of consciousness, and in particular memory. If the soul of a prince (to use Locke's own example), carrying with it the consciousness of the prince's past life should enter the body of a cobbler after the departure of the cobbler's own soul, the new entity would be the same person as the prince, but the same man as the cobbler (II. xxvii. 15). It might seem from this that Locke was placing identity of persons in the continuity of an immaterial or spiritual substance, but other passages show clearly that he did not. For personal identity consciousness of past actions is what matters, not continuity of any substance, whether material or immaterial. Locke remarked that he had himself known someone who was convinced that his own soul had formerly been the soul of Socrates (II. xxvii. 14), but even if this were possible, the absence in him of any memories of what Socrates had done would mean that he could not be the same person as Socrates.

Book II finishes with a chapter on the association of ideas, added in the fourth edition of 1700. It is an aspect of human psychology that seems not to have been previously described, and Locke's account was to be extremely influential, often in ways that might have surprised and even disconcerted him. Chance or custom can link two ideas together so that the appearance of one in the mind inevitably summons up its associate. Locke saw this tendency of the human mind to link together ideas that have no rational connection as a form of madness, albeit one to which we are all liable to a greater or lesser extent. It is something that we can guard against, and those who are responsible for the education of young children should do their best to prevent such associations being formed. There is in Locke no trace of the view found in Hume that the association of ideas is normal and needs to be invoked to explain how the mind acquires its natural beliefs about causation and the existence of the external world. For Locke the whole phenomenon is pathological.

Words, and what they signify

In Book III Locke laid aside his primary concern, the relation between our ideas and the things they represent, in order to consider two other problems: the relation of words to ideas, and the relation of words to things. Present-day philosophers educated in the analytic tradition are often inclined to see the relation of language to the world as among the most important problems addressed by philosophers, and the theory of meaning as one of the central areas of philosophy. It is wrong to suppose that Locke was similarly motivated. He was certainly concerned with the differences between meaningful and meaning-less utterance, and with the distressing tendency of human beings to deviate into the latter, but it is anachronistic to suppose that he saw himself as investigating problems in the philosophy of language.

One of the most striking features of Locke's account of how words have meaning is that it relies on a single basic notion, that of *signification*. Most writers who have made a systematic investigation of these problems have found it necessary to use two such terms: the logicians in the thirteenth and fourteenth centuries used *significatio* and *suppositio*; John Stuart Mill, following earlier scholastic writers, used *connotation* and *denotation*; Frege used *Sinn* and *Bedeutung*, standardly (although not entirely uncontroversially) translated as *sense* and *reference*. These distinctions do not precisely coincide, but in every case the first term is used (approximately) for the meaning of the word in general, the second for the word's naming or designating entities in the world. Locke could have found distinctions of this kind in the writings of the scholastic logicians, but he despised them too much to seek any help in that quarter.

The central thesis of Locke's semantic theory is set out in III. ii. 2: "*Words in their primary or immediate Signification, stand for nothing, but the* Ideas *in the Mind of him that uses them*". This does not mean that each of us uses words only to refer to the contents of his or her own mind. Language-users also suppose words to have

> a secret reference to two other things. *First, they suppose their Words to be Marks of the* Ideas *in the Minds also of other Men, with whom they*

communicate ... Secondly, Because *Men* would not be thought to talk *barely* of their own Imaginations, but of Things as really they are; therefore they often suppose their Words to stand also for the reality of Things.   (III. ii. 4, 5)

Some of the consequences of Locke's central thesis are immediately apparent: words used as signs of obscure and confused ideas have "a very loose and undetermined, and consequently obscure and confused signification" (III. ix. 9), and words used by a speaker who has no ideas in his mind corresponding to them have no meaning at all (III. x. 26, 31). For Locke the primary purpose of language is communication. It is not the only purpose – language is also needed for the recording of thoughts, as an aid to memory – but it is the most important. There is no suggestion that human beings need language in order to think, although the possession of language does make it much easier for them to put together certain kinds of very complex ideas; an example would be the triumph awarded in ancient Rome to a successful general. The idea is given its lasting duration by the name: "Though therefore it be the Mind that makes the Collection, 'tis the Name which is, as it were the Knot, that ties them fast together" (III. v. 10). The idea of a triumph is a useful idea, but the abstract ideas that our possession of language enables us to form are often positively harmful, and it is best to dispense with language altogether: "the examining and judging of *Ideas* by themselves, their Names being quite laid aside, [would] be the best and surest way to clear and distinct Knowledge" (IV. vi. 1).

Given that each of us necessarily has to understand anything that someone else has said by using our own ideas, it is quite common for communication to break down. Sometimes it is obvious that this has happened. If a speaker uses a word for which he has an idea but his hearer does not, then for the hearer the word lacks any signification: an example of this would be "cohobation" (II. xviii. 7), a chemical term that Locke – no doubt rightly – thought would be unknown to most of his readers, and has not gained in familiarity since. If the speaker and the hearer both attach ideas to the word, but not the same idea, then successful communication of the speaker's thought is not achieved; sometimes this soon becomes apparent, but sometimes not. An example that Locke himself gave took place "in a Meeting of very learned and ingenious Physicians, where by chance there arose a Question, whether any Liquor passed through the Filaments of the Nerves" (III. ix. 16). The issue was debated fruitlessly until Locke himself suggested that they stopped to consider what the word "liquor" signified, whereupon it turned out – unsurprisingly – that none of the participants to the dispute shared the same conception. Such occurrences are far from uncommon, especially where the educational system has been placed in the hands of those who value "Subtilty" and skill in disputation (III. xi. 5, 7). The effect of using obscure and equivocal terms is that many controversies are nothing but "noise and wrangling about Sounds" (III. xi. 6). If there is no agreement between speaker and hearer about the idea that a word they are using stands for, then their dispute ceases to be about things and becomes merely a dispute about names.

Words immediately signify ideas in the mind of their user, but they can also be used to refer to other things. Some words, such as "Peter" and "James", are proper names, but a language consisting entirely of such words would be quite useless; general words such as "man" and "animal" are also needed. There are, however, no general *things* corresponding to these general words. Locke was a nominalist in the tradition of Ockham, Gassendi and Hobbes. Everything that exists is an individual, even the things that can act as universal signs:

> *General and Universal*, belong not to the real existence of Things; but
> ... *concern only Signs*, whether Words, or *Ideas*. Words are general ...
> when used, for Signs of general *Ideas*; and so are applicable indifferently to many particular Things; And *Ideas* are general, when they are
> set up, as the Representatives of many particular Things: but universality belongs not to things themselves, which are all of them particular in their Existence, even those Words, and *Ideas*, which in their
> signification, are general. (III. iii. 11)

General words caused no great problems for Locke, but general ideas did. Human beings can use language, unlike non-human animals, because they have the psychological capacity to form abstract ideas: "the having of general *Ideas*, is that which puts a perfect distinction betwixt Man and Brutes; and is an Excellency which the Faculties of Brutes do by no means attain to" (II. xi. 10). These abstract general ideas are a special kind of idea, capable of representing other more particular ideas. How they do this is never adequately explained: Berkeley was to seize with evident glee on Locke's description of the general idea of a triangle as "neither Oblique, nor Rectangle, neither Equilateral, Equicrural [isosceles], nor Scalenon; but all and none of these at once" (IV. vii. 9). Such an idea cannot be a sense-image or a copy of such an image, but no clear account is provided of what else it might be.

Locke's rejection of any kind of real universals had immediate consequences for his account of essences. For the scholastic realists the essence of something made that thing what it was, but it was also the modification of some more general essence, and as such was a universal of some kind. For example the species *homo* (man, or human being) falls under the genus *animal*, and is formed from it by the addition of the differentia *rationalis*. What is happening here is not merely a quasi-biological classification of man as a rational animal; it is also a metaphysical account of how human nature is made from a more universal nature. Locke considered this way of thinking barely intelligible and wholly mistaken. If we are to think about these matters properly we need to make a distinction between two entirely different kinds of essence. The *real essence* of something is "the real internal, but generally in Substances, unknown Constitution of Things, whereon their discoverable Qualities depend"; the *nominal essence* is "that abstract *Idea*, which the General, or *Sortal* ... Name stands for" (III. iii. 15). The real essence of something, like the thing of which it is the essence, is a particular. Thus the real essence of the particular lump of gold in front of me is (according to the best available hypothesis) the unknown arrangement of the sub-microscopic corpuscles in the gold that is causally responsible for its observable qualities of yellowness, malleability and the like. The nominal essence of gold (the species, not the individual lump) is the abstract idea of gold that I have in my mind.

Several consequences follow directly from this account. One is that there is no reason why all the individual bodies to which we apply the name "gold" should have the same real essence. Locke did not think that this was something that would surprise anyone with experience of investigating the natural world, as opposed to scholastic logicians and metaphysicians trained merely to discourse about essences and properties: "Chymists especially are often, by sad Experience, convinced of it, when they, sometimes in vain, seek for the same Qualities in one parcel of Sulphur, Antimony, or Vitriol, which they have found in others" (III. vi. 8). Another is that different people put together different nominal essences in accordance with their own knowledge and their own interests. Someone who knows some chemistry may put solubility in *aqua regia* as part of the nominal essence of gold; somebody who has never even heard of *aqua regia* (a mixture of nitric and hydrochloric acids, although in the seventeenth century its composition was not well understood) will certainly not do this, but they may still have an idea of gold as a heavy yellow metal that does not tarnish and can be beaten into gold leaf. For the first person, solubility in *aqua regia* is part of the nominal essence of gold; for the second person it is not. Neither is wrong; they merely have different ideas. There is, properly speaking, no such thing as *the* nominal essence of gold; different users of the word associate it with different ideas, and every distinct abstract idea is a distinct essence (III. iii. 14).

This account of real and nominal essences has profound consequences for the theory of classification. The boundaries of species are not made by nature, but are "the Workmanship of the Understanding" (III. iii. 14). This is not to say that our classifications are arbitrary; there is a natural world that exists independently of us, and the individuals that exist in it resemble and do not resemble one another in various ways. Nevertheless the classifications that we make are governed by our own knowledge and our own interests; if they are to be of any use they need to respect the resemblances and differences that exist in nature, but are not determined by them.

Knowledge and opinion

Book IV falls into two main parts: Chapters i–xiii are concerned with knowledge and Chapters xiv–xx with the cognitive states that fall short of knowledge, such as faith and opinion; the final chapter (xxi), "Of the Division of the Sciences", serves as a conclusion to the *Essay* as a whole.

Locke's account of knowledge is the culmination of the *Essay*, and the part of his achievement about which he was most proud. As he explained to Stillingfleet, many authors had written about the mind,

> yet nobody, that I had met with, had, in their writings, particularly set down wherein the act of knowing precisely consisted. To this reflection upon the actions of my own mind, the subject of my Essay concerning Human Understanding naturally led me; wherein, if I have done any thing new, it has been to describe to others more particularly than had been done before, what it is their minds do, when they perform that action which they call knowing ...
>
> (*Works* (1824), III: 143–4)

Locke's analysis of that action is given at the beginning of the first chapter: "*Knowledge* then seems to me to be nothing but *the perception of the connexion and agreement, or disagreement and repugnancy of any of our Ideas*" (IV. i. 2). There are four kinds of agreement or disagreement: identity or diversity, relation, co-existence or necessary connection, and real existence. These in turn produce four kinds of knowledge: "Thus *Blue is not Yellow*, is of Identity. *Two Triangles upon equal Basis, between two Parallels are equal*, is of Relation. *Iron is susceptible of magnetical Impressions*, is of Co-existence. *GOD is*, is of real Existence" (IV. i. 7).

Locke also distinguished between what he called different degrees of knowledge. Sometimes we can perceive the agreement or disagreement of two ideas immediately, without the intervention of any other ideas. This kind of knowledge is *intuition* and is "the clearest, and most certain, that humane Frailty is capable of " (IV. ii. 1). Often, however, we cannot perceive the agreement or disagreement of two ideas without bringing other intermediate ideas. This kind of knowledge is *demonstration* and is less "clear and bright" than intuition, especially when a long chain of intermediate ideas is involved, even though the individual steps of the proof may all be intuitively certain.

All our knowledge of general truths comes only from intuition and demonstration, but truths about particular things can be known in another way: there is "another *Perception* of the Mind, employ'd about *the particular existence of finite Beings* without us; which going beyond bare probability, and yet not reaching perfectly to either of the fore-going degrees of certainty, passes under the name of Knowledge" (IV. ii. 14). This is *sensitive knowledge*. Its introduction at the end of the chapter and the curiously oblique wording that Locke chose to use might suggest that it is an afterthought, but in fact it is one of the oldest parts of his system: unlike the account of intuition and demonstration it is clearly present in the two 1671 drafts. Our confidence in our senses requires no independent rational justification, as Descartes had supposed: "the greatest assurance I can possibly have, and to which my Faculties can attain, is the Testimony of my Eyes, which are the proper and sole Judges of this thing, whose Testimony I have reason to rely on" (IV. xi. 2). The scope of sensitive knowledge is, however, quite limited: it extends only to things actually present to our senses, although Locke did also allow memories of past perceptions to count as knowledge (IV. xi. 11).

It is not obvious that Locke's account of sensitive knowledge is compatible with his official account of knowledge as the perception of agreement or disagreement between ideas. The knowledge that there was a sheet of paper in front of him that Locke describes himself to have had when writing this section of the *Essay* (IV. xi. 2) does not appear to have arisen from the comparison of two ideas, one of the paper, and the other – presumably – of existence. A similar criticism can be made of Locke's account of how he knew that he himself exists. We have, according to Locke, "*an intuitive Knowledge of our own Existence*, and an internal infallible Perception that we are" (IV. ix. 3). It is not very plausible to say that we obtain this knowledge by comparing two ideas, of ourselves and of existence, and seeing (fortunately) that they agree.

Two consequences immediately follow from Locke's account of knowledge. One is that we cannot have any knowledge of things of which we have no ideas. There may well be other beings in the universe that are "not tied down to the dull and narrow Information ... received from some few, and not very acute ways of Perception, such as are our Senses" (IV. iii. 6). Locke was always aware that a very large part of what he called "the vast Ocean of *Being*" lay as much beyond our thought as our knowledge. The second consequence is that we are often incapable of acquiring knowledge even when we do have ideas, if we are unable to perceive any agreements or disagreements between the ideas. This is especially important in natural philosophy. Our idea of gold is of a body that is yellow, heavy, malleable, fusible and fixed (i.e. chemically unreactive), but we cannot discover any necessary connection between these ideas. The main reason for this is the weakness of our senses and their consequent inability to reveal to us the minute parts of bodies. If we did know the arrangement of these parts, then "The dissolving of Silver in *aqua fortis* [nitric acid], and Gold in *aqua Regia*, and not *vice versa*, would be then, perhaps, no more difficult to know, than it is to a Smith to understand, why the turning of one Key will open a Lock, and not the turning of another" (IV. iii. 25). The arrangements of the minute parts of bodies are not intrinsically unknowable or unintelligible to us, but this is not a kind of knowledge we are ever likely to have: "our Faculties are not fitted to penetrate into the internal Fabrick and real Essences of Bodies" (IV. xii. 11). We must be content to glean what we can from particular experiments, and avoid system-building. Experimental natural philosophy can produce useful results, but there is no prospect of it becoming a science as Locke and his contemporaries understood that term: a system of universal, rigorously demonstrated propositions.

Our inability to perceive connections between ideas has consequences in other areas of philosophy. We have an idea of matter and an idea of thinking, but we do not know whether a purely material being can or cannot be capable of thinking. Apart perhaps from the rejection of innate ideas, this was the claim in the *Essay* that received the largest amount of hostile comment from Locke's contemporaries, and in successive editions he rewrote and added so much to §6 of Chapter iii that it became the longest section of the whole work. Locke did not think that materialism in the full sense could be true; he was quite insistent that God's existence was demonstrable, and that he could not possibly be made of matter. What we do not know is whether the thinking thing that exists within each of us is material or immaterial. Locke assured his readers that he was not writing to lessen belief in the soul's immateriality, and indeed maintained that the opinion that it is immaterial is much more probable (II. xxvii. 25, IV. iii. 6), but he insisted that it was not something that we could rightfully claim to *know*.

The account of knowledge set out in the opening chapters of Book IV is open to one very obvious objection, as Locke saw. If our knowledge is only of the agreements and disagreements of ideas, how could we have knowledge of things that are not ideas? Locke's reply was that we do not know things immediately, but we can know them mediately, by the intervention of the ideas we have of them, and that our knowledge is real when there is conformity between ideas and things.

This generates another question: "How shall the Mind, when it perceives nothing but its own Ideas, know that they agree with Things themselves" (IV. iv. 3)? As Locke admitted, this is a difficult question, and his answer to it falls into several parts. Simple ideas of sensation are the product of external things "operating on the mind in a natural way ... and so carry with them all the conformity which is intended; or which our state requires" (IV. iv. 4). (The claim in Chapter viii of Book II that our ideas of primary qualities *resemble* those qualities is not mentioned.) Complex ideas of modes and relations are "voluntary Collections of simple *Ideas*, which the Mind puts together, without reference to any real Archetypes, or standing Patterns, existing any where" (II. xxxi. 3) and are necessarily therefore both real and adequate: a mathematician considers the ideas of a triangle or a circle, and it does not matter if nothing precisely corresponding to those shapes exists in the world (II. xxx. 4; IV. iv. 6). A similar analysis can be given of moral modes such as justice and murder: "If it be true in Speculation, *i.e.* in *Idea*, that *Murther deserves Death*, it will also be true in Reality of any Action that exists conformable to that *Idea* of Murther" (IV. iv. 8). Locke felt confident enough of his own account to announce that moral knowledge can be as certain as mathematical knowledge, and indeed that morality is as capable as demonstration as mathematics (III. xi. 16; IV. iii. 18, iv. 7, xii. 8).

No demonstrative science of nature would seem to be possible for human beings, and the main reason for this is that our ideas of substances are not their own archetypes, or – to use the language of Book III – the real and nominal essences of substances are not the same. We have no idea of the real essence of a substance like gold. Almost everyone has some idea of gold, and these ideas give the word "gold" the meaning it has for each of us, but they are different for different people. One person has an idea of gold as a body that is yellow, heavy, malleable and fusible, while another person has an idea of it as a body that is yellow, heavy, malleable, fusible and fixed. Since no connection is discernible between fixedness and the other qualities, the first person does not know whether all gold is fixed. The second person does know this, but only because he has already included fixedness in his idea of gold: all he is doing is explicating the meaning of the word (IV. vi. 8, 9). These are the kinds of propositions that Kant was to label "analytic", but Locke's description of them is more unkind: they are "trifling" or "barely verbal" (IV. viii. 4–5, 12–13).

The second part of Book IV is concerned with rational belief. The areas of potential concern to us in which knowledge is possible are quite limited, but we still have to live, and this involves making decisions under conditions of uncertainty: anyone who declines to act unless he is certain "will have little else to do, but sit still and perish" (IV. xiv. 1). The religious themes that are in the background of so much of Locke's thinking are clearly visible here: "in the greatest part of our Concernment, he [God] has afforded us only the twilight, as I may so say, of *Probability*, suitable, I presume, to that State of Mediocrity and Probationership, he has been pleased to place us in here" (IV. xiv. 2).

When knowledge is not available we have to use our judgement, which Locke defines as "the putting *Ideas* together, or separating them from one another in the Mind, when their certain Agreement or Disagreement is not perceived, but *presumed* to be so" (IV. xiv. 4). As we judge things to be more or less probable so the assent we are rationally entitled to give varies "from full *Assurance* and Confidence, quite down to *Conjecture*, *Doubt*, and *Distrust*" (IV. xv. 2). Probable propositions fall into two classes: those that concern particular matters of fact that can be observed and hence are the subject of human testimony, and those that concern matters that lie outside the range of our senses (IV. xvi. 6). Locke's concern was mainly with the first of these. He did have a little to say about the use of analogical reasoning in natural philosophy (IV. xvi. 12), but there is nothing about the kinds of theory-based inferences to unobservables that occupy the attention of modern philosophers of science; no such theories existed when Locke was writing the *Essay*, and he had no reason to think that any would ever be produced. Most of his account is concerned with the evaluation of testimony, whether given by ancient historians or modern travellers in remote parts of the world.

One group of propositions was of particular concern to Locke, and to a large number of his readers. On some matters the testimony that we rely on is not human but divine and, unlike human witnesses, God cannot lie or be deceived. This kind of testimony is called "revelation", and our assent to it "faith". Locke was, however, quite explicit that although God cannot be mistaken in what he reveals, human beings can be very badly mistaken about whether something that is claimed to be divine revelation really is one:

> Faith . . . leaves no manner of room for Doubt or Hesitation. Only we must be sure, that it be a divine Revelation, and that we understand it right: else we shall expose our selves to all the Extravagancy of Enthusiasm, and all the Error of wrong Principles, if we have Faith and Assurance in what is not divine Revelation.   (IV. xvi. 14)

Whether something that claims to be a divine revelation really is one has to be decided by reason, and here "our Assent can be rationally no higher than the Evidence of its being a Revelation" (IV. xvi. 14). The existence of God is something that Locke thought could be demonstrated (IV. x. 6) and cannot properly be a matter of faith; faith is founded on the testimony of God revealing something to us, and is therefore irrational if it has not previously been established by reason that God exists.

In Chapter xviii Locke set out to draw the boundaries between faith and reason. By the latter he did not mean only intuition and demonstration; reason here means "the discovery of the Certainty or Probability of such Propositions or Truths, which the Mind arrives at by Deductions made from such *Ideas*, which it has got by the use of its natural Faculties". Faith "is the Assent to any Proposition, not thus made out by the Deductions of Reason; but upon the Credit of the Proposer, as coming from GOD, in some extraordinary way of Communication" (IV. xviii. 2). It can never be as certain as knowledge, and we should never assent to anything as a revealed truth that is "directly contrary to our clear and distinct Knowledge" (IV. xviii. 5). The example that Locke gave was the proposition that the same body cannot be in two distant places at once, and although this might appear to be purely a truth of natural philosophy, its relevance to the doctrine of transubstantiation would not have escaped many of his readers, either Catholic or Protestant.

"*Faith* can never convince us of any Thing, that contradicts our Knowledge" (IV. xviii. 5), but the situation is entirely different with regard to matters that are merely probable, or about which our natural faculties can provide us with no evidence one way or the other. "*Revelation*, where God has been pleased to give it, *must carry it*, *against the probable Conjectures of Reason*" (IV. xviii. 8). Provided that we have rational grounds for believing that a purported revelation does indeed come from God, and that the words by which it has been conveyed to us mean what we suppose them to mean, then we ought to give it our assent, even if in the absence of revelation we would have judged some of the propositions revealed to be more or less improbable. Additional (divine) testimony is now available, and the balance of probabilities is therefore altered.

The reception of Locke's thought

The epistemological doctrines of the *Essay* were subjected to acute criticism by other philosophers from Berkeley onwards, but this did little to shake their acceptability to the educated public, who saw Locke as having given a plain unmetaphysical account of the workings of the human mind that could serve as a complement to Newton's account of the physical universe. Many of his doctrines were far from unprecedented. The denial of innatism, the empiricist account of concept acquisition and its attendant semantic theory can all be found in earlier authors, notably Hobbes, although Locke's account was far more thoroughly worked out, and such features as the distinction between real and nominal essences were entirely new. Other features of the *Essay* that had a profound impact on later thought include the accounts of personal identity, of the association of ideas, and of faith and reason. Perhaps the most original aspect of the *Essay* is, however, the conception of philosophy which it embodied. Locke abandoned the whole enterprise of first philosophy, as practised from Aristotle to Descartes. He did not see himself as laying a metaphysical foundation on which natural philosophers could then build, but rather as undertaking a critical enquiry into the limits of the human understanding, and (as he put it in the Epistle to the Reader) acting "as an Under-Labourer ... clearing Ground a little, and removing some of the Rubbish, that lies in the way to Knowledge".

Further reading

Locke's main philosophical work is *An Essay concerning Human Understanding*. There are many editions of this – some abridged – that can be used, including A. D. Woozley (ed.), *An Essay Concerning Human Understanding* (Glasgow: Fontana, 1977) and John W. Yolton (ed.), *An Essay Concerning Human Understanding* (London: Everyman, 1985), but for more advanced study the only satisfactory edition of the *Essay* is the one edited by Peter Nidditch (Oxford: Clarendon Press, 1975); this contains both a very accurate text and full details of all the changes that Locke made after the first edition. There is much interesting material in the three very long letters that Locke wrote to Edward Stillingfleet in 1697–99. There is no modern edition of these, but they are included in all the old collected editions of Locke's works, of which the 1823 edition (London: Thomas Tegg, 1823; reprinted Aalen: Scientia, 1963) is probably the most widely available. This also contains two works originally planned as part of the *Essay*: the *Conduct of the Understanding* and the *Examination of Malebranche*.

E. J. Lowe, *Locke on Human Understanding* (London: Routledge, 1995) is a good elementary introduction. J. L. Mackie, *Problems from Locke* (Oxford: Clarendon Press, 1971) is a little more advanced; it is philosophically stimulating but deeply unhistorical in approach. Roger Woolhouse, *Locke* (Brighton: Harvester Press, 1983) is accessible and pays more attention to the context in which Locke wrote, but perhaps the best introduction is Nicholas Jolley, *Locke: his Philosophical Thought* (Oxford: Oxford University Press, 1999). Jonathan Bennett, *Locke, Berkeley, Hume: Central Themes* (Oxford: Oxford University Press, 1999) is lively but sometimes brutal in its interpretative approach; the same characteristics are present in his more recent *Learning from Six Philosophers* (Oxford: Oxford University Press, 2003). An older but still useful general works is Richard I. Aaron, *John Locke* (3rd edn, Oxford: Clarendon Press, 1971). The most elaborate (but demanding) and recent books on Locke's philosophy are Michael Ayers, *Locke, vol. I: Epistemology* and *Locke, vol. II: Ontology* (London: Routledge, 1991). Vere Chappell (ed.), *The Cambridge Companion to Locke* (Cambridge: Cambridge University Press, 1994) contains chapters on the main aspects of Locke's philosophy, with a very full bibliography.

More specialized books on particular aspects of Locke's philosophy include John W. Yolton, *Locke and the Compass of Human Understanding* (Cambridge: Cambridge University Press, 1970), Nicholas Jolley, *Leibniz and Locke* (Oxford: Oxford University Press, 1984) and Walter R. Ott, *Locke's Philosophy of Language* (Cambridge: Cambridge University Press, 2004). Peter Alexander, *Ideas, Qualities, and Corpuscles: Locke and Boyle on the External World* (Cambridge: Cambridge University Press, 1985) has a very thorough discussion of the primary–secondary quality distinction.

There are many collections of essays on Locke. A recent collection (with a very good up-to-date bibliography) in the Oxford Readings in Philosophy series is Vere Chappell (ed.), *Locke* (Oxford: Oxford University Press, 1998); an earlier but still valuable volume in the same series is I. C. Tipton (ed.), *Locke on Human Understanding* (Oxford: Oxford University Press, 1977). Another older collection with some good articles is D. M. Armstrong & C. B. Martin (eds), *Locke and Berkeley* (London: Macmillan, 1969). More extensive collections of reprinted journal articles can be found in Richard Ashcraft (ed.), *John Locke: Critical Assessments* (London: Routledge, 1991) and Udo Thiel (ed.), *Locke: Epistemology and Metaphysics* (Aldershot: Ashgate, 2002).

There are a number of volumes of published essays on Locke, including John W. Yolton (ed.), *John Locke, Problems and Perspectives* (Cambridge: Cambridge University Press, 1969), Reinhard Brandt (ed.), *John Locke: Symposium Wolfenbüttel* (Berlin: De Gruyter, 1981), G. A. J. Rogers (ed.), *Locke's Philosophy: Content and Context* (Oxford: Clarendon Press, 1994), M. A. Stewart (ed.), *English Philosophy in the Age of Locke* (Oxford: Clarendon Press, 2000) and Peter R. Anstey (ed.), *The Philosophy of John Locke: New Perspectives* (London: Routledge, 2003).

There is no satisfactory biography of Locke. Maurice Cranston, *John Locke: A Biography* (Oxford: Oxford University Press, 1985) gives a general account of Locke's life, but is often inaccurate on points of detail. A shorter but more reliable account can be found in the *Oxford Dictionary of National Biography* (Oxford: Clarendon Press, 2004).

6

George Berkeley

A Treatise Concerning the Principles of Human Knowledge

Tom Stoneham

George Berkeley published the *Principles of Human Knowledge* Part 1 in 1710, when he was just 25 years old. He never published the projected Part 2, on free will and the self, claiming to have lost the manuscript while travelling in Italy. Part 1, now known simply as the *Principles*, defends the apparently shocking thesis that there is no material world; all that exists are immaterial minds and the ideas that are their objects of consciousness. At the stroke of a pen, this bold move did away with all the problems that had beset the materialist philosophies dominant during the seventeenth century. Few philosophers of the period denied the immateriality of the mind (Hobbes did, and Locke was accused of doing so), but all agreed that the external, non-mental world consisted of inanimate matter governed by mechanical principles of motion. Such a mechanism seemed unavoidable given the scientific discoveries of the time, but it faced two major problems. One was the interaction between mind and matter, a problem that had plagued Descartes. The other was scepticism: either we could not know what the external world was like, because all we perceived were ideas, or if we had some other route to knowledge, be it scientific induction or rational intuition, it revealed to us that the world was very different from what our perceptual experiences had led us to believe. In his *Three Dialogues between Hylas and Philonous* (1713), Berkeley describes a sceptic as one who "denies the reality of sensible things, or professes the greatest ignorance of them" (DHP1 173), and it was this consequence of materialism that his *Principles* seeks to avoid by the dramatic move of denying the existence of the material world; if there is no

137

material world, then there is nothing about which our sense-experiences might give us inadequate knowledge. Of course, having denied the existence of matter, the problem of the interaction of mind and matter also disappears.

There are two obstacles to understanding Berkeley's *Principles*. The first is the distinction between denying the existence of the material world and denying the existence of the physical world of ordinary objects. Failure to grasp this distinction can take two forms. It can be mere ignorance, as was displayed by the lexicographer Samuel Johnson, who, according to Boswell, kicked a stone and said "I refute him [Berkeley] thus". Or it can be more sophisticated, when it takes the form of the charge that, despite his efforts, Berkeley fails to reconcile his metaphysics with our common-sense conception of the world. Here misunderstanding is dressed up as criticism, but it is misunderstanding nonetheless, for it imposes on Berkeley a peculiarly twentieth-century conception of the philosophical project. We shall see that Berkeley's primary concern was not to preserve common sense, but to produce a coherent metaphysics that was acceptable to common sense. That is a subtle difference but an important one. In what follows I try to give a more sympathetic account of Berkeley's philosophy.

The second obstacle to understanding the *Principles* is the rapidity and confidence with which Berkeley takes himself to have established his most important claim; namely, that the ordinary objects of perception, such as tables and trees, cannot exist unperceived. This is an obstacle because it is hard to find an argument in the text that adequately proves this claim. One explanation is that Berkeley is arguing *ad hominem* against, for example, Locke, showing how Locke's claims about perception are not consistent with his materialism. Another explanation is that he sees himself as pointing out how to accept two apparently incompatible but widely held beliefs; namely, the common-sensical view that we perceive physical objects, and the theoretical view that the objects of perception are ideas. The trouble with interpreting Berkeley in either of these ways is that it leaves his work incomplete, and dependent upon what other philosophers have said, in a way that the text does not suggest. Furthermore, it leaves Berkeley with a primarily historical significance that is at odds with the almost universal interest and curiosity that his writings inspire. In the later sections below I look at what arguments against matter can be extracted from the text.

Immaterialism

In the Third Dialogue (DHP3 254) Berkeley first describes his view as "immaterialist". He did not use this term in the *Principles*, but once introduced, it can be seen to be more appropriate than recent alternatives such as "idealist", for, as we shall see, Berkeley is not denying that there is a real world of daffodils and ducks, but merely that this real world is material. "Idealism" suggests that the world is subjective, a product of our minds, whereas "immaterialism" makes clear that it is only the materiality of the world that is being denied. It is crucial to see that Berkeley denies the existence of matter only in so far as it is *defined* as unthinking substance (PHK 7–11, 76). If the materialist wants to claim that minds are also material, he is committed to there being two kinds of matter, thinking and unthinking, and it is only the existence of the latter that Berkeley is concerned to deny. However, Berkeley is committed to the denial of *physicalism*, which is, roughly, the thesis that everything that exists can be accounted for by the physical sciences, the sciences that describe the physical world of daffodils and ducks.

So Berkeley holds that minds exist and so do daffodils: that minds are thinking substances, but daffodils are neither thinking substances nor unthinking substances. What then are daffodils? Berkeley's answer, in the very first paragraph of the *Principles*, is that they are collections of ideas. And here Berkeley's philosophy begins to look like a form of idealism, since it seems that ideas must be subjective/mental; philosophers might argue whether pains and after-images are mental objects or modes of experiencing, but they agree that they are mental, and thus, if Berkeley is claiming that daffodils are collections of ideas, he is claiming that daffodils are mental. This line of thought explains why so many commentators on Berkeley take his immaterialist doctrine that all that exists are minds and ideas, as equivalent to the doctrine that everything is mental. But it is mistaken.

It will be instructive to demonstrate one source of the mistake. Immaterialism sounds like a purely negative doctrine, and the predominant form of materialism that Berkeley was rejecting had a tri-partite metaphysics (Fig. 1).

The mind perceives, or perhaps just "has" ideas, which are caused by and represent the world. This view, called "representative realism", is motivated by the thought that the senses can mislead us about the nature of the world, and that the best explanation of this is that what is given in sense-experience is not the world itself, but a realm or veil of ideas that represent, and can thus misrepresent, the world. It is held, in very different forms, by the three seventeenth-century philosophers who had greatest influence on Berkeley: Descartes, Malebranche and Locke. Now it is undeniable that Berkeley thought this view was deeply misconceived, and much of the argument in the *Principles* is directed against it. The objection he took most seriously was that it conflicted with the obvious, everyday opinion that the real world is given in sense-experience. Although Berkeley did argue that the representative realist is left unable to know whether his "real" world exists (PHK 18–20), the view is sceptical in a

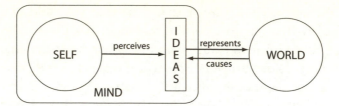

Figure 1 Representative realism. In the terminology of "Appearance and reality" below, there are in fact three options for the representative realist: (a) an act–object account of the perception of ideas, that is, ideas are the objects of an act of perceiving; (b) an adverbial account, that is, ideas are ways of perceiving; and (c) an adverbial account of the perception of ideas combined with an act–object account of the perception of material objects.

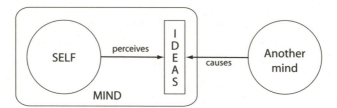

Figure 2 Idealist metaphysics.

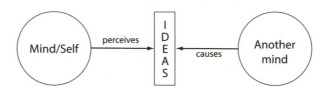

Figure 3 Berkeley's immaterialist metaphysics.

different sense, which Berkeley found equally invidious, for it denies that what people ordinarily take for reality *is* real. The representative realist is committed to saying that when we ordinarily say we see a daffodil, we are wrong, for what we see are ideas caused by the "real" but not perceptible daffodil, if such a thing even exists.

Berkeley found this consequence intolerable and sought to avoid it by denying that there is a material reality distinct from our minds and the ideas they perceive. He did not deny that ideas had to have an external cause, but this must be another mind (PHK 29), and the ideas we have do not represent anything beyond themselves (PHK 8). It would seem then that Berkeley has accepted two-thirds of the representative realist picture, and substituted a mind for the material world (dropping the relation of representation between ideas and their cause along the way) (Fig. 2).

This story of what Berkeley is up to makes it almost inevitable that we should see him as an idealist, for if you take the representative realist framework and remove the material world, all you are left with is mental: the only options for what ideas might be are those available to the representative realist. To find the realist strand in Berkeley's thinking, we must stop thinking of immaterialism as representative realism minus the material world, and start instead thinking of it as a positive doctrine (Fig. 3).

What then are ideas for Berkeley? The *Principles* opens with some very clear statements:

> It is evident to any one who takes a survey of the objects of human knowledge, that they are either ideas actually imprinted on the senses; or else such as are perceived by attending to the passions and operations of the mind; or lastly, ideas formed by help of memory and imagination – either compounding, dividing, or barely representing those originally perceived in the aforesaid ways. (PHK 1)

> For, what are [houses, mountains, rivers, and in a word all sensible] objects but the things we perceive by sense, and what do we perceive besides our own ideas or sensations ...? (PHK 4)

> By sight I have the ideas of light and colours, with their several degrees and variations. By touch I perceive hard and soft, heat and cold, motion and resistance, and of all these more and less either as to quantity or degree. Smelling furnishes me with odours; the palate with tastes; and hearing conveys sounds to the mind in all their variety of tone and composition. (PHK 1)

> And it seems no less evident that the various sensations or ideas imprinted on the sense, however blended or combined together (that is, whatever objects they compose), cannot exist otherwise than in a mind perceiving them. (PHK 3)

There are four claims about the nature of ideas in these passages:

1. Ideas are the objects of knowledge, that is, all our knowledge is *about* ideas (there will need to be a qualification here to make clear that knowledge of minds is not included).
2. Ordinary things such as houses and mountains are among the objects of knowledge.

141

3. Ideas presented to the senses are not objects such as houses but qualities, specifically qualities of appearance.

4. Ideas presented to the senses cannot exist unperceived.

In the fourth passage quoted (from PHK 3), Berkeley says that ideas exist "in a mind". Understanding this phrase is of utmost importance in understanding his immaterialism. In PHK 2 he talks of the mind as a thing "wherein [ideas] exist", and throughout his works he denies that ideas exist "without the mind". There is a subtle ambiguity in this language that is rarely noticed and can lead to misunderstanding: the antonym of "without" can either be "within" or "with". So to deny that ideas exist without the mind could be either to assert that they must exist within the mind, or merely that they must exist *with* a mind, that is, that ideas only exist when related to a mind. Rather than making this distinction, Berkeley makes a stipulation that the former is to be understood in terms of the latter; that what it is for an idea to exist within the mind, is for it to be perceived by that mind, which is for it to be related to that mind, and thus with it, but not necessarily part of it (e.g. PHK 3, 49; DHP3 250; see also passages such as PHK 33 where the "or" of paraphrase is used to force a synonymy between "in" and "perceived by" a mind). So we should be very careful to read Berkeley's talk of things existing in minds as meaning no more than that they are perceived or known by those minds. Had Berkeley been writing after Kant, he may well have chosen to express the relation between minds and ideas by saying that ideas exist *for* a mind. After all, his famous slogan, that "their *esse* is *percipi*" (PHK 3), amounts to no more than that; what is perceived necessarily exists for the mind that perceives it, but not necessarily within that mind, so merely claiming that it is the essence of ideas to be perceived does not entail that ideas are elements or aspects of the perceiving mind.

To show, as I hope I have done, that Berkeley's immaterialism is not trivially a form of idealism is not to show that it is not ultimately a form of idealism. To do that I shall need to show that he can account for the distinction between appearance and reality ("Appearance and reality" below), and that he can allow for the common-sense belief in public, persistent objects ("Persisting public objects" below). But it is not possible to make much progress in these directions until we have considered Berkeley's argument for the existence of God.

The existence of God

Before considering Berkeley's argument for the existence of God, it is worth clearing away some misconceptions: misconceptions encouraged by a tendency to refer to him as "Bishop Berkeley". In the eyes of the British establishment, his becoming a bishop was his most significant achievement, but the 25-year-old Berkeley who wrote the *Principles* showed no desire for the episcopacy, nor even much intention to pursue a career in the Church. He had been ordained in 1709, since ordination was a requirement on all Fellows of Trinity College, but his ambitions at the time, and for the next 25 years, seemed to be more academic and literary than pastoral. He accepted the lucrative Deanship of Derry in 1724, but was an absentee and merely used the large income to assist with his plan to found a College in Bermuda. While it does seem true that he had a strong religious belief, it would be a mistake to see Berkeley's early philosophy as merely exploring the options within the context of that belief. Rather he is, like Descartes before him, trying to construct a free-standing philosophical system and thus, if that system is to include God, he must give an argument for the existence of God from suitably neutral premises.

Berkeley's argument for the existence of God in the *Principles* is very simple (there is another more complex argument discernible in the *Three Dialogues*). He has already established to his own satisfaction that all that exists are minds and ideas. He then argues that ideas are "visibly" inert (PHK 25), they have no causal powers, whereas minds are active and can cause ideas to "arise" (PHK 28) in thought and imagination. Then he observes: "But whatever powers I may have over my own thoughts, I find the ideas actually perceived by sense have not a like dependence on my will ... There is therefore some other will or spirit that produces them" (PHK 29). While this establishes that Berkeley is not alone in the universe, it falls short of showing that the other mind is God. Berkeley makes this transition in the very next sentence:

> The ideas of sense are more strong, lively, and distinct than those of the imagination; they have likewise a steadiness, order, and coher-ence, and are not excited at random, as those which are the effects of human wills often are, but in a regular train or series, the admirable connexion whereof sufficiently testifies the wisdom and benevolence of its Author. (PHK 30)

So Berkeley's argument has two stages. The first is a demonstrative proof that there must be some other mind that causes my ideas of sense. The second is a much less certain inference from the character of the effects to the nature of the cause. The second stage is weak in two respects. First, we may be less confident than Berkeley that the world we experience is the one a wise and benevolent God would create. (See PHK 152, where he suggests that natural disasters "are not without their use, in that they make an agreeable sort of variety, and augment the beauty of the rest of creation"!) Secondly, the evidential force of the premise that the natural order "enables us to regulate our actions for the benefit of life" (PHK 31) is undermined by the observation that were it not so, we would not be here to experience it. However, Berkeley's theological ambitions outstrip what is needed for his philosophy, so we should concentrate our attention on his proof that there is some other mind that is the cause of our ideas of sense. Even if we follow him in calling that mind "God", we need attribute to it no more properties than are necessary for it to have the effects it does.

The problem with this proof is its major premise: that only minds can be causes. This will be attacked from two directions, both by those who think the things we perceive, which for Berkeley are ideas, can be causes, and by those who think that if ideas are inert, so must minds be.

To argue that ideas lack causal powers, Berkeley appears simply to appeal to observation:

> All our ideas, sensations, or the things which we perceive, by whatsoever names they may be distinguished, are visibly inactive; there is nothing of power or agency included in them. So that one idea or object of thought cannot produce, or make any alteration in, another. To be satisfied of the truth of this, there is nothing else requisite but a bare observation of our ideas. For since they and every part of them exist only in the mind, it follows that there is nothing in them but what is perceived. But whoever shall attend to his ideas, whether of sense or reflexion, will not perceive in them any power or activity; there is therefore no such thing contained in them.   (PHK 25)

But on this point Berkeley seems simply mistaken. We can see this by considering an illusion of cause and effect. Imagine that you are looking at a large metal container being lifted by a fork-lift truck and you marvel at the power of the truck. However, were you to be told that the truck was not doing the lifting, that in fact the container was being pulled upwards by an electromagnet, the impression would persist; it would still seem as if the truck were doing the lifting. This suggests that the relation of cause and effect is part of our perceptual experience, for if it were a judgement we made on the basis of experience of perceived correlations, then the impression ought to go away when we no longer make the judgement. (I have adapted this example from Peacocke (1986: 156).) So an appeal to introspection alone will not make Berkeley's point. Either he must give a theoretically motivated account of what are the possible contents of perceptual experiences, or he must give an argument for the inertness of ideas that would show all impressions of cause and effect to be mistaken.

144

He makes a step in the latter direction when he follows the introspective argument with: "A little attention will discover to us that the very being of an idea implies passiveness and inertness in it, insomuch as it is impossible for an idea to do anything, or, strictly, to be the cause of anything" (PHK 25). This suggests that Berkeley has an *a priori* argument for the inertness of ideas, but it is not spelled out in enough detail for us to know what it is. Perhaps he had in mind something like Hume's argument (1978: I. iii. 3–6) that a cause must necessitate its effect, but any two ideas are only ever contingently related.

What then of the worry that any argument against the causal potency of ideas will generalize to minds? This was certainly what Hume thought, and Berkeley was famously criticized by Mill (1996: 462) for failing to spot the point. However, it is far from clear that Hume's argument about the contingency of all relations between ideas does apply to the relation between volitions and actions. Berkeley would have been familiar with Malebranche's argument that only God's volitions are causally efficacious, because only they cannot fail to have their effects, and thus only they can be said to necessitate their effects:

> It is clear that no body, large or small, has the power to move itself … Thus, since the idea we have of all bodies makes us aware that they cannot move themselves, it must be concluded that it is minds which move them. But when we examine our idea of all finite minds, we do not see any necessary connection between their will and the motion of any body whatsoever …
>
> But when one thinks of about the idea of God, i.e. of an infinitely perfect and consequently all-powerful being, one knows there is such a connection between His will and the motion of all bodies, that it is impossible to conceive that He wills a body to be moved and that this body not be moved. (Malebranche 1980: VI. 2. iii)

But something much weaker would suffice to block the Humean argument. Volitions may not necessitate actions in the strong sense Malebranche wants, but the connection is far from contingent: my intention to type a "p" would not be the intention it is if it did not, in normal circumstances and in the absence of conflicting intentions, usually result in my typing a "p". Berkeley never offers this sort of consideration in favour of his view that minds have causal power. Instead, in PHK 26 he seems to argue by ruling out the alternatives: something causes our ideas; it is not ideas, so it must be a substance; substances are either thinking or unthinking; there is no unthinking material substance, so it must be a thinking substance, that is, a mind. What he never even seems to contemplate is a position that denies the very first step in this argument. Perhaps our ideas of sense, those not caused by us, are uncaused; perhaps it is just a basic fact about the universe, which has no explanation, that we have the ideas of sense we do when we do. But that is hardly an attractive view.

Appearance and reality

Berkeley tells us that what we perceive are ideas, that for an idea to exist it must exist in a mind, and what it is for an idea to exist in a mind is for it to be perceived by that mind. Unfortunately, he does not help us out of this tight little circle of inter-definitions by telling us what it is for a mind to perceive an idea. Almost all commentators who have tried to say something about this have made a significant, but rarely explicit (a notable exception is Henry 2000) assumption; namely, that in perceiving an idea, the perceiving mind is *receptive*. That is to say, when a mind perceives an idea, there is a mental event, which is the reception of that idea by the mind, a mental event we can call the "perception". This assumption is related to the Aristotelian thought that if A causes a change in B, then B must have the capacity to be affected by A. Perceiving minds must have the capacity to receive ideas, which capacity is exercised in each episode of perception.

If we make the receptivity assumption, there are two possible interpretations of what Berkeley means by "perception": the act–object and the adverbial accounts. The former distinguishes the event of perceiving from the object perceived, in this case an idea. Thus when I look at the daffodils, there is a yellow idea that I perceive, and also an event of my perceiving that idea. The latter does not make this distinction, for on the adverbial account, when I see the yellow of the daffodils, there is an event that is my perceiving "yellowly". Perceiving a yellow idea is just having a "yellow" perceptual event. The difference between the act–object and the adverbial accounts is clearest when applied to bodily sensations such as pains. According to the former, feeling a pain consists in being aware of a mental object, a pain, which is distinct from the mental state of awareness (although it may only exist when I am aware of it). According to the latter, feeling a pain is just having an experience with a certain quality, namely painfulness; there is no such thing as a pain for which we can even raise the question of whether it can exist unfelt, there are just feelings that are painful or not. This is called the "adverbial account" because it holds that being a pain is a property not of an object, but of an event, and is thus best expressed as an adverb modifying the verb "to feel": "he felt painfully" is better than "he had a painful feeling".

Unfortunately, neither of these can be the correct account of what Berkeley meant by "perceiving an idea". Against the act–object model we have Berkeley's own testimony (DHP1 194–7). Furthermore, once we introduce an act–object model, it becomes hard to explain two fundamental Berkeleian theses: that ideas cannot exist unperceived (PHK 3–5, 22–3); and that ideas cannot be misperceived (PHK 25). The adverbial account has no trouble explaining why Berkeley made these claims, and is never explicitly discussed, and thus never rejected, by Berkeley. However, it is inconsistent with the account of Berkeley's immaterialism that I sketched earlier (Fig. 3), for it makes ideas aspects of perceivings, which are mental events, and thus ideas are aspects of the perceiving mind, not objects distinct from that mind that are perceived by it. While it is possible to square the adverbial account with PHK 49, it is harder to square it with Berkeley's persistent talk of ideas as things; for example, in PHK 39 he says that he would have used "thing" instead of "idea", except that minds are things as well and he is keen to mark a distinction between minds and ideas. Finally, if the adverbial account is correct, then Berkeley is undoubtedly an idealist, and protestations such as PHK 41 and 84 are disingenuous.

It seems then that we must reject the receptivity assumption. To perceive an idea is to have that idea before one's mind, that is, for there to be a relation between the mind and the idea. Certain mental acts and operations may follow as a consequence of that relation holding, but the mere holding of that relation does not require any event in the perceiving mind; there is no exercise of a capacity of receptivity. (In Stoneham 2002: 54 I called this the "simplest model of perception".) Given that ideas themselves do not represent anything, there can be no errors within perception: either the relation holds or it does not. Yet it would be ridiculous for Berkeley to deny that there are such things as perceptual illusions, dreams and hallucinations.

In order to provide an appearance–reality distinction, Berkeley needs first to distinguish genuine sense-experience from dreams and imaginings, and secondly to make a distinction within sense-experience between the veridical and the illusory. He makes the first distinction at PHK 33, but does not make the second in the *Principles*, so we will have to draw on the Third Dialogue to understand that. The first distinction has several strands, which need separating:

> The ideas imprinted on the senses by the Author of Nature are called *real things*: and those excited in the imagination, being less regular, vivid and constant, are more properly termed *ideas*, or *images of things*, which they copy and represent. But then our sensations, be they never so vivid and distinct, are nevertheless *ideas*, that is, they exist in the mind, or are perceived by it, as truly as the ideas of its own framing. The ideas of sense are allowed to have more reality in them, that is, to be more strong, orderly, and coherent than the creatures of

the mind; but this is no argument that they exist without the mind. They are also less dependent on the spirit or thinking substance which perceives them, in that they are excited by the will of another and more powerful spirit. (PHK 33)

One interesting thing to note about this passage is that Berkeley shows an awareness of the original meaning of the word "idea" – namely, an image – and makes explicit that it is extended to include the objects of sense-experience, not because he holds a representative theory of perception, but merely because of the connotation within philosophical writing that ideas "exist in the mind". So one distinguishing mark of imaginings is that the ideas perceived in imagining, unlike those perceived by sense, are images of other ideas. While this might have been a fruitful avenue for Berkeley to explore, he in fact offers three rather different criteria:

- Ideas of sense have greater order and intensity.
- Ideas of sense have an external cause.
- Ideas of sense are less dependent upon the mind that perceives them.

While the second entails the third, they are not equivalent because the third is a matter of degree but the second is not. However, since the distinction between the second and third only surfaces in the *Three Dialogues*, we can concentrate on the first and second here. (The third is explored in detail in Stoneham 2002: Ch. 5)

The first criterion looks more like a rule of thumb than a necessary condition, since regularity, orderliness and coherence are relational properties, and thus whether a given experience exhibits them depends upon what other experiences that person has had, whereas whether a given idea is a sense-perception or not does not depend upon what other sense-experiences the subject has had. The intrinsic properties of vividness, constancy and strength seem more appropriate as a necessary condition, but are hard to define in ways that do not make them immediately subject to counter-examples; the experience of a man dying of thirst who dreams of drinking water may be considerably more vivid than my experience when I sip from my glass while concentrating on my work, and yet I have the experience of real water. It seems that the first criterion offers neither necessary nor sufficient conditions.

In contrast, the second criterion is more promising. The reference to the "Author of Nature" is a distraction, since, as we have seen above (p. 143), the argument that ideas of sense are caused by God takes the fact that they have an external cause as a premise. All that is crucial to the criterion of reality being offered here is that ideas of sense have an external cause. Berkeley takes himself to have shown that that external cause is God, and thus phrases his criterion in those terms, but we need not. I shall briefly mention two problems for this criterion: dreams and my own actions.

Some dreams seem to have an external cause, at least, they do not seem to be voluntary in the way that what I imagine is under my voluntary control (although there may be exceptions to this as well). Appeal to a lack of vividness and coherence with the rest of my experience will not help here, partly because these criteria are not decisive, and partly because some dreams are quite vivid and some dreams cohere well with the rest of my experience. So Berkeley must either say that such dreams are perceptions of reality, or allow that some of my experiences may not have an external cause, despite appearing to. As Freud made clear, the latter strategy for explaining dreams requires us to postulate an unconscious agency within the mind, a suggestion Berkeley would have rejected. Furthermore, once we have such an unconscious agency, it can be cast into doubt whether *any* of our experiences have an external cause, leaving Berkeley with no way of proving the existence of God or avoiding the charge that the poet Yeats made; namely, that he "proved all things a dream". But that leaves Berkeley no choice other than to say that some dreams turn out to be perceptions of reality. Once he has the second distinction in place, that between veridical and illusory sense-perceptions, he will be able to argue that if there are such dreams they are entirely illusory.

The second problem derives from the observation of our own actions. If I wave my hand in front of my face, then what I see, my hand's moving, is my voluntary action and thus caused by me. But that means it does not have an external cause, rendering it an imagining rather than a sense-perception by the second criterion. (To the best of my knowledge, this problem was first mentioned in Ayers (1975: xix).) Being an action of mine it must be voluntary, but being a sense-perception it must be involuntary; however, it cannot be both.

Whether this is a problem or not depends upon Berkeley's theory of action: do I have the power to move my hand myself, or do I merely form the volition that it move and rely upon God to actually move the hand? Berkeley seems to endorse the latter option:

> For it is evident that in affecting other persons, the will of man has no other object, than barely the motion of the limbs of his body; but that such a motion should be attended by or excite any idea in the mind of another, depends wholly on the will of the Creator. He alone it is who, *upholding all things by the Word of his Power*, maintains that intercourse between spirits whereby they are able to perceive the existence of each other. (PHK 147)

So when I perform an action such as drinking from a glass of water, the ideas other people have, of my arm lifting the glass to my lips and tipping, and presumably the ideas I have as well, are caused directly by God. Hence they are not under my voluntary control.

While this theory of action appears to solve the problem, it also creates new problems of its own. For example, Berkeley says that the object of my volition is the motion of my limbs, but given his immaterialism, the motion of my limbs must consist in ideas perceived by myself or others. Since it is not me but God who is the actual cause of those ideas, it follows that my volition is impotent. I can cause ideas of imagination in myself, but I am not able to cause anything else, merely to prompt God to cause it. Even if Berkeley was happy to accept such an occasionalism about action on its own merits, it appears to have serious consequences for his religion; we know people sometimes succeed in wicked actions, but on this occasionalist theory of action, if someone forms the unkind volition to steal from a child, it is God not the unkind person who actually takes the sweets away from the child. The man would still be culpable for his unkind volition, but we might rightly ask whether God might not also bear some of the blame, since He actually performed the unkind act. Of course, there may be ways to get around this difficulty, but the obviousness of the problem, its seriousness for Berkeley and his silence on the matter, together suggest that he did not endorse occasionalism about action. So there remains a problem for his criterion of reality.

Having offered us a distinction between sense-perceptions and imaginings, Berkeley now needs to distinguish veridical from illusory sense-perceptions. He does this in response to an objection in the Third Dialogue:

> HYLAS: What say you to this? Since, according to you, men judge of the reality of things by their senses, how can a man be mistaken in thinking the moon a plain lucid surface, about a foot in diameter; or a square tower, seen at a distance, round; or an oar, with one end in water, crooked?
>
> PHILONOUS: He is not mistaken with regard to the ideas he actually perceives; but in the inferences he makes from his present perceptions. Thus in the case of the oar, what he immediately perceives by sight is certainly crooked; and so far he is right. But if he thence conclude, that upon taking the oar out of the water he shall perceive the same crookedness; or that it would affect his touch, as crooked things are wont to do: in that he is mistaken.   (DHP3 238)

Hylas thinks he has a good objection here because he thinks that the only way to explain a perceptual illusion is by saying that the perception does not correspond to reality. If Berkeley rejects both the act–object and the adverbial accounts of perception, then the perception just is the idea, and so if the perception fails to correspond to reality, the real oar must be something other than the ideas perceived. Philonous, speaking on behalf of immaterialism, offers an ingenious response: when we see an oar in water, what we see really is crooked, that is, among the ideas we perceive are ideas of crookedness, so the perception is not illusory or in any other way an inadequate take on reality. However, our past experience has taught us certain correlations between things looking crooked at one time and how they will feel or look at another time, and if we use these to infer that the oar in water will still look crooked when taken out of the water, or will feel crooked if we plunge our hands below the surface, then we will have made a mistake. So the oar in water is an illusion in that, if you did not know it was an exception to a generalization about the correlations between sense-experiences, you would be led to make a false judgement.

Now Hylas might reasonably complain that this misses the point, for it is the common-sense view that, although the oar looks crooked to me now, it is not really crooked right now; yet Philonous is saying that it *is* crooked right now, although it will not be crooked when I feel it or look at it later. To answer this concern fully we would have to develop Berkeley's immaterialism much further than he did, but we can give an indication of how that development would go. The first move to make is to distinguish descriptions of ordinary objects like oars and trees from descriptions of ideas. If an oar is crooked, then it does not merely look crooked at one moment from one particular perspective: it must also look crooked at other times and to other observers, and feel crooked as well. The predicate "crooked" applies to oars and trees but the predicate "looks crooked" applies to ideas of sight. The latter *appears* to be semantically complex and thus mean something like "looks like a crooked thing does", but in fact it is primitive: it describes a property of ideas. So let us introduce "crooked*" for this property. Then what Philonous is saying is that the oar half in water is crooked* but is not crooked. Normally, what is crooked* is also crooked, so we are led to conclude from the crookedness* that the oar is crooked. But this is a mistake, since if it were crooked, it would be crooked* when out of the water and be crooked** (= "feel crooked") as well. So with a little care separating the description of the oar from the description of the ideas that we perceive at a given time, Berkeley can allow for the common-sense thought that the oar is not crooked despite appearing so, without saying that there is a real oar distinct from the ideas we perceive.

But this commits him to saying that several different experiences, some crooked*, some not, some crooked**, possibly had by different people and cer-tainly had at different times, are all experiences *of the same oar*. The materialist

151

can explain how all these experiences are of the same oar by saying that there is a single, material oar that causes all of them. Berkeley cannot.

Persisting public objects

In PHK 45 Berkeley considers the objection that on his principles "things are every moment annihilated and created anew … Upon shutting my eyes all the furniture in the room is reduced to nothing, and barely upon opening them it is created again". Many commentators take this to be the point at which Berkeley is addressing the criticism that his view is inconsistent with the common-sense conception of ordinary objects. Before considering his reply to the objection, we should note that Berkeley is happy to suggest that "common sense" is mistaken or confused (PHK 55), so for him it is not a decisive objection that his immaterialism is inconsistent with a widely held belief or intuition. Rather, what matters is that, upon reflection, immaterialism offers revisions of common sense that are acceptable to people in general, where the standard of acceptability is practical; namely, that everything they *care about* remains. Thus the objection that, according to immaterialism, my table ceases to exist when I leave the room, is only an important objection in so far as it is important to me that my table should exist unperceived. If all that matters to me about my table is consistent with its being annihilated and created anew, then the mere fact that I believe it persists between episodes of my perceiving it, carries no weight with Berkeley. Furthermore, he might argue that, since a table can only affect me through my senses, an unperceived table could have no effect on me, and thus be of no importance.

Berkeley's first response to the objection (PHK 45) is to remind the reader that he has already given plenty of arguments for the claim that ideas cannot exist unperceived, and thus the objection amounts to charging him with "not assenting to those propositions which at bottom have no meaning in them". So his initial reaction is to face out the objection: it is more absurd to think that ideas should exist unperceived than that the table should cease to exist when I leave the room.

However, Berkeley is sensitive to the fact that many will find this response unpersuasive, so he offers a series of further considerations. The arguments of PHK 46–7 are largely *ad hominem*, aiming to show that the materialist is equally committed to sensible objects failing to exist unperceived. The postulation of a material table that exists when I am out of the room is of little help if that material table lacks all the qualities, such as size, shape and solidity, that I care about in my table.

In PHK 48 Berkeley offers a new consideration in response to the objection, and readers have seized upon this as an indication that he did have a positive account of the table existing when I leave the room:

> For though we hold indeed the objects of sense to be nothing else but ideas which cannot exist unperceived; yet we may not hence conclude they have no existence except only while they are perceived by us, since there may be some other spirit that perceives them, though we do not. (PHK 48)

When this is combined with PHK 3 – "The table I write on, I say, exists, that is, I see and feel it; and if I were out of my study I should say it existed, meaning thereby that if I was in my study I might perceive it, or that some other spirit actually does perceive it" – and the proof of the existence of God, Berkeley can deny that on his principles the table ceases to exist when he leaves the room. Of course, *his* ideas cease to exist, but the table does not, because God continues to perceive it.

Before further exploring this proposal for the continued existence of objects, it is important to point out that Berkeley does not explicitly endorse it. In PHK 48 he is only pointing out that his ceasing to perceive the table does not entail that the table is unperceived. If, as he leaves the study, a mouse comes out of the skirting board, that mouse will perceive the table, which suffices for the table to exist. The claim that "some other spirit" must refer to God is driven by the thought that it is possible that no mouse or other creature is in his study to perceive the table *and yet it continues to exist*. But Berkeley never commits himself to the claim that the table does continue to exist when unperceived by any finite spirit; this is a piece of "common sense" that he is at liberty to reject. In PHK 6 he does mention the possibility that things unperceived by finite minds "subsist" in a God-like mind, but this is not endorsed and may only be included for the completeness of his enumeration of the options (it is also worth noting that an idea's *subsisting* in God's mind may not involve God *perceiving* the idea): "so long as they are not actually perceived by me, or do not exist in my mind or that of any other created spirit, they must either have no existence at all, or else subsist in the mind of some eternal spirit" (PHK 6).

Assuming for the time being that Berkeley does want to give an account of what it is for the table to exist unperceived by any finite spirit, there are three different ways that God's perceptions could achieve this:

(a) The table consists of ideas, some in our minds and some in God's mind.
(b) The "real" table is a collection of ideas in God's mind, and some of these are shown to us (so they are perceived by both us and by God).

(c) The "real" table is a collection of ideas in God's mind, and our ideas represent it.

To discuss these options properly would be beyond the scope of this essay, so I shall just make a comment about each in turn. Option (a) makes God's perception of things unperceived by us serve no other purpose than to make true the belief that they exist unperceived by finite minds, so the account looks very ad hoc. Furthermore, unlike (b) and (c), (a) offers no account of how two people can perceive the same table. Option (b) has the attraction of placing the table in an independent (although mental) reality, but requires Berkeley to make sense of two spirits perceiving one and the same idea. Perhaps he could make sense of that, but he in fact often uses the possessive pronoun when talking about ideas: "my ideas", "our ideas", "your ideas". Option (c) avoids the objections to (a) and (b), but commits Berkeley to a position structurally identical to representative realism. While some of Berkeley's objections to representative realism turn upon the materiality of the world beyond the veil of perceptions, others focus upon the conflict between it and the important common-sense belief that sensible things, the objects of our perception, are the real things: "A piece of sensible bread, for instance, would stay my stomach better than ten thousand times as much of that insensible, unintelligible, real bread you speak of" (DHP3 229). This objection would hold equally well if the alleged real bread was merely insensible to us, although perceived by God.

Given these problems with (a), (b) and (c), we should take seriously the possibility that Berkeley thought that, if no other finite mind perceives the table while I am out of the room, then it ceases to exist. In a letter written only months after the publication of the *Principles*, he does say that what it was for God to create the world was for him to make it perceptible to finite minds (1948–57: Vol. 8, 37). This has the clear corollary that the mark of real existence for physical objects is perception by finite minds, and not perception by God. Of course, should Berkeley take this line about existence unperceived, then he needs to explain why we say that, despite having been annihilated and created anew, it is the very same table that he will find in his study tomorrow. But this is another point at which he may choose to challenge the correctness of common sense, for at DHP3 245–6 he suggests that there is an equivocation on "same" in the common-sense view that it is the same table.

Where's the matter?

In the Introduction to the *Principles*, Berkeley attacks the doctrine of abstract ideas, using Locke as his primary target. This attack is part of a wider project in the Introduction to "prepare the mind of the reader" by discussing "the nature and abuse of language" (PHK Intro 6). Berkeley's thought is that people are led into errors such as materialism because they take singular and general terms to work in the same way: that is, to act as signs for ideas in the mind. For example, the words "extension" and "colour" have different meanings, so if each signifies an idea, we have an idea of extension that is distinct from our idea of colour, and that would allow us to conceive of something extended but not coloured. But Berkeley thinks that one cannot conceive of something with extension and no colour (PHK 10). Since we could never see something as extended without seeing it as coloured, the idea of extension that was not coloured would have to be an abstract idea. So by showing how abstract ideas are impossible, Berkeley has shown how a misunderstanding of the nature of language leads to errors in philosophy. However, while this argument helps undermine one reason for accepting materialism, it does not show that materialism is false. The arguments for that conclusion come in the main body of the *Principles*.

Berkeley's negative claim that matter does not exist is in fact the rejection of more than one position. For the materialist might hold that:

(i) The objects of perception are material.
(ii) The objects of perception, while themselves not capable of existing "without the mind", subsist or inhere in an unperceived material substance.
(iii) The objects of perception, while themselves not capable of existing "without the mind", are caused by and represent an unperceived material substance.

Berkeley takes himself to have rejected all three of these in the first 24 paragraphs of the *Principles*. This would be a striking achievement, but few readers have found his arguments as compelling as he did.

The first argument he offers is an objection to (i) based on what we mean when we talk of the existence of the things we perceive:

> I think an intuitive knowledge may be obtained of this, by any one that shall attend to what is meant by the term *exist* when applied to sensible things. The table I write on, I say, exists, that is, I see and feel it; . . . There was an odour, that is, it was smelt; there was a sound, that is to say, it was heard; a colour or figure, and it was perceived by sight or touch. This is all that I can understand by these and the like expressions.   (PHK 3)

Now, if this is intended to be a piece of conceptual analysis, it seems obviously wrong, for "unperceived table" is not an oxymoron like "round square".

Someone who talks of sensible things existing unperceived has not simply misunderstood what we all mean by the word "exist", otherwise there would be no controversy. It is likely then that Berkeley did not see this claim as something akin to offering a dictionary definition of "exist", after all, he was writing before Johnson had produced the first such dictionary. Furthermore, he had ended the Introduction to the *Principles* with the warning: "Unless we take care to clear the first principles of knowledge from the embarras and delusion of words, we may make infinite reasonings upon them to no purpose (PHK Intro 25).

The argument here must then be rather different. And it seems that there is another sense of the "meaning" of an assertion that could be what Berkeley intended; namely, the point or purpose of that assertion. Thus someone who asserted that there are an odd number of stars in the universe, while knowing it is impossible for anyone to count them, would be saying something meaningless, if only in the sense that she would have made an assertion that could have no point (which does not *entail* that it is meaningless is the twentieth-century sense of being nonsense). Similarly, Berkeley might be best understood as saying that the only point in talking about sensible things is to talk about them in so far as they affect some mind, and the only way they can affect a mind is through perception. When he tells us what he "means" by saying that his table exists while he is out of his study, he is not offering a piece of conceptual analysis, rather he is telling us what the point or purpose of such an assertion would be; namely, either to mark the fact that were he to return to his study he would perceive the table, or to point out that some other creature perceives it. There can be no other *practical* point in saying that the table exists unperceived. Thus Berkeley is not making a trivial semantic point, but a substantive claim that one might come to believe on the basis of reflection, that is, by unsuccessfully seeking counter-examples.

Berkeley concludes PHK 3 with his famous slogan, that, for sensible things, "*esse* is *percipi*". Sometimes this is misquoted as "*esse est percipi*", a Latin translation of "to be is to be perceived". But Berkeley did not write that, and not for lack of Latin, so we should take his careful choice of words as significant. "*Esse*" is a technical term in scholastic philosophy for the nature or being of something, so by using this term Berkeley is saying that his earlier point about the meaning or purpose of talk about sensible things reveals their true nature; namely, that they are objects of perception. It is this claim that he uses in PHK 4 and 6 to hammer home his objection to (i): think hard about what sensible things "mean to you" – that is, about what impact they have on your or anyone else's lives – and you will see that their nature is to be perceived, that they are essentially objects of perception.

At first sight, this line of argument is wildly implausible, because even if sensible things such as daffodils and ducks were only contingently perceived, if they had a material nature, it could still be the case that our interest in them was exhausted by what we perceived, that is, *so far as we are concerned* they only exist to be perceived. Effectively, Berkeley has moved from how things are for us to how they are in themselves, and this is unjustified. However, we should not be happy with this criticism, since it leaves the puzzle of why Berkeley found this unjustified move so attractive (cf. DHP3 234). The resolution of that puzzle lies in noting that Berkeley is arguing against (i) here, so his concern is with the true nature of the immediate objects of perception, which he is calling ideas. Now, if the objector holds that such things might have a nature distinct from what is revealed in perception, then she needs an account of what it is to perceive an idea that allows a gap between appearance and reality. But we have seen that Berkeley allows no such gap within perception, so how sensible things seem just is how they are: they can have no "true" nature that is not part of how they are for us. We can call this property of ideas "transparency".

A very common criticism of Berkeley is that he first of all makes a terminological stipulation in specifying that the objects of sense-perception are ideas, then draws on a philosophical theory of ideas, which holds that they are mind-dependent and transparent, to conclude that the objects of perception are not material. But the inference is invalid, because when "idea" is stipulated to mean "object of perception", there is no implication of mind-dependence or transparency. Transparent ideas are special sorts of objects introduced for special purposes by philosophers, so the identification of these with what we ordinarily take to be the objects of sense-perception is a substantive thesis that needs an argument. Berkeley appears to offer no argument and instead make the identification by stipulation.

Perhaps Berkeley did make this rather silly mistake, or perhaps he was simply arguing *ad hominem* against Locke and his followers, in the belief that they would accept the stipulation as true. Perhaps, but there is another explanation: if Berkeley's view of what it is to have a sense-perception entails the transparency of the objects of perception, whatever they are, then the argument is enthymematic but not invalid. We saw above (in "Appearance and reality") why Berkeley cannot accept the act–object or adverbial accounts of perceiving an idea, and that instead he needs to reject the receptivity assumption. But once that has been rejected, the transparency of the objects of perception, whatever they are, is a consequence. So if we are to be charitable in reading the argument of PHK 3–4, we must see it as premised on the rejection of the receptivity of perception: trees and mountains are among the objects of perception; the objects of perception are transparent, not because they are stipulated to be ideas but because of the nature of perception, and they can be seen not to exist without the mind (cf. Fogelin 2001: 29–30); so trees and mountains only exist when perceived.

PHK 5 introduces an explanation of why someone might mistakenly endorse (i), which is that they abstract the existence of sensible things from their being perceived, which would only be possible if one could conceive or imagine such things existing unperceived, but one cannot do that because one's "conceiving or imagining power does not extend beyond the possibility of real existence or perception" (PHK 5). That is, one cannot conceive or imagine what one cannot perceive, and one cannot perceive a sensible object existing unperceived. This last point is taken up again in PHK 22–3, which I shall discuss in the next section.

Supposing that we find this as persuasive a line of argument against (i) as Berkeley did, what of (ii) and (iii)? The argument against (ii) occurs in PHK 7, 16 and 17, and amounts to saying that this form of materialism is vacuous, for the relation of subsistence or inherence is never explained, but even if anyone could make sense of it, it would amount to a simple confusion. For sensible qualities are said to inhere in material substance but, as has already been shown, sensible qualities are necessarily perceived, and so they cannot subsist, inhere or otherwise exist in unthinking material substance.

One line of response to this would be to say that ideas, that is the objects of sense-experience, are the appearances of things (e.g. Lennon 2001). An appearance is always an appearance *to* some perceiving mind, so Berkeley's rejection of (i) is correct, but an appearance is also an appearance *of* some thing or things, and these are the material objects. What is the relation between an appearance and that which it is an appearance of? The proponent of (ii) takes it to be the relation of predicate to subject, e.g. "the daffodil is yellow" predicates yellowness of the daffodil (whereas the proponent of (iii) takes it to be resemblance or representation.) Since Berkeley thinks that the daffodil we perceive is a collection of the qualities we perceive (PHK 1), he does not think that ordinary predications describe a relation of inherence between a property and a distinct kind of thing, a substance (PHK 49). So if the yellowness is an appearance of something in this sense, it is not an appearance of the seen and felt daffodil, but of some unperceived material substratum, and the accusation of vacuity or incoherence stands.

The materialist must then take ideas to be appearances of material things in the sense of being effects of those things that represent their causes. This is representative realism. Berkeley has two objections. The first is simply that "an idea can be like nothing but an idea" (PHK 8). Since ideas are necessarily perceived and the material is unperceived, an idea cannot be like something material, and so ideas cannot be appearances of matter. The second is slightly more complex. Berkeley, like many others, thinks that conflicts of perceptual experience, such as something looking black to one person but blue to another, give reason to doubt that our perceptual experiences taken as a whole represent a material world. He then argues that if there is reason to doubt that some perceived qualities represent the true nature of the world, then this doubt will spread to all of them, undermining representative realism. One way the doubt will spread is from the fact that we cannot know which, if either, of two conflicting experiences is the "true" one. Suppose the coat looks blue to me and black to you; we cannot both be right but, according to Berkeley, nor can we ever know which, if either, of us is right (PHK 15). This forces us to treat them all as equally mistaken, and thus undermines the thought that our colour experiences represent the nature of the world to us.

Some representative realists accept the point about colour and other "secondary qualities", but insist that there are some "primary" qualities we perceive that can be understood as representing the nature of the material world to us (PHK 9). Colours, sounds, tastes and textures are secondary qualities; shape, size, motion and solidity are primary qualities. Berkeley's objection here is, first, that we cannot in fact conceive of a reality that has size and shape but no colour (PHK 10) and, secondly, that the arguments that lead us to doubt that the secondary qualities represent the true nature of the world apply equally well to the primary qualities (PHK 11–14).

The "Master Argument"

In PHK 22–3 Berkeley offers a very famous argument. He tries to show that it is impossible to even conceive of a tree or a book existing unperceived. This is often called Berkeley's Master Argument, after Gallois (1974). Some (e.g. Pappas 2000) think that it is the culmination of a single strand of argument that reaches back to PHK 3–7 and even, via the references to abstraction, to the Introduction. The argument goes like this:

1. If I cannot imagine a tree existing unperceived, I cannot conceive of a tree existing unperceived.
2. If I cannot conceive of a tree existing unperceived, it is impossible for a tree to exist unperceived.
3. If it is impossible for a tree to exist unperceived, materialism is false.
4. If I try to imagine a tree existing unperceived, I always imagine a tree which is perceived by me.
5. So I cannot imagine a tree existing unperceived.
6. So materialism is false.

Every premise of this argument has been challenged by some philosopher or other, except for 3. Premise 1 expresses the implausible view that to conceive of something is to form an image of it in one's mind (Pitcher 1977: 67; McGinn 1983: 80–81), premise 2 overlooks the fact that many things once inconceivable have turned out not merely to be possible but true (e.g. human beings on the moon), and the error of premise 4 has been diagnosed in many different ways, for example, it confuses the fact that when we visualize something we always do so from a point of view, with the claim that the point of view is part of what we visualize (Williams 1973; Noordhof 2002), or it confuses conceiving that some tree exists unconceived with conceiving of some tree that it exists unconceived (Urmson 1982: 45). But before discussing the merits of the argument, we should consider whether it can really be attributed to Berkeley.

It is not clear that 3 is a premise of the argument in PHK 22–3, since Berkeley writes: "if you can but conceive it possible for one extended moveable substance, or in general, for any one idea or anything like an idea, to exist otherwise than in a mind perceiving it, I shall readily give up the cause" (PHK 22). This conditional says: if you can imagine a tree existing unperceived, then materialism is true; whereas the conjunction of premises 2 and 3 only entails: if you cannot imagine a tree existing unperceived, then materialism is false. If we substituted what Berkeley actually wrote for premises 2 and 3, then the argument would commit the fallacy of affirming the consequent. Rather, what Berkeley says here suggests that he sees the Master Argument as a response to an objection rather than an argument for immaterialism. His claim that he is "content to put the whole upon this issue" (PHK 22) is a gambling metaphor and need mean no more than that, if he loses this point, he loses everything: again making his argument a reply to an anticipated objection.

In the first four sentences of PHK 22, Berkeley appears to repeat the argument of PHK 3–4. Then, with the gambling metaphor, he offers a challenge: if you can conceive of an idea or anything like an idea existing unperceived, he will accept the truth of materialism. In PHK 23 he imagines someone rising to the challenge, and tries to show that she will unavoidably fail. None of this needs Berkeley to accept premises 2 and 3. However, at the end of PHK 23 he writes: "A little attention will discover to anyone the truth and evidence of what is here said, and make it unnecessary to insist on any other proofs against the existence of material substance". Given that what has been "here said" is that we cannot conceive of ordinary things such as trees and books existing unperceived, this sentence suggests that he takes himself to have given an argument with the conclusion that materialism is false. Perhaps Berkeley is overstating his case here, for when he reprises the argument in the First Dialogue (DHP1 200) it is quite clearly a reply to an objection; or perhaps he is thinking back to the argument of PHK 3–4, repeated in PHK 22, which does give him a reason to draw conclusions about the nature of objects such as trees from what is or is not contained in our conception of them. One thing is clear, though: it is unclear from the text what Berkeley took himself to be arguing at this point.

If Berkeley is not giving a knockdown argument *for* immaterialism in PHK 23, we can search for a more sympathetic interpretation. Consider the argument in full:

> But say you, surely there is nothing easier than to imagine trees, for instance, in a park, or books, in a closet, and no body by to perceive them … But do not you yourself perceive or think of them all the while? … When we do our utmost to conceive the existence of external bodies, we are all the while only contemplating our own ideas. But the mind taking no notice of itself, is deluded to think it can and doth conceive bodies existing unthought of or without the mind; though at the same time they are apprehended by or exist in itself.
>
> (PHK 23)

If this argument really aimed to show that any idea I can conceive or think of is necessarily perceived by me, it would be far too strong, for it would make the sense-experiences of other people literally inconceivable (Tipton 1974: 161; Pitcher 1977: 112–13). This would in turn make inconceivable Berkeley's claim that the table might exist when unperceived by me because it is perceived by "some other spirit". Clearly there is a need to distinguish between thinking that someone else has ideas similar to mine, and perceiving those ideas of theirs. The question then is why does Berkeley think that the obvious impossibility of perceiving an idea and yet that idea being unperceived entails that I cannot conceive of an idea that is unperceived by anyone. Is this just an error or confusion on his part?

We can come at this question indirectly. Someone who argues along the lines of 1–6 must think that there are facts about what is conceivable that can be determined independently of what is possible and thus be used to draw metaphysical conclusions. But in the few places where Berkeley relates conceivability and possibility, he appears to be suggesting the reverse; namely, that we should argue from something being impossible to its being inconceivable: "But I deny that I can abstract one from another, or conceive separately, those qualities which it is impossible should exist so separated" (PHK Intro 10, cf. PHK 5). If we are to argue from impossibilities to inconceivabilities, then the undeniable fact that there cannot be an idea before my mind that is unperceived, that is, before no mind, could only lead us to think that it is inconceivable that an idea should exist unperceived *via* showing that it is impossible that an idea should exist unperceived, and that would lead us back to the argument of PHK

3–4. Underlying that argument is a conception of possibility that is broadly Aristotelian: some propositions are necessarily true because some properties are essential. To say that ideas are necessarily perceived is to say that being perceived is essential to the nature of an idea (Winkler (1989: 76–100) disagrees).

In PHK 23 Berkeley is considering an objector who thinks that it is conceivable that an idea should exist unperceived. The objector must show that it is possible for some idea to exist unperceived, which she does by claiming to imagine an unperceived idea, such as a book in a closet. If this imagining is to establish a possibility on the broadly Aristotelian account, it is by showing that being perceived is not part of the nature or *esse* of the idea. And to show that, the objector must produce an idea that is unperceived, which cannot be done, so the objection fails. We can reveal this line of argument by a slight rephrasing of the crucial sentence from PHK 23:

> This therefore is nothing to the purpose: it only shows you have the power of imagining or forming ideas in your mind; but it does not show that *it is* possible the objects of your thought may exist without the mind: to make out this, it is necessary that you *have an idea before your mind which is also not before any mind*, which is a manifest repugnancy.

So Berkeley's Master Argument is either a fallacious argument for immaterialism, or a valid response to an objection, resting upon the doctrine that one can only grasp the *esse* of an idea by having it before one's mind. As he said in the Introduction: "I do not see how [the reader] can be led into an error by considering his own naked, undisguised ideas" (PHK Intro 25).

Concluding comments

When I was an undergraduate I was encouraged to think that Berkeley had spotted the fundamental flaws in representative realism, but that his own view rested on bad arguments and was obviously unacceptable. Thus the task posed to philosophers by Berkeley's writings was to find a reasonable middle-way between two extremes. I later came to the view that Berkeley is no extremist. He certainly does not think he is offering an extreme or implausible view, so either he is self-deceived or his real view is not *obviously* unacceptable. My main objective in this chapter has been to find a reading of the *Principles* that displays the moderate Berkeley. This is not easy and has required us to pay attention to fine distinctions and detailed textual analysis.

The discussion has been structured around two questions: how can Berkeley's denial of matter not amount to a denial of the objective world of ordinary objects, and what arguments could have led Berkeley to such a strong conviction in his views? The key to answering the first question was to see that ideas are not necessarily items within the mind, and are in that sense not even mental. Rather, they are items, objects of perception, that are necessarily related to minds. Berkeley argues that our ideas fall into two categories – those that we cause and those that we do not cause – and that the latter must be caused by some other mind, which Berkeley takes to be God. This distinction also enables Berkeley to distinguish between sense-perceptions and imaginings, although not between veridical and illusory sense-perceptions. To do the latter he needs to make a further distinction between what we perceive with our senses and what we judge on the basis of those perceptions. That still leaves the question of what happens to ordinary objects when there is no one there to perceive them. Some things Berkeley says suggest that God plays some role in sustaining unperceived objects, perhaps by perceiving them in our absence. But other things he says suggest he did not take the problem to be particularly important because objects unperceived by any finite creature would make no practical difference to us (remember that only minds have causal powers).

From Berkeley's very rapid argument for immaterialism in the first few pages of the *Principles*, it is clear that he believed there is something very wrong about the thought that the sort of thing we perceive by sense might exist unperceived. The opening sections of the *Principles* suggest that this is something to do with the meaning of the word "exist", but it is unclear what the connection is since "unperceived table" is not an oxymoron. If "*esse* is *percipi*" is not a semantic claim, it could be based on the following line of thought: the true nature of the objects of perception is revealed in perception; actual or potential existence unperceived is not revealed in perception; so it is not part of their nature to exist unperceived.

Most famous of all Berkeley's arguments against existence unperceived is the claim that it is impossible to conceive of an unconceived tree. This is normally construed as an attempt to prove that materialism is false and has been roundly criticized for failing to do so. But if we read it as responding to an objection, as defending immaterialism against the claim that materialism is true because we can conceive of an unconceived tree, then it looks more plausible. But so construed it seems to rely upon the earlier argument for "*esse* is *percipi*", and thus adds no new reason to accept immaterialism.

When properly understood, immaterialism is a coherent and not implausible metaphysics. But in the *Principles* Berkeley gives us no clear, let alone clearly compelling, arguments for accepting it. What seems to be really driving his immaterialism is a strong sense of the inadequacy of the alternatives, so it is not surprising that in the *Three Dialogues* he frames the debate in terms of which view, the materialist or the immaterialist, has fewest unacceptable consequences.

Note on references

References to the *Principles* are given by section number, thus PHK 49 means *Principles of Human Knowledge* section 49. References to the *Three Dialogues* are given by dialogue number and page number in Berkeley (1948–57); thus DHP2 214 means page 214 of the second of the *Three Dialogues between Hylas and Philonous*.

Bibliography

Ayers, M. 1975. "Introduction". In G. Berkeley, *Philosophical Works*, M. Ayers (ed.). London: J. M. Dent (Everyman).

Berkeley, G. 1948–57. *The Works of George Berkeley Bishop of Cloyne*, A. A. Luce & T. E. Jessop (eds). London: Thomas Nelson.

Berkeley, G. 1975. *Philosophical Works*, M. Ayers (ed.). London: J. M. Dent (Everyman).

Berkeley, G. 1998. *A Treatise Concerning the Principles of Human Knowledge*, J. Dancy (ed.). Oxford: Oxford University Press.

Dancy, J. 1987. *Berkeley: An Introduction*. Oxford: Blackwell.

Fogelin, R. 2001. *Berkeley and the Principles of Human Knowledge*. London: Routledge.

Foster, J. & R. Robinson(eds) 1985. *Essays on Berkeley*. Oxford: Clarendon Press.

Gallois, A. 1974. "Berkeley's Master Argument", *Philosophical Review* **83**, 55–69.

Henry, D. 2000. "Berkeley's Passive Mind", *Minerva* **4**, www.ul.ie/~philos/ (accessed Dec. 2004).

Hume, D. 1978. *A Treatise of Human Nature*, L. A. Selby-Bigge (ed.), P. H. Nidditch (rev.). Oxford: Clarendon Press.

Lennon, T. 2001. "Berkeley on the Act-Object Distinction", *Dialogue* **40**, 651–67.

Luce, A. 1945. *Berkeley's Immaterialism*. London: Thomas Nelson.

Malebranche, N. 1980. *The Search After Truth*, T. M. Lennon & P. J. Olscamp (trans.). Columbus, OH: Ohio State University Press.

McGinn, C. 1983. *The Subjective View*. Oxford: Clarendon Press.

Mill, J. S. 1996. "Berkeley's Life and Writings". In *Collected Works of John Stuart Mill, XI: Essays on Philosophy and the Classics*, J. M. Robson (ed.). London: Routledge.

Muehlmann, R. (ed.) 1995. *Berkeley's Metaphysics*. University Park, PA: Pennsylvania University Press.

Noordhof, P. 2002. "Imagining Objects and Imagining Experiences", *Mind and Language* **17**, 426–55.

Pappas, G. 2000. *Berkeley's Thought*. Ithaca, NY: Cornell University Press.

Peacocke, C. 1986. *Thoughts: An Essay on Content*. Oxford: Blackwell.

Pitcher, G. 1977. *Berkeley*. London: Routledge.

Stoneham, T. 2002. *Berkeley's World*. Oxford: Oxford University Press.

Tipton, I. C. 1974. *Berkeley: The Philosophy of Immaterialism*. London: Methuen.

Urmson, J. O. 1982. *Berkeley*. Oxford: Oxford University Press.

Williams, B. 1973. "Imagination and the Self". In *Problems of the Self*. Cambridge: Cambridge University Press.

Winkler, K. 1989. *Berkeley: An Interpretation*. Oxford: Clarendon Press.

Further reading

The best modern edition of the *Principles* is the Oxford Philosophical Texts edition edited by Jonathan Dancy (1998), although the Everyman edition edited by Michael Ayers (1975) is also very good and contains much else besides the *Principles*. Short and accessible overviews of Berkeley's thought can be found in Dancy, *Berkeley: An Introduction* (1987) and Urmson, *Berkeley* (1982). Fogelin, *Berkeley and the Principles of Human Knowledge* (2001) is a stimulating commentary on the *Principles* aimed at students. Foster and Robinson's *Essays on Berkeley* (1985) contains interesting papers on a wide range of themes in Berkeley's thought.

7

David Hume

A Treatise of Human Nature

P. J. E. Kail

David Hume's *A Treatise of Human Nature: Being an Attempt to introduce the experimental Method of Reasoning into Moral Subjects* is an immensely complex, endlessly fascinating and hugely influential work. It is a bold attempt to give a secular account of the nature of human minds, based on the methods of science, an attempt that is tinged with sceptical lessons about the extent of human knowledge. Its full meaning remains controversial to this day and here I attempt to give a flavour of the work and its difficulties.

The work comprises three volumes (now referred to as "Books"): "Of the understanding", "Of the passions" and "Of morals". The first two books were published anonymously in January 1739, the third (by a different publisher but again anonymously) in November 1740. The Advertisement to the first two books tells us that the "subjects of the understanding and the passions make a compleat chain of reasoning by themselves", whereas the Advertisement to Book III suggests some measure of independence of this book from the first two. The ambition of the work is shown by Hume's intention, expressed in the first Advertisement, to produce a further volume (or perhaps volumes) on politics and criticism. This intention was derailed, or at least redirected, by the failure, in Hume's view, of the *Treatise*. It "fell dead-born from the press", he records in *My Own Life* (a brief autobiography penned in April 1776). Although the first two books of the *Treatise* were not entirely ignored, their early reception was not to Hume's liking. In March 1740 he published an *Abstract* (again anonymously) of the first two books of the *Treatise* in an effort, perhaps, to clarify and promote their central claims. He seemed to be unhappy with the *Treatise* at an early stage: before Book III was published, Hume wrote to Francis Hutcheson in March 1740 expressing "some impatience for a Second Edition". There was to be no second edition, although Hume added an *Appendix* that makes some additions, corrections and confesses to some difficulties. Many of the topics of all three books of the *Treatise* were, as Hume puts it in *My Own Life* "cast ... anew" later in his career. Book I transformed into *An Enquiry concerning Human Understanding*, published in 1748 (its original title, *Philosophical Essays concerning Human Understanding*, being changed to its now familiar one in 1756). The topic of the passions was treated in "Of the Passions", published in the 1757 *Four Dissertations*. This work, which later became called "A Dissertation on the Passions", contains much verbatim material from the *Treatise*. The topics of Book III are treated in the 1751 *An Enquiry concerning the Principles of Morals*.

The complexity and subtlety of the *Treatise* have occasioned very different readings and endless scholarly debate. L. A. Selby-Bigge, writing in 1893, says:

> Hume's philosophic writings are to be read with great caution. His pages, especially those of the Treatise, are so full of matter, he says many different things in so many different ways and different connexions, and with so much indifference to what he has said before, that it is very hard to say positively that he taught, or did not teach, this or that particular doctrine ... This makes it easy to find all philosophies in Hume, or, by setting one statement against another, none at all. (Hume 1975: Editor's introduction, vii)

There is much to this cautionary note, and, indeed, some have despaired of finding any coherent system in the *Treatise*. John Passmore accuses Hume of being a "philosophical puppy-dog, picking up and worrying one problem after another, always leaving his teeth-marks in it, but casting it aside when it threatened to become wearisome" (1968: 87–8). Furthermore, there has been a recent trend to take Hume's *Enquiry concerning Human Understanding* as the definitive statement of his philosophy, a trend accompanied by an insinuation that the *Treatise* is an unsystematic work (see e.g. Buckle 2001; Millican 2002a).

Two things need to be said at this early stage. Since this series is devoted to works rather than philosophers, we have already a reason to concentrate on the *Treatise* rather than the first *Enquiry*. The *Treatise* is the work that has attracted the bulk of philosophical attention and thus constitutes a central work of philosophy (I shall, though, say a little about the relation of the *Treatise* to the first *Enquiry* later). We shall also concentrate on Book I of the *Treatise* rather than the work as a whole. The excuse for concentrating on Book I is again its canonical status. Outside scholarly circles, most of Book II is little read by philosophers and Book III is often read independently of Book I. This is not to say that a unified reading of the *Treatise* cannot be given or is undesirable. It is merely to record a fact about the role of the *Treatise* in the philosophical canon (for two systematic readings of the *Treatise*, see Norman Kemp Smith (1941) and Annette Baier (1991)).

Influences

Although we shall touch on some of the influences on the *Treatise* when we look at particular topics, it is worth giving a brief overview of them. After a sojourn in France, predominately in La Flèche in Anjou, Hume returned to England with a manuscript in 1737 and secured a publishing contract for the first two volumes in 1738. From France, in a letter dated 26 August 1737, he wrote to a friend advising him what to read in preparation for the *Treatise*. The list comprises Malebranche's monumental *Recherche de la Vérité* (*The Search After Truth*), Berkeley's *Principles of Human Knowledge*, "some of the more metaphysical articles" of Bayle's *Dictionary*, and Descartes's *Meditations*. In the same letter, Hume writes that the bulk of his ideas have "so little dependence on all former systems of Philosophy, that your natural Good Sense will afford you Light enough to judge of their Force and Solidity". That Hume mentions four authors in this letter by no means implies that they are the only important influences on the *Treatise*. As David Fate Norton writes, Hume's "breadth of study and reading" suggests that "no single writer or philosophical tradition can be relied upon to provide a comprehensive key to his thought" (1993a: 1–2). We can identify connections between the doctrines of the *Treatise* and many early modern thinkers, including Arnauld, Hobbes, Mandeville, Butler, Boyle, Pascal, Samuel Clarke and many others.

Some major figures absent from the list in Hume's letter who are often claimed as influences on Hume are Hutcheson (with whom Hume corresponded during the writing of some of the *Treatise*), Locke and Newton. In all three cases the influence is real enough, but can be overstated and may sometimes be vicarious. This is especially true of Newton. Certainly Hume is fond of Newtonian-sounding metaphors and phrases, and refers to him at a number of places, but appeal to Newton in the period was fairly commonplace and need not speak of any deep knowledge (Barfoot 1990: 161; for a contrary view, see Buckle (2001: 69ff)). A better case can be made for Locke, but it can be overstated. An impressive case for Locke's relation to Hume in his discussion of reason can be made (see e.g. Owen 1999), but with some topics about which Locke had a lot to say (e.g.

personal identity, substance and essence), there is surprisingly little evidence of any direct engagement with Locke's arguments or concepts by Hume. Locke's discussion of the derivation of the idea of power does not get considered by Hume until the *Appendix*. Furthermore, Hume's conception of secondary qualities such as heat and cold as "nothing but perceptions in the mind" has more affinity with Malebranche's and Bayle's conception of secondary qualities than Locke's view of them as corpuscular powers. Hutcheson's influence on Hume was emphasized by Kemp Smith, who argued that Hume's purpose is inspired by Hutcheson's theory of moral feeling to show that all reason is to be subordinated to feeling, but both the thesis and the extent of the influence are now viewed as overstated.

Returning to the list, evidence of Pierre Bayle's influence can be found in Hume's discussion of space, time and the void, his treatment of secondary qualities and the immateriality of the soul. Bayle was a French sceptic, concerned to undercut the pretensions of reason to make way for fideism, the doctrine that belief in the end depends on faith rather than reason. Berkeley's treatment of abstract ideas is referred to by Hume with approval. As for Malebranche, much of Hume's vocabulary bears the influence of Malebranche's monumental *Search After Truth*, as well as his treatment of particular topics (especially causation). Indeed, there are paragraphs of the *Treatise* that are almost word for word translations of Malebranche (see e.g. Wright 1983; McCracken 1983), giving some weight to Dr Johnson's remark that Hume's prose style is not English but French. This influence is extensive and rather interesting, since Hume and Malebranche are of very different philosophical tempers. Malebranche claimed to introduce a "science of man", but went on to produce a highly baroque, and deeply Christian metaphysical system. Hume, who took on the same project, came to a rather different conclusion. For Malebranche, our God-like nature is expressed in reason, which, because of original sin, has become trapped in the corporeal body. Human beings are sinful creatures, misled and trapped by the senses, passions, the imagination and mechanical sympathy. These faculties pollute pure reason and, although useful, constitute a stain on our true nature. For Hume, whose lifetime concern was on the harmful effects of religious thinking on human life, Malebranche is fundamentally mistaken; the science of man shows that the senses, imagination, passion and sympathy are the very stuff of human nature, and not something that we should attempt to transcend.

What is the project of the *Treatise*?

There are a number of different views of the project of the *Treatise*, each of which emphasizes the importance of different and detectable strands of thought therein. These strands are *naturalism*, *scepticism* and a certain *analytical* or *conceptual* project, involving a thesis about concepts and their relation to experience. We begin with naturalism.

If we take the introduction to the *Treatise* at face value, then it seems that naturalism is in the driving seat. There, Hume announces his project as a "science of human nature". Any science, says Hume, must have a solid foundation, and that must be "experience and observation". Through the use of "careful and exact experiments", we can derive a number of general explanatory principles for mental phenomena. Such a science, however, should not be confused with complete and transparent knowledge of the workings of the mind. "Any hypothesis", he writes, "that pretends to discover the ultimate original qualities of human nature, ought at first be rejected as presumptuous and chimerical" (T *Introduction* 8; SBN xvii). The "essence of the mind" is unknown to us. Once we have derived our general principles, we can understand better the operations of the mind, and crucially, its limits. We can then "sit down contented", aware that "we can give no reason for our most general and refin'd principles, besides our experience of their reality" (T *Introduction* 9; SBN xviii).

This brief statement of Hume's intentions is sufficient to give it a Newtonian flavour. For Newton, the correct experimental method in natural philosophy (roughly, physics) is to start with experience and observation and derive by induction some more general principles. Newton's famous slogan, *hypotheses non fingo* ("I frame no hypotheses") is an injunction against taking some relatively determinate *a priori* conception of physical body as a starting-point for investigation and attempting to derive the laws of motion from it. Instead we start with observable facts and draw general principles from them. This marks a key departure from Cartesian physics, which, although highly experimental, adheres to an *a priori* conception of matter as a substance whose essence is pure extension. To a great extent, Hume applies the same "experimental method" to the mind, whose essence, he says is "unknown to us with that of external bodies" (T *Introduction* 8; SBN xvii), thus applying the same schematic method in "moral philosophy" (which we now call philosophy) as Newton's in natural philosophy, that is, natural science. The "Newton of the mind" proposes in the *Abstract* "to anatomize nature in a regular manner, and promises to draw no conclusions but where he is authorized by experience. He talks with contempt of hypotheses" (T *Abstract* 2; SBN 646).

This feature makes for a naturalism that is methodological. The methods that have brought success in our knowledge of the natural world should be applied to the mental. Hume will also pursue an explanatory project, explaining the operations of the mind and the formation of certain key beliefs, by appeal to more minimal, and more tractable, ingredients. By appeal to the association of ideas, Hume will attempt to explain why we form beliefs in causal powers, in enduring selves, in space and time and in an external world. We shall look at some of these explanations a little later, but his attempt to explain the operations of reason is a vital part of this project. Before Hume, philosophers had thought (or assumed) that reason was an inherently normative "faculty". (For a good discussion see Owen (1999) and Hatfield (1990: Ch. 1).) The "faculty" was supposed to explain how such and such beliefs are derived from other beliefs in the mind of the thinker. Furthermore, being a product of the "faculty" bestowed upon beliefs positive normative status: that is, it makes them the justified, rational or best thing to believe. But talk of "faculties" was one of the favourite targets of early modern philosophers, most memorably summed up by Molière's satire on a related notion of "virtue". If one asks why opium puts people to sleep, the response that it has some "dormitive virtue" is vacuous, since it does not specify any details of the mechanism by which it has that effect. Hume thinks he can do better. Given a closer look at the mechanisms of the mind, he can offer genuine explanations of how we come to believe things. But this account does not make reason inherently normative. It explains *how* we infer, but that we do so does not show that those inferences are *correct* or the *right* thing to infer. Hume's causal explanation of inference is often neutral on that issue.

Armed with a broadly Newtonian methodology, Hume intends to offer a new, explanatory theory of human nature. This tradition of interpretation has given us two classic works, Kemp Smith's *The Philosophy of David Hume* (1941) and Stroud's *Hume* (1977), as well as impressive recent works (e.g. Baier 1991; Garrett 1997; Owen 1999). Indeed, recent work has taken Hume to be instigating a form of cognitive science. But if there is one "ism" that is most associated with the *Treatise*, and Hume's philosophy in general, it is scepticism. So far the science of human nature does not seem sceptical and, moreover, talk of a "science of human nature" seems set against anything we might recognize as sceptical.

The extent and nature of Hume's scepticism is one of the most difficult topics in Hume scholarship. An extreme sceptical reading comes from Thomas Reid, who claimed that the *Treatise* was "a system of scepticism which leaves no ground to believe any one thing rather than its contrary" (Reid 1997: 4). On this view, Hume is not only interested in explaining *how* we come to have our beliefs and how we make inferences, but also delivers a negative evaluation of them: they are all unjustified, or all the inferences we make are irrational. Few these days would concur with Reid's extreme reading, but that some form of scepticism plays a significant role in Hume's thought is undeniable, and is emphasized by, among others, Robert Fogelin (1985). Furthermore the image of Hume as a sceptic – especially his supposed formulation of "the problem of induction" –

had an influence on twentieth-century Anglo-American philosophy that is difficult to overestimate.

Certainly Hume does not deny that he was a sceptic: quite the reverse. But it does not follow from this that Hume's teachings yield the conclusion Reid claims for them. The accusation of scepticism was levelled very early at Hume, together with a charge of atheism. These contributed to his failure to secure the Chair of Moral Philosophy at Edinburgh in 1745. In a letter penned during the controversy surrounding his attempt to secure the Chair, Hume defended himself against a number of charges, and wrote that the purpose of scepticism is:

> to abate the Pride of *mere human Reasoners*, by showing them, that even with regard to the Principles which seem the clearest, and which they are necessitated from the Strongest Instincts of Nature to embrace, they are not able to attain a full Consistence and absolute Certainty. (Hume 1967: 19).

This suggests that the function of scepticism is to tell us something about the nature of "mere human reasoners", pricking its pretensions by showing that certain standards of "absolute Certainty" cannot be met, rather than offering the extreme conclusion that all belief is irrational. The relation between scepticism and naturalism will be taken up when we discuss some of the particular movements of the *Treatise*, but the reader is warned that this remains a controversial topic.

The same is true of the final strand in the *Treatise*, which I have called the analytical or conceptual. Hume adopts, as we shall see, something known as the "Copy Principle": roughly the thesis that all our simple ideas or concepts are derived from experience. Hume will use the Copy Principle to examine our ideas to reveal "their true meaning", and to expose other putative terms as "meaningless" when no appropriate experience can be linked to them. In the heyday of logical positivism, this strand of Hume's thinking was greatly appealing, offering a way to expose metaphysical questions as devoid of content. Thus in the *Abstract*, Hume writes:

> when he [the author of the *Treatise*] suspects that any philosophical term has no idea annexed to it (as is too common) he always asks, *from what impression that pretended idea is derived*? And if no impression can be produced, he concludes that the term is altogether insignificant. (T *Abstract* 7; SBN 648–9, original emphasis)

This doctrine about meaning has also suggested to many that Hume ultimately rejects causal powers (see e.g. Rosenberg 1993) and, to some, that he adopts a phenomenalism about the external world. To parody this view of Hume's philosophy, A. J. Ayer's *Language, Truth and Logic* constitutes a 1930s update of the *Treatise*, making Hume an "anti-realist". If one can't properly mean anything by "causal powers", no question about their existence can even be raised. Asking whether linglops exist, or whether there really are linglops, is pointless, since "linglops" is totally meaningless (I have just made the term up). The term "causal power", although it may sound as if it has a meaning, is really in the same semantic boat as linglops, and it is equally as pointless to ask whether there really are causal powers as it is to ask whether linglops exist. Recently, considerable scholarly pressure has been put on this reading by a number of interpreters under the label "sceptical realism" (see Wright 1983; Craig 1987: Chs 1 & 2; Strawson 1989; Read & Richman 2000; Kail, forthcoming). Talk of "lacking a meaning" picks up on a lack of an adequate understanding of, for example, the power connecting causally related objects, not that no thought at all can be formed. This, and other issues, will be picked up when we discuss some of the details of the *Treatise*.

Treatise Book I, Part I:
"Of ideas; their origin, composition, connexion, abstraction, & c"

Book I comprises four parts. The first, "Of ideas", concerns the materials of thought, ideas, and their relation to impressions, and how ideas are connected and associated in the mind. There is also a discussion of memory and abstract ideas. Part II, "Of the ideas of space and time", contains Hume's account of how we come to form the ideas of space and time, and includes discussions of the void and existence. Part III, "Of knowledge and probability", is the centrepiece of the work, focusing on probable (inductive) inference, reason and causation. Part IV, "Of the sceptical and other systems of philosophy" discusses scepticism about reason, and about the external world, ancient and modern philosophy, the immateriality of the soul and personal identity, and finishes with a highly dramatic conclusion. It is obvious that there is far too much to handle in an essay of this length. I shall not discuss Hume's treatment of our ideas of space and time (see e.g. Frasca-Spada (1998) for a discussion), and much of the detail of the remaining parts will not get the attention it deserves.

In this section we shall look at the key theses of Book I, Part I, which deals with the fundamentals of Hume's conception of the mind. There is a certain bold simplicity to Hume's theory of in what thinking consists, which has been much criticized, and much of this criticism is well placed (but for a defence of a neo-Humean theory of thought see Fodor (2003)). Book I opens with the claim that all "the perceptions of the human mind resolve themselves into two distinct kinds, which I shall call IMPRESSIONS and IDEAS" (T 1.1.1.1; SBN 1). What is an impression and what is an idea? Hume thinks that the two correspond to feeling and thinking, respectively, and his intention in the opening sections is clear enough, although the distinctions he draws are notoriously slippery. Both impressions and ideas are perceptions, and Hume has a sustained tendency both to reify perceptions and treat them as images. Perceptions are mental "things" or "objects", constituted by sensory properties that the mind manipulates (for a contrary view see Yolton (1984)). The perceptions we have when we sense something are impressions; the perceptions we have when thinking are ideas. As well as sensory impressions and ideas, there are impressions and ideas "of reflection": those passions or attitudes like desire and fear that arise from sensory impressions and ideas. All thinking and feeling is a matter of having "perceptions".

Things start becoming problematic when the difference "betwixt" feeling and thinking is discussed by Hume. Impressions are distinguished from ideas in virtue of the former having greater "force", "vivacity" and "liveliness". But what is force and vivacity? On one interpretation, impressions have a greater *phenomenological* intensity than ideas: they are somehow "brighter" images. But this is a dreadful way of capturing the distinction between feeling and thinking, for one can certainly have a very vivid idea in one's imagination on the one hand and sensory experiences with little phenomenological intensity on the other (e.g. looking at the sea on a murky day – see Pears (1990: Pt 1)). A second view is to take the notion of "force" as an immediate tendency to effect behaviour as central, and think of sensory experiences as having such a force to a greater degree than mere thought (see e.g. Everson 1988). It seems in the end that Hume wants the "intensity" of an image to account for its tendency to affect the mind, which in the end is rather unsatisfactory. The issue of force and liveliness will return when we come to discuss Hume's theory of belief, but even if we can draw the distinction between impressions and ideas, the next question is why this should be important to him.

Hume wants to claim that ideas derive from sensory impressions. More precisely, he is aiming for his "first principle" in the science of human nature, the Copy Principle, whereby all *simple* ideas "are derived from simple impressions, which are correspondent to them, and which they exactly represent" (T 1.1.1.7; SBN 4). Ideas are "copies" of impressions: fainter "images" of their correspondent impressions. To get to this claim Hume will need to distinguish impressions from ideas in a non-circular way, and his unsatisfactory "vivacity" story is his attempt to do so. Notice, however, I mentioned simple ideas, and this introduces a further division between simple and complex perceptions.

Perceptions are typically complex. One's ordinary visual experience involves a complex of colours and shapes, but the elements of these can be extracted in thought into their simple elements (red and square, say). These simple elements of impressions can be manipulated and recombined to form complex ideas for which there is no corresponding complex impression. A somewhat simplistic example will help to get the point across. We can combine our idea of a wing, derived from an impression of a bird, with the idea of a horse, to produce the idea of Pegasus, even though no one has experienced – had an impression of – Pegasus. The Copy Principle then amounts to the claim that the simple or basic elements of thinking are derived from simple sensory impressions. All the materials of thought are thus derived from sensory experience.

The Copy Principle seems to be related to a claim about meaning. Determine the true meaning of an idea by finding its source impression, and if no impression can be found, the term attached to the "pretended idea" is meaningless. So Hume will then argue that we have no impression of self, or of causal power, and so these terms are "meaningless". But as commentators are fond of pointing out, Hume's actual formulation of the Copy Principle makes it a poor polemical weapon. Not only does he present the Copy Principle as a contingent, *a posteriori* claim, thus leaving it prone to counter-examples, but he also introduces his own counter-example, the missing shade of blue. Hume asks us to imagine someone who has experienced every shade of blue except for one, laying all those shades out in his imagination so that the gap in the spectrum becomes apparent to him. He then claims that it is plausible to suppose that this person could furnish an idea of this missing shade of blue, even though he has not had the corresponding impression. Hume is not worried about this "contradictory phenomenon", but should he be? Given that he has admitted a counter-example, can't his opponents say that they have an idea of causal power or self even though there are no relevant impressions? Adding to that the contingent status of the Copy Principle has been thought by some to make it useless as a criterion of meaning.

A common response to these worries is revisionary. Convert a genetic thesis to an analytic claim about meaningfulness (see e.g. Bennett 2001: 215). So although the imagined person has not actually *encountered* the missing shade of blue, Hume's insight about meaning and experience are untouched, since the missing shade of blue is something that *could* be encountered in experience, whereas causal power and selves cannot be, for reasons we shall examine below (see also Fogelin 1992a).

Standing back from the details of Hume's Copy Principle, we should ask what is at stake here. Why is it important to Hume? The key contrast between the so-called rationalists and empiricists turns not on the doctrine of innate ideas, but on whether human beings are equipped with *pure intellect*, a non-sensory mode of apprehension, which facilitates an, in principle, perspicuous grasp of the fundamental nature of the world external to sensory experience. That is to say, our minds can understand how the world is in itself rather than merely how it shows up to us in sensory experience. The rationalists subscribe to such a faculty and empiricists do not. According to the empiricists, we are limited to the deliverance of the senses. For Hume, on some readings, this means that the nature of the external world is closed off from us because of this deep, but contingent, limitation on our faculties.

How are ideas related in Humean minds? Two kinds of relation are introduced: philosophical and natural. The former comprise the seven relations in which ideas can be arbitrarily compared by a kind of mental inspection. These relations are identity, resemblance, relations of space and time, quantity and number, degree of any quality, contrariety and cause and effect. One can be consciously aware of *A* resembling *B*, or *A* being to the left of *B* and so on. The relation of cause and effect is the most complicated, and occupies a great deal of Hume's attention later in the *Treatise*.

Natural relations, on the other hand, are not a matter of arbitrary comparison. Instead, irrespective of any mental activity on our part, ideas become related together in minds in virtue of one of three general "principles of association" (or their combination). These relations comprise *resemblance, contiguity* and *cause and effect*. So if *A* resembles *B*, they become associated in the mind, so that when *A* occurs one will naturally think of *B*. Alternatively, if one has had frequent experience of, say, a cat sat on a chair (contiguity), one will naturally think of the cat when one thinks of the chair. Finally, frequent experience of *A* and *B* standing in the relation of cause and effect will set up habits of thought: when one has experienced, say, fire causing pain, one will think of the pain when one thinks of the fire. Causation is the "most extensive" relation, responsible for much of what is orderly in our patterns of thought.

These principles of association are clearly important for Hume. He writes in the *Abstract*:

> Thro' this whole book, there are great pretensions to new discoveries in philosophy; but if any thing can intitle the author to so glorious a name as that of an inventor, 'tis the use he makes of the principle of the association of ideas, which enters into most of his philosophy … 'Twill be easy to conceive of what vast consequences these principles must be in the science of human nature, if we consider, that so far as regards the mind, these are the only links that bind the parts of the universe together … these are the only ties of our thoughts, [and] they are really *to us* the cement of the universe.
>
> (T *Abstract* 35; SBN 661–2, original emphasis)

But such vast consequences seem to flow from rather flimsy premises, for Hume's introduction of the principles is rather brief and has the distinct air of unargued announcement. One explanation of this brevity is that the principles of association are explanatory postulates, which will be made good in the body of the *Treatise* (see Owen 1999: 77). Another is the fact that similar doctrines were widespread in the early modern period, and Hume expects his audience to be familiar with them. We can find associationism – although not always under that name – in Hobbes, Descartes, Malebranche, Spinoza, Leibniz, Locke and many others. Such mental habits were seen by many philosophers as inevitable and often useful. But they were thought to be second class and due to our animal nature and, very importantly, explicitly contrasted with reason. Hume will attempt to explain the vast proportion of our inferential practices with the principles of association, and all but obliterate this contrast between reason and association.

Before we turn to examine the relation between reason, association and the idea of cause and effect, which comprise the topics of Part III, we need to draw attention to a couple of features of section 7, "Of abstract ideas". The first is his broad agreement with Berkeley's criticism of Locke's notion of abstract ideas. General thinking, both with respect to properties and to kinds, does not owe itself to the formation of abstract general ideas. Hume augments Berkeley's positive account that particular ideas come to stand for general thought with his theory of association of ideas. Rather than there being some single general idea that is supposed to stand for, say, triangularity itself, a particular triangle is associated, by resemblance, with other triangles. When I reason concerning a triangle, and make some claim supposed to apply to all triangles, the ideas associated with the particular idea with which I am reasoning will be revived and serve to correct, or falsify, the claim. This associational practice is supposed to ensure that my thought about triangles extends to all the general facts about triangles.

The second feature of note is a theory of conceivability and its relation to possibility. The account of conceivability Hume exploits involves the "Separability Principle" (for a discussion see Garrett (1997: Ch. 3). Hume writes: "We have observ'd, that whatever objects are different are distinguishable, and whatever objects are distinguishable are separable by the thought and imagination" (T 1.1.7.3; SBN 18). These notions of difference and separability are difficult to determine in a non-circular way, but one suggestion is this. Imagine a particular globe of a particular colour. These are not separable, according to Hume, although we may make a "distinction of reason" with the help of abstract ideas. That is to say, we can understand the colour alone in light of its resemblance to other colours, and, similarly, the shape alone. Hume states, however, that the shape and colour of this particular are neither distinct nor separable, which in turn suggests that separability is a quasi-spatial notion of images occupying visual or tactile space. The particular itself comprises an array of extensionless coloured points, or *minima sensibilia*, which are the true atoms or simples of experience, upon which the phenomenal extension depends. Since any particular figure or extension is composed of these *minima sensibilia*, one cannot separate the shape from the colour. But two non-overlapping objects in phenomenal space can be "separated" in the sense that one can *imagine* the one without the other. To conceive it possible that *A* exists independently of *B* is then to be able to imagine *A* without *B*.

What kind of possibility is revealed by such separations? Hume talks about "metaphysical" and "absolute" possibility and impossibility, and seems to allow a straightforward move from conceivability to metaphysical possibility, when our ideas are "clear" and "adequate" representations of "objects". So we can gain insight into the modal structure of the world – what is possible and what is necessary – through the exercise of our imagination. Plenty in the text seems to suggest this, but things may not be as straightforward as they seem. For ideas may be clear or adequate representations of impressions, but it is not clear that *impressions* are clear or adequate representations of "external objects". If there is a world beyond sensory impressions (and plenty suggests that Hume assumes so), our imagination cannot reveal its modal structure. The importance of this matter will emerge later.

Treatise Part III: "Of knowledge and probability"

The main concerns of Part III are an account of causal inference, the nature of belief and our idea of cause and effect. Hume divides reason into demonstrative reason, which involves "intuition", and probable reason. Hume's conception of intuition and demonstration is notoriously complex (the reader should consult Owen (1999)), but a number of things can be said here. The operative conception of reason is non-formal, or semantic, depending, as it does, crucially on an awareness of the *contents* of ideas and their relations. For example, the idea "Socrates moves" is contained in the idea "Socrates runs" and reason can display this connection, so one can move validly from "Socrates runs" to "Socrates moves". A formal or syntactic conception of deduction would involve an addition premise – "anything that runs, moves" – to render this move valid by appeal to form, either syllogistically or by appeal to quantification. Relatedly, when Hume talks of "arguments", he often moves between what we would express as relations between premises and conclusions on the one hand, and the mental inferences drawn from idea, on the other.

Demonstration involves a more basic cognitive state, namely "intuition". Here, the mind is intimately aware of some *philosophical* relation among ideas. This cognitive state is knowledge, and Hume shares with his contemporaries a conception of knowledge different from the modern conception as true belief plus some other factor, like justification, reliable causation or what have you. Demonstrative reason again yields knowledge, and involves a chain of inference from idea to idea, mediated by an intuitive awareness of some connection holding between their contents. A puzzling feature of demonstrative reason and argument is that their conclusions are not merely necessitated as a consequence of the relevant relations among ideas, but seem to yield conclusions that are necessary truths. One of Hume's favourite moves is to undermine the claim that there can be a demonstrative argument for some proposition by appealing to the fact that conceiving the contrary of that proposition implies no contradiction, thereby revealing that the proposition is *contingent*. Again, this is subject to controversy. For different views see Bennett (2001: 309–12), Millican (2002b: 132–6) and Kail (forthcoming).

The account of probable reason is a little more tractable. All reasoning, says Hume, "consists in nothing but a *comparison*, and a discovery of those relations, either constant or inconstant, which two or more objects bear to each other" (T 1.3.2.1; SBN 73). His first question concerns what *philosophical* relation is the basis for forming beliefs about what we do not presently perceive, and he pitches on the philosophical relation of cause and effect. For example, perceiving now that there is an acrid smell I can infer to what I presently do not perceive (e.g. my dinner is burning). So it looks, at first sight, that the mind can go beyond its present ideas by probable reasoning, reasoning based upon the relation of cause and effect. I reason from my present experience or impression of an acrid smell to the conclusion or idea that my dinner is burning on the basis of the fact that burning food *causes* an acrid smell. But what is our idea of cause and effect?

Hume's initial examination reveals that causes are spatiotemporally contiguous to effects, and temporally prior to them. A further component seems to be that of "necessary connection", or "power", but he immediately notes that the "known qualities" of objects do not reveal power or necessary connection to the senses, and so proposes to approach that aspect of causation obliquely. Hume argues that we cannot have demonstrative knowledge of the proposition that every event must have a cause (T 1.3.3), and in "Of the inference from the impression to the idea" (T 1.1.6) we arrive at a key move in his account of causal inference. When we have an impression of an object, we infer its effect. What is the nature of this inference?

I said above that, since all reasoning consists in comparing objects standing in relations, we might think that we can move from one's present impression to the idea of its effect by comparing the two objects with respect to the relation of cause and effect. But this is what Hume denies in this section. First, he argues that the inference from cause to effect is not explained in terms of our grasp of the essences of objects (T 1.3.6.1). Were we able to do that, we could simply "read off" the effect that some object necessitates, rendering it impossible to *conceive* of the cause without its effect. That is to say, knowledge of essence would allow us to infer *demonstratively* that such and such an effect must "flow" from its essence. But since the ideas involved in cause inference are distinct, we can separate one from the other and thus conceive cause without effect. So, for example, prior to experience of its effect, we cannot tell whether fire might be followed by the freezing of water, the production of honey or a ticking sound, rather than its usual effects of burning wood, heating rooms and so on.

Instead, our inference from cause to effect depends on repeated experience of a cause and its usual effect (T 1.3.6.2). We remember that *A* has been followed by *B* in the past (in relations of contiguity and temporal succession), and, further, that *A* and *B* have been constantly conjoined. Hume then says that constant conjunction is to be added to the idea of causation. But we are not yet to the bottom of things. For how do we become aware that *A* and *B* have been so related? Remember, Hume's question is how we move beyond the present contents of the mind, and experience of *A* and *B* standing in the causal relation seems to presuppose that we have already moved beyond the present contents of our minds. This brings us to Hume's deepest question. How does experience produce the idea of effect *B* when we perceive cause *A*? Are we determined to make this transition by reason or by the association of ideas? Hume then says: "If reason determin'd us, it would proceed upon that principle, *that instances of, which we have had no experience, must resemble those of which we have had experience, and that the course of nature continues uniformly the same*" (T 1.3.6.4; SBN 89) . Call this principle the Uniformity Principle (UP). If "reason determin'd us", our inference would depend on a grasp of the principle, but Hume argues that reason cannot determine a grasp of the UP. First, demonstrative reason cannot produce such a belief. If it did, we would find a change in the course of nature inconceivable, but since we can conceive of such a change, we cannot demonstrate it (see Owen 1999: Ch. 5). Secondly, probable reason – reasoning from cause and effect – cannot itself determine a grasp of the UP, since probable reasoning *is* inference based on a grasp of the UP:

> probability is founded on the presumption of a resemblance betwixt those objects, of which we have had experience, and those, of which we have had none; and therefore 'tis impossible that this presumption can arise from probability. The same principle cannot be both the cause and the effect of another.   (T 1.3.6.7; SBN 90)

Instead, what causes the mind to infer B when A is experienced is the natural or associative relation of cause and effect, the passively acquired habit discussed in the previous section. Reason is not what explains our inferential habits, it is instead explained by association in the imagination.

There are two broad interpretations of this: sceptical and naturalistic (for survey and discussion, see Garrett (1997: Ch. 4)). According to the latter, we have an account of the causal processes of the mind, which attacks the notion of reason as an autonomous and unexplained "normative faculty" productive of inferential transitions. Since there can be no arguments for the UP, something else must explain the inference. On the sceptical reading, Hume is telling us that the inference from past experience to future belief is epistemically worthless. For one cannot justify the use of probable reason by probable reason because such an attempt is circular. The first reading takes the causation of probable inference to be Hume's main concern, the second a conclusion that we can have no justification for it. The former seems closer to the truth. Hume is arguing that no argument can be causally responsible for our inferential practice, and so reason itself cannot be the fundamental source of inference. But this causal fact does not itself undermine the status of such inferences. After all, Hume relies on the experimental method throughout the *Treatise*, and so if he does not trust induction he must distrust his own work, as Baier puts it (Baier 1991: 55). Certainly awareness that our inferential practice is not determined by reason leaves scope to raise a sceptical question, but Hume never declares that probable reason is evidentially worthless.

So much for Hume's account of causal inference. What of his account of belief? Hume thinks that no one has properly addressed the issue of in what the difference between belief and mere conception consists, and he is proud of raising the question, even if, as the *Appendix* attests, he is unhappy with the answer. Somewhat anachronistically, we can distinguish between the content of some attitude and the attitude taken towards that content. Sarah takes the attitude of disbelief to the idea or content that Edmund is in the kitchen, whereas, disagreeing with her, I take the attitude of belief. I think Edmund is in the kitchen, and she does not, but clearly there is a sense in which our different attitudes are about the same idea. Any change of idea would be a change of content, and so Hume argues that a difference in belief cannot be an additional idea: two persons can take different attitudes, of belief or unbelief, to the very same content, so the difference must lie elsewhere. In the body of the *Treatise*, the difference between belief and mere conception parallels the difference between impressions and ideas. Belief involves a higher degree of force and vivacity than mere conception. This vivacity is transferred from the present impression to the idea connected to it, so when I have an impression of A, the imagination produces the idea of B, and the vivacity from A is transferred to B, thus accounting for my *believing* that B will occur when I experience A.

Here again is the issue we touched upon with respect to the difference between impressions and ideas. Is the distinguishing feature some phenomenological feature (vivacity) or is it more to do with the causal effects of the relevant mental state (force)? Hume shows some awareness of this issue in the *Appendix*, but affirms that it is a "peculiar feeling", different from, but analogous to, that which marks impressions. What Hume seems to be looking for is some intrinsic and introspectible feature of belief in virtue of which it has its tendency to affect behaviour, and this is perhaps his key mistake (for a good discussion and further complexities, see Broackes 2002).

The position so far is this. Our reasoning from cause and effect is, at bottom, a matter of brute association, involving the natural relation of cause and effect. The philosophical relation of cause and effect at this stage has been resolved into contiguity, temporal priority and constant conjunction. The associative tracks set up in the imagination thus, in favourable cases, mirror perceivable regularities in experience. The tracks allow for the transference of force and vivacity from present impressions to connected ideas, facilitating belief in future events. This basic story is augmented by a reflective capacity of the mind to form higher-order habits of inference, or general rules, which produce a stable network of inferential patterns, and there is much nuanced discussion of the interplay of probabilities and the transfer of vivacity. All this leads up to an issue that Hume has so far left aside, namely our idea of a necessary connection between cause and effect (T 1.3.14).

A hint of what Hume has to say is dropped earlier, where he writes "Perhaps 'twill appear in the end, that the necessary connexion depends on the inference, instead of the inference's depending on the necessary connexion" (T 1.3.6.3; SBN 88). The thought that the inference could depend on the necessary connection or causal power is that, were we *aware* of the causal power connecting A with B, we could infer *a priori* what causal upshots an object has, rather than having to discover them *a posteriori*. But Hume thinks that we can never do this. So what then explains our idea of necessary connection, since we do not perceive it? Repeated association in the mind not only produces a habit of inference, but also an internal impression or determination of the mind, which is the source of our idea of necessary connection, which is then projected onto objects. So we have an impression of necessity *because* we make certain inferences, rather than making certain inferences *because* we have an impression of genuine causal necessity.

The nature and role of the impression is the topic of much dispute (see e.g. Stroud 1977: 78–9; Pears 1990: 110–19; Bennett 2001: 274–6). Much more vexed, however, is what we should take Hume to be saying about causation. For many, Hume's conclusion is that causation reduces, ontologically speaking, to constant conjunction, temporary priority and contiguity: a form of regularity theory. Given the conceptual strands in Hume's impression and ideas doctrine, mentioned much earlier, it seems that since we don't have an impression of power "in the objects", the most that can be meant by "necessary connection" is the elusive internal determination of the mind. More subtly, the additional idea of necessity is some non-cognitive reaction to this metaphysical baseline, but this still does not represent anything in the objects (see Blackburn 2000).

Some resist this reading, and point to various places where Hume seems to be saying that we are ignorant of necessary connection. The source of our idea of necessity is not that which we expected (namely an experience of genuine causal power), but instead the idea has its origin in the imagination. But this claim about where our ideas come from is compatible with the existence of hidden and unknowable connections "out there". Hume's lesson is one of deep ignorance not rejection (see Wright 1983; Craig 1987; Strawson 1989).

The issue ultimately turns on whether one takes Hume's account of conceivability to extend to the world beyond impressions. If we really can conceive of cause and effect objects separately, it is metaphysically possible for a cause to exist without necessitating its effect, and so there can be no real necessary connections "out there". Alternatively, one may take Hume simply to be saying that since the only objects available to the mind are impressions and ideas, our imagination allows us to conceive of the ideas of our cause and effect separately, and hence we cannot be in a position to know the "real connection" between causally related objects (for discussion, see Kail (2003)). Since sensory experience does not reveal the real nature of objects (supposing that there are such things – see below), what we find possible in our imagination may not be really possible metaphysically speaking. So perhaps we are not really conceiving cause and effect separately, but merely what we *know* about them, namely their appearances.

Hume also offers us two notorious definitions of "cause", which are neither extensionally nor intensionally equivalent: they don't pick out just the same objects or mean the same. On the one hand, causation is roughly defined as the constant conjunction of objects, on the other, constant conjunction together with the subjective determination of the mind. Given their lack of equivalence, it is difficult to determine whether he favours one over the other, accepts both or ultimately rejects both as "defective" (for discussion see Garrett (1997: Ch. 5)). Much ink has been spilt on this topic, but it is useful to think of these "definitions" in the following way. Causation as "constant conjunction" is the "input" into the mind, whereas the second definition also specifies the "output", namely the belief in necessary connection (see Craig 1987: Ch. 2).

Part III rounds off, after a discussion of the rules by which to judge cause and effect, with a section entitled "Of the reason of animals" (T 1.3.16). There, Hume takes his account of our causal inferences to be confirmed by the fact that it is equally applicable to animal reasoning. One of the many interesting aspects of this relatively neglected section is that Hume's account of human and animal reasoning is no different from other accounts of animal inference that were present in the period (see e.g. Leibniz *Monadology* (§§26–30) for an epitome). What is different, however, is that earlier authors always refrained from calling such inferences "reason". Instead, association and reason were explicitly contrasted, the former being merely "mechanical", and the latter often conceived of as a normatively and ontologically distinct faculty. What Hume's science of the mind concludes is that our inferential capacities, when explored empirically, do not differ from the mechanical natures that govern other animals. Malebranche's "science of man" views human beings as ontologically dualistic, as owners of a distinct "reason", in virtue of which we resemble God, conjoined to a mechanically governed beast machine. That there is no such distinction to be drawn is Hume's most provocative conclusions.

Treatise Part IV:"Of the sceptical and other systems of philosophy"

Part III yields a naturalistic theory of probable inference, which greatly resembles the conception of animal inference favoured by Hume's predecessors. Probable reason in human beings is not different in kind from this "mechanical force", and certainly does not involve any insight into causal powers. This is augmented by a theory of belief as vivacity. Aside from the section on necessary connection, Hume's tone is not very sceptical. Instead, arguments are exploited to show that probable reason is based upon the associative relation of cause and effect, reflective awareness of which allows us to reason causally: "Thus tho' causation be a *philosophical* relation ... 'tis only so far as it is a *natural* relation, and produces an union among our ideas, that we are able to reason upon it, or draw any inference from it" (T 1.3.6.16; SBN 94). Part IV differs in a number of respects, and here reflective awareness of the sources of belief has a destabilizing effect. First, each section discusses different topics, including scepticism with regard to reason, scepticism with regard to the senses, ancient philosophy (the notions of causation and form), "modern philosophy" (the primary and secondary quality distinction), the immateriality of the soul and personal identity. Secondly, Hume's tone undergoes a progressive shift, whereby he becomes less and less confident about the status of the beliefs he is examining. The final section, the conclusion, is a dramatic record of the sentiments which these

185

"intense reflections" have "wrought upon" Hume the philosophical reflector, and how he reacts to them. Thirdly, intertwined in this discussion, are a number of causal explanations of beliefs, including not merely those of ordinary, or "vulgar", common sense but of philosophical doctrines.

Clearly, then, Part IV is an immensely complex, polyvalent text, making it difficult to summarize (for an interesting discussion of the faces of Part IV, see Livingston (1998)). A running theme is that reason and the senses cannot be sources for fundamental beliefs like that of an external world or an enduring self. The imagination is responsible for much of our cognitive lives, and reason operating alone would all but extinguish belief. During this part, Hume's tone changes in light of his growing awareness that the imagination governs belief to a far greater extent than had been expected, and reason to a much less extent.

It is important to emphasize that in light of the discussion in Part III, probable reason itself has been assimilated to the operations of the imagination, namely the associative relation of cause and effect. But it is during the dialectic of Part IV that Hume draws a distinction in the imagination, between the "permanent, irresistible, and universal" principles and the "changeable, weak and irregular" (T 1.4.4.1; SBN 225). The former seem to be candidates for reason, but without the latter all belief would be extinguished (T 1.4.7.7; SBN 267–8), and this issues in a dilemma Hume faces in the conclusion. Should we follow reason alone, reject the "trivial suggestions of the fancy" (T 1.4.7.7; SBN 267), and remove all belief, or save ourselves from scepticism by yielding to such trivial suggestions? Outside the study our natures make this psychologically impossible to do so, but this by itself does not tell us that we are justified in doing so. The conclusion of the book seems to offer some form of practical appraisal of what principles and products of the imagination are to have normative weight, appealing implicitly to his conception of virtue (see e.g. Owen 1999: Ch. 9).

The sections of Part IV that have attracted the most attention are "Of scepticism with regard to the senses" (T 1.4.2) and "Of personal identity" (T 1.4.6), and I shall concentrate on these, although I shall touch upon some other sections. Part IV opens with "Of scepticism with regard to reason". Hume's naturalistic conclusion is contained in the opening paragraph: "reason must be consider'd as a kind of cause, of which truth is the natural effect" (T 1.4.1.1; SBN 180). The sceptical aspect to this section involves a twofold argument to the effect that "knowledge degenerates into probability", and reasoning can extinguish all probable belief. The general idea is that first-order judgements must involve second-order judgements to maintain our "assurance", but this leads to a regress of iterated judgements, each of which diminishes our confidence. The more we reflect on a claim, the less and less is our idea of it attended with the vivacity characteristic of belief. Whatever the merits of this argument, Hume's stated intention in exploiting it is to show that "belief is more properly an act of the sensitive, than of the cognitive part of our natures" (T 1.4.1.8; SBN 183). So he does not recommend the sceptical conclusion, but thinks it shows that our natural belief productive faculties depend less on the demands of reason than had been previously thought.

"Of scepticism with regard to the senses" is a complex and celebrated section (H. H. Price (1940) devoted a lengthy book to it). Hume starts with a claim that we must take for granted the existence of body, and that he merely intends to investigate the causes of our belief in an external world, but towards the end of the section he reports a "contrary sentiment", an inclination to "repose no faith at all in my senses". So his reflections on the causes of the belief seem to destabilize his original confidence. We shall return to why this might be so, but first sketch the account. There are two beliefs that concern Hume, or two versions of the same belief: the vulgar or common-sense perceptual belief and the sophisticated philosophical belief. The first is an extreme form of direct realism, whereby the direct and immediate objects of acquaintance are taken to continue to exist when not perceived and to be spatially distinct from the perceiver. The three possible sources for the belief are the senses, reason and the imagination, but the first two are rejected. Why these two sources are rejected is a complicated matter, but one key consideration is the notion of continuity, namely the continued existence of a presently unobserved object; clearly we cannot observe the continued existence of an unobserved object.

How does the imagination produce the belief? Hume identifies two features of perceptions conducive to the belief, which he calls "constancy" and "coherence". The former is very close qualitative similarity among interrupted perceptions. If I stare at a glass, close my eyes briefly and reopen them a set number of very similar perceptions greet me. This is constancy. However, the objects we suppose to exist when we do not perceive them can change quite drastically over time. To use Hume's example, the fire left blazing in the hearth when I leave my study will have decayed into embers when I return a few hours later. Clearly there is no constancy on either side of my perception of it, yet we think the fire continues to exist when I am not perceiving it. But, Hume thinks, I recognize a certain kind of coherence holding between perceptions of the relevant type, which prompts this judgement.

However, we only get sufficient coherence among such perceptions if we suppose those objects to continue, and this belief rests on a certain trick of the mind constancy plays. The mind has a strong tendency to view qualitatively similar but numerically distinct perceptions as two experiences of a single object that continues between gaps in experience. Yet at the same time, the mind is

aware (somehow) that there are two distinct objects on either side of the inter-
ruption, that is, two perceptions. This sets up an uncomfortable dissonance in
the mind, and in order to remove it the mind simply yields to the first tendency.
The bottom line is that we suppose objects to continue to exist because it is too
uncomfortable to think otherwise.

This vulgar version of the belief is false. We think that the objects of immediate acquaintance continue to exist unperceived, but the objects of immediate
acquaintance are perceptions and these do not exist unperceived. Philosophers,
aware of this fact, then replace the vulgar view with the "doctrine of double
existence". Here the immediate objects of acquaintance are perceptions, but
perceptions resemble and are caused by external objects that are continuous and
distinct. But this version of the belief is no improvement; indeed, in many
respects, it is worse. First, the belief is not caused by reason, but instead is partly
the result of the grip that the ordinary belief still has on the imagination of the
philosophers: nature "is obstinate, and will not quit the field, however strongly
attack'd by reason" (T 1.4.2.52; SBN 215). The philosopher's belief is the
"monstrous offspring" of the imagination (*ibid*.). Secondly, there is a worry
about the very content of the belief. We cannot conceive of anything except
perceptions, or things like perceptions, and so the notion of anything different
from perceptions – which is how philosophers suppose "external objects to be"
– looks vacuous.

Whether Hume denies the existence of everything other than perceptions,
and offers a nascent phenomenalism is still a matter of controversy (for a realist
discussion of this matter, see Wright (1983: Ch. 1)). But as we said, Hume's
survey of the causes of the belief induces in him the "contrary sentiment",
reported towards the end of the section. This is because his investigation makes
it clear that the causation of a fundamental belief of human nature rests on
"trivial qualities of the fancy" (T 1.4.2.56; SBN 217): their causation does not
constitute a good reason for the belief. This is a particular instance of the general
drift in Part IV of the fundamental importance of the imagination in the gen-
eration of belief. Hume reports of this worry that "carelessness and in-attention
alone can afford us any remedy" (T 1.42.57; SBN 218), but this is a staging post
on the route to the pragmatic resolution offered in the conclusion.

Hume then gives debunking accounts of the beliefs of "antient philosophy",
namely the fictions of "sympathy" and "antipathy", exposes a "contradiction"
between reason and the senses, resting on the primary–secondary quality
distinction in "Of the modern philosophy", and examines the immateriality of
the soul. "Of personal identity", wherein Hume presents his "bundle theory"
of the mind, stands with "Of scepticism with regard to the senses" as the most
famous section of Part IV. Here Hume repudiates the notion of the self as an

"owner" of perceptions. On that view, perceptions are related to selves in the manner of modes of substances. His initial observation is that such an "owner" is not given in experience, so our idea of self cannot be thus derived: introspection just reveals perceptions. "For my part", says Hume, "when I enter most intimately into what I call *myself*, I always stumble on some particular perception" (T 1.4.6.3; SBN 252, original emphasis). But this introspective move is not his most powerful weapon. Instead, there is a modal argument that builds upon a move in "Of the immateriality of the soul". Since we can conceive of perceptions having independent existence, and what we can conceive reveals metaphysical possibility, it is metaphysically possible for perceptions to exist independently. But if perceptions were modes of substances, they could not have an independent existence, for modes are characterized as precisely as a class of beings dependent on substances for their existence. So either perceptions are substances – that which may exist by itself – or we can have no conception of substance.

Instead, Hume famously proposes that the "true idea" of the human mind is of a collection or bundle of perceptions, related primarily by the association relations of resemblance and causation. So there is no self, no "owner" of experiences. This Hume thinks has consequences for the issue sparked off by Locke's famous discussion of what personal identity consists in. Whether bundle of perceptions *A* is the same person as bundle of perceptions *B*, is, for Hume, little more than a "grammatical dispute". He also has an account of how we come to the mistaken belief in an owner of perceptions. Hume thinks that responsible for the belief is a propensity similar to the one in his account of the vulgar belief in continuing bodies to mistake resembling perceptions for an experience of a unity item. This causes us to "feign" the idea of a unitary owner of perceptions.

One of the most vexed exegetical issues in the history of philosophy concerns Hume's confession of failure of his account of the self in the *Appendix*. He reports that he has found himself in a "labyrinth". Having reviewed the arguments that caused him to deny the "simplicity of the soul", he worries about what unites our perceptions in thought. He writes: "In short there are two principles, which I cannot render consistent; nor is it in my power to renounce them, viz. *that all our distinct perceptions are distinct existences*, and *that the mind never perceives any real connexion among distinct existences*" (T *Appendix* 21; SBN 636, original emphasis). The problem is that these two principles *are* consistent, and it is difficult to see how this generates a problem for Hume's account of self. There are many different accounts of what worry Hume voices here, but no consensus has emerged (see Garrett (1997) for a survey of different views and his own, and Kail (forthcoming) for my own suggestion).

The *Treatise* and the first *Enquiry*

A word should be said about the relation of the *Treatise* to the first *Enquiry*. Hume's claim that the *Treatise* "fell dead-born from the press" is an exaggeration but, for some, telling. It is an allusion to Pope's *Epilogue to the Satires* ("All, all but truth, drops dead-born from the press"; see Frasca-Spada (1998: 86)), and this is seized upon as evidence that Hume later took the failure of the *Treatise* to be a deserved one. In the spring of 1751, Hume wrote to Gilbert Minto, saying that he had "published too precipitately", and had "repented [his] Haste a hundred, & a hundred times". On top of that, the 1777 edition of Hume's *Essays and Treatises on Several Subjects* includes an Advertisement, written by him in 1775, which declares that the "following pieces", including the *Enquiry concerning Human Understanding*, "may alone be regarding as containing his philosophical senti-ments and principles". It is these considerations that partly motivate the call from some scholars to concentrate on the first *Enquiry* rather than the *Treatise*. The first *Enquiry* also differs in substance and style in a number of ways. Gone is the com-plex psychological accounts of key beliefs; the account of self and the theory of belief are offered somewhat more apologetically. It also includes material on explicitly religious matters, including the famous section "Of miracles", which Hume had originally intended for inclusion in the *Treatise* (for discussion, the reader should consult the papers in Millican (2002a)).

So why concentrate on the *Treatise* rather than the First *Enquiry*, if Hume effectively disowns the former? Part of the answer has already been given, namely that it is the work that has attracted the most attention. More importantly, its very complexity is, of itself, fascinating. Complexity, however, is not to be confused with a lack of system. The *Treatise* is certainly a systematic work. Perhaps in the end its relentless attention to detail, its irony, ambition and passages of sheer beauty are what makes it a highly attractive and instructive work of genius.

Editions and referencing

Referencing Hume's works has recently become a complicated matter. Oxford University Press publishes a student edition, edited by David Fate Norton and Mary J. Norton (Oxford: Oxford University Press, 2000). At the time of writing, a critical edition of the *Treatise* is about to be published by Clarendon Press. Prior to these editions, the standard edition was edited by L. A. Selby-Bigge, revised by P. H. Nidditch (2nd edn, Oxford: Oxford University Press, 1978), to which around 100 years' worth of secondary literature refers. All three differ in pagination, although the first two number each paragraph. The following referencing convention, adopted by the journal *Hume Studies*, is followed in this chapter. Following the "T", the book, part, section and paragraph numbers are given (e.g. T 1.2.1.4), followed by the Selby-Bigge page number (e.g. SBN 31). When the Introduction, Abstract and Appendix are cited, they are flagged as such.

Acknowledgement

Thanks to John Shand, Dan Navon and Marie-José Freier for their invaluable suggestions on drafts of this chapter.

Bibliography

Baier, A. 1991. *A Progress of Sentiments: Reflections on Hume's* Treatise. Harvard, MA: Harvard University Press.

Barfoot, M. 1990. "Hume and the Culture of Science". In *Studies in the Philosophy of the Scottish Enlightenment*, M. A. Stewart (ed.), 151–90. Oxford: Clarendon Press.

Bennett, J. 2001. *Learning from Six Philosophers*, vol. 2. Oxford: Clarendon Press.

Blackburn, S. 2000. "Hume and Thick Connexions". In *The New Hume Debate*, R. Read & K. Richman (eds), 100–112. London: Routledge.

Broackes, J. 2002. "Hume, Belief, and Personal Identity". In *Reading Hume on Human Understanding*, P. Millican (ed.), 187–210. Oxford: Oxford University Press.

Buckle, S. 2001. *Hume's Enlightenment Tract: The Unity and Purpose of* An Enquiry Concerning Human Understanding. Oxford: Oxford University Press.

Chappell, V. (ed.). 1966. *Hume: A Collection of Critical Essays*. New York: Doubleday.

Craig, E. J. 1987. *The Mind of God and the Works of Man*. Oxford: Clarendon Press.

Everson, S. 1988. "The Difference Between Feeling and Thinking", *Mind* **87**, 401–13.

Fodor, J. 2003. *Hume Variations*. New York: Oxford University Press.

Fogelin, R. 1985. *Hume's Skepticism in* A Treatise of Human Nature. London: Routledge.

Fogelin, R. 1992a. "Hume's Missing Shade of Blue". In *Philosophical Interpretations*, R. Fogelin, 70–80. Oxford: Oxford University Press.

Fogelin, R. 1992b. *Philosophical Interpretations*. Oxford: Oxford University Press.

Frasca-Spada, M. 1998. *Self and Space in Hume's* Treatise. Cambridge: Cambridge University Press.

Garrett, D. 1997. *Cognition and Commitment in Hume's Philosophy*. New York: Oxford University Press.

Hatfield, G. 1990. *The Natural and the Normative: Theories of Spatial Perception from Kant to Helmholtz*. Cambridge, MA: MIT Press.

Hume, D. 1967. *A Letter from a Gentleman to his Friend in Edinburgh*, E. C. Mossner & J. V. Price (eds). Edinburgh: Edinburgh University Press.

Hume, D. 1975 [1777]. *Enquiries concerning Human Understanding and concerning the Principles of Morals*, L. A. Selby-Bigge (ed.), 3rd edn. P. H. Nidditch (rev.). Oxford: Clarendon Press.

Kail, P. 2003. "Conceivability and Modality in Hume", *Hume Studies* **29**(1), 43–61.

Kail, P. forthcoming. *Projection and Realism in Hume*. Oxford: Oxford University Press.

Kemp Smith, N. 1941. *The Philosophy of David Hume*. London: Macmillan.

Livingston, D. 1998. *Philosophical Melancholy and Delirium: Hume's Pathology of Philosophy*. Chicago, IL: University of Chicago Press.

McCracken, C. 1983. *Malebranche and British Philosophy*. Oxford: Clarendon Press.

Millican, P. 2002a. "The Context, Aims and Structure of Hume's First *Enquiry*". In *Reading Hume on Human Understanding*, P. Millican (ed.), 27–65. Oxford: Oxford University Press.

Millican, P. 2002b. "Hume's Sceptical Doubts Concerning Induction". In *Reading Hume on Human Understanding*, P. Millican (ed.), 107–73. Oxford: Oxford University Press.

Millican, P. (ed.) 2002c. *Reading Hume on Human Understanding: Essays on the First* Enquiry. Oxford: Oxford University Press.

Mossner, E. 1980. *The Life of David Hume*, 2nd edn. Oxford: Clarendon Press.

Noonan, H. 1999. *Hume on Knowledge*. London: Routledge.

Norton, D. F. 1993a. "An Introduction to Hume's Thought". In *The Cambridge Companion to Hume*, D. F. Norton (ed.), 1–32. Cambridge: Cambridge University Press.

Norton, D. F. (ed.) 1993b. *The Cambridge Companion to Hume*. Cambridge: Cambridge University Press.

Owen, D. 1999. *Hume's Reason*. New York: Oxford University Press.

Passmore, J. 1968. *Hume's Intentions*, rev. edn. London: Duckworth.

Pears, D. 1990. *Hume's System: An Examination of Book I of his* Treatise. Oxford: Clarendon Press.

Penelhum, T. 1975. *Hume*. London: Macmillan.

Price, H. H. 1940. *Hume's Theory of the External World*. Oxford: Clarendon Press.

Read, R. & K. Richman (eds) 2000. *The New Hume Debate*. London: Routledge.

Reid, T. 1997. *An Inquiry into the Human Mind on the Principles of Common Sense*, D. Brookes (ed.). Edinburgh: Edinburgh University Press.

Rosenberg, A. 1993. "Hume's Philosophy of Science". In *The Cambridge Companion to Hume*, D. F. Norton (ed.), 64–89. Cambridge: Cambridge University Press.

Strawson, G. 1989. *The Secret Connexion: Causation, Realism and David Hume*. Oxford: Clarendon Press.

Stroud, B. 1977. *Hume*. London: Routledge.

Wright, J. P. 1983. *The Sceptical Realism of David Hume*. Manchester: Manchester University Press.

Yolton, J. W. 1984. *Perceptual Acquaintance from Descartes to Reid*. Oxford: Basil Blackwell.

Further reading

References to preferred editions of the *Treatise* are given above. There is also an abridgement edited by John P. Wright, Robert Stecker and Gary Fuller (London: Everyman/Dent, 2003), which is short enough to make it possible to gain an impression of reading all three books in concert without becoming too bogged down in detail. Barry Stroud's *Hume* (1977) remains not merely a wonderful introduction to the *Treatise* but an independently excellent piece of philosophy. Harold Noonan's *Hume on Knowledge* (1999) is shorter but a lucid introduction to the topics of Book I. There is forthcoming a collection of papers edited by Elizabeth Radcliffe in the *Blackwell Companion to Hume* (Oxford: Blackwell), which should be very useful for students at a more advanced stage.

8

Jean-Jacques Rousseau
The Social Contract

Jonathan Riley

Introduction

Perhaps the most quoted line of Jean-Jacques Rousseau's *The Social Contract* begins its first chapter: "Man is born free, and everywhere he is in chains" (*SC* i.1 [1]; Rousseau 1997b: 41).[1] Man is naturally free in the sense that he is born without any genuine obligations to others to refrain from doing whatever he judges is necessary for his self-preservation, once he acquires the capacities for judgement. Yet everywhere he is subjected to positive laws administered by some government whose leaders claim to be his rightful masters.

The author of that provocative line, which echoes similar statements by the great seventeenth-century English social contract theorists Hobbes and Locke, was born in Geneva in 1712 to parents who were native citizens of the small republic. His mother died within days of his birth, and his watchmaker father left Geneva in 1722, forcing Jean-Jacques to find work as an apprentice to a notary and then an engraver. He wandered away in 1728 and found shelter with Mme de Warens at Annecy in Savoy. Aside from a brief stint in Turin, where he converted from Calvinism to Roman Catholicism (although he reconverted to Calvinism in 1754), he spent the next dozen years living with her, educating himself at her salon and becoming her lover as of 1733. In 1740, he moved to Lyon to tutor the children of M. de Mably and became acquainted with Mably's elder brother, Etienne Bonnot (later the Abbé de Condillac), whom Patrick Riley calls "with Voltaire the greatest 'Lockean' in post-Regency France" (2001:

3). In 1742, Rousseau moved to Paris. There, after a few years, he began his lasting partnership with Thérèse Lavasseur, whom he eventually married in 1768, after she had apparently borne him five children, all said by him to have been abandoned at a home for foundlings (rather as he had been left to the care of others by his parents). He also met Denis Diderot and Jean d'Alembert and became a contributor to their famous *Encyclopedia*. Its fifth volume, for instance, published in 1755, included his *Discourse on Political Economy*. But his distinctive moral and political ideas led to tensions with them and other French Enlightenment philosophers, notably Voltaire, culminating in a decisive break in 1758, when he published his *Letter to M. d'Alembert*. In that work, he rejected d'Alembert's suggestion, which at the urging of Voltaire had been inserted into an article on "Geneva" published in 1757 in the seventh volume of the *Encyclopedia*, that Geneva's culture would be improved if a theatre was established to stage Parisian imports.

Rousseau's reputation as a leading philosopher was made in 1750, when his *Discourse on the Sciences and Arts* won the prize of the Academy of Dijon with a dazzling argument to the effect that the "purification of morals" depended on a recovery of natural virtue, whose simple principles were "engraved in all hearts" by a beneficent god. This natural virtue is displayed in the rustic and martial culture of Sparta and early Rome, he insists, but it is incompatible with the rebirth of sophisticated learning, urbane taste and refined manners associated with wealthy and civilized Athens. He went on to produce a steady stream of writings on an amazing range of topics until he died suddenly in 1778, on an estate in Erménonville not far from Paris. *The Social Contract* was published in 1762, the same year in which his other best-known work, *Émile*, a treatise on education, came out. Both books were immediately banned by the French civil and ecclesiastical authorities, and publicly burned in Paris. Warrants were issued for his arrest. The books were similarly treated in Geneva, where he was charged with impiety. He was forced to take refuge in Neuchâtel (part of Prussia) and spent the next few years under serious threat, taking extraordinary steps to avoid arrest, including moving to England in 1765 (with the help of the great Scottish philosopher David Hume, although he quarrelled with Hume and returned to France in 1767) and living under the assumed name Renou (as he was when he married Thérèse). He permanently renounced his Genevan citizenship in 1764, and thereby chose to spend the remainder of his life as an individual without a country. In 1794, however, as the French Revolution descended into a reign of terror under the violent Jacobin leader Maximilian Robespierre, France decided to recognize him as one of her heroes. With great ceremony, his ashes were carried in a procession from Erménonville to Paris and placed in the Pantheon next to Voltaire's remains.

Why did Rousseau's best-known works cause so much offence to the authorities in contemporary France and Geneva? The question brings us back to the famous line that opens *The Social Contract*. He indicates that his purpose in the treatise is not to explain how men have actually gone from the state of natural freedom into societies where they are bound by chains. In other works, notably his *Discourse on Inequality* (1755), he emphasizes that the move has usually taken place in an illegitimate way: that is, wealthy and powerful men, motivated by vanity (*amour-propre*), have repeatedly fought to determine which of them sets up and runs a tyrannical government whose positive laws and orders trample over the basic interests of the inhabitants of some given territory. But his purpose in *The Social Contract* is different. He proposes to clarify how the move ought to occur for it to be morally legitimate. How should men give up their natural freedom in order to create a genuine civil society with a non-tyrannical government that legitimately employs force to compel them to obey positive laws? The answer does not depend on how frequently the proper way of making the move has been observed in history. To forestall the objection that it is simply not feasible, however, Rousseau allows that fortune has permitted it to occur now and then, even in the midst of an Hobbesian state of war among vainglorious rulers. Admittedly, "we have scarcely anything but conjectures" to explain why it has taken place in some contexts but not others (*SC* iv. 4 [1], 127). But that explanatory problem is not Rousseau's concern. It is enough for him that genuine communities with non-tyrannical governments, including Sparta, the ancient Roman republic, and his native Geneva, have emerged and flourished, however briefly, despite the odds against them.

Rousseau is concerned to show that reasonable men can all promote their own basic interests as well as the common good if all consent to give up their natural freedom in order to mutually cooperate as *citizens*. Citizens are free and equal members of a political association that has full authority to enact a special type of positive laws, namely, "general wills" that are, by definition, directed at the common good. The association has no authority to enact anything else, however, since nothing but a general will can be a genuine law. Although the idea of a "general will" requires clarification, these genuine laws include fundamental political laws that establish a non-tyrannical form of government entrusted by the citizens with power to draft, administer and enforce valid laws. The fundamental political laws themselves are drafted by an extraordinary "lawgiver", or founder of the constitution, a wise leader (not necessarily a citizen but perhaps a foreigner) who must be able to persuade the citizens that his proposals are divinely inspired so that the popular majority will ratify them. If he persuades the people and the constitution endures, the lawgiver can expect that he will eventually be venerated as a god himself, as Lycurgus was venerated by the Spartans. Each citizen is obliged to obey all general wills enacted by the body politic, and any recalcitrant citizen can be forced to obey by government officials, if necessary. More importantly, each citizen ought to feel obliged to obey because each has had an equal right to vote in a general assembly, and any general will – any genuine law – passed by a majority of citizens necessarily promotes the basic interests of each.

Under these conditions, Rousseau claims, a legitimate political association exists "that will defend and protect the person and goods of each associate with the full common force, and by means of which each, uniting with all, nevertheless obeys only himself and remains as free as before" (*SC* i.6 [4], 49–50). The upshot is that it is advantageous for each associate to contract with the others to convert his natural freedom into another kind of freedom, namely, the moral and political freedom of a citizen who wills the laws that he is obliged to obey (*SC* i.8 [1–3], 53–4). By mutually cooperating in this fashion, the citizens:

> have only made an advantageous exchange of an uncertain and precarious way of being in favor of a more secure and better one, of natural independence in favor of freedom, of the power to harm others in favor of their own security, and of their force which others could overwhelm in favor of right made invincible by the social union.
>
> (*SC* ii. 4 [10], 63)

Rousseau's theory of how men can advantageously give up their natural freedom in order to create a legitimate polity in which their political and moral freedom is secure, implied that the sitting King of France, Louis XV, who claimed absolute power by divine right, was merely a tyrant who had no proper authority. So it is hardly surprising that the king and his minions viewed the contract theory as a seditious and blasphemous libel. Even at Calvinist Geneva, where the republican leaders did not claim absolute power (although authority seems to have become increasingly concentrated in an upper council that rarely bothered to consult the citizenry), his repeated assertions that good Christians cannot be good citizens of a republic could hardly fail to strike the leadership as seditious and blasphemous.

But there is no reason for us to side with the French and Genevan rulers of Rousseau's day. Properly understood, his theory gave encouragement to all those who opposed absolute monarchy. Moreover, his defence of a "civil religion" combined with what is essentially a form of deism implied that divine purposes would be served by a rebirth of simple natural virtue. That in turn gave encouragement to all those who opposed the clergy's use of God as a source of justification for tyrannical government that trampled over the basic interests of the people. As a result, during the course of the French Revolution, Rousseau's arguments could continue to inspire the different parties that rose to prominence in the fight against tyranny by divine right. His theory could inspire constitutional monarchists who merely wished to limit the power of the king, no less than republicans who wished to abolish the monarchy and its official Church altogether. This may help to account for the wide and enduring appeal of *The Social Contract*.

Rousseau's theory is best interpreted as a reconfiguration of Locke's liberalism, in my view, but I shall not argue for that reading here. Rather, my purpose is confined to clarifying what Rousseau says in *The Social Contract*. I shall focus on that text, without referring to his other writings to any significant extent. Moreover, I cannot pretend to offer a full discussion of the vast secondary literature that is relevant to my purpose. It will emerge that Rousseau's ideal polity is a fairly small self-sufficient republic, typically allied with others in a confederation for military defence, with a "tempered" form of government that is neither a simple "democracy" nor a simple "aristocracy" but rather a mixture of both as he understands those terms. The ideal public culture is liberal in the sense that equal basic claim-rights and correlative duties for all citizens are among the most weighty social norms.[2] This liberal culture is rigorously taught and enforced by the state as a civil religion such that the rights and duties of citizens are linked to the existence of a beneficent god and an afterlife in which the just are rewarded and the wicked punished. Yet Rousseau's preference for such an ideal republic does not imply that he thinks the ideal is attainable by a sudden revolution in any given social context, independently of such factors as the size and location of the country, the customs and traditions of the people, and so forth.

The social contract and the people

For Rousseau, any legitimate political association is formed by unanimous consent. Each associate expressly promises, by taking a public oath that includes affirming his belief in a beneficent god, to cooperate with the others by putting his natural life, liberty and possessions (including land) under the complete control of the united body. The united body is an artificial "public person" that takes the name of "*Republic* or of *body politic*, which its members call *State* when it is passive, *Sovereign* when active" (*SC* i.6 [10], 50–51, original emphasis). The republic in action (that is, the sovereign) has a will of its own, namely, a general will that (as I shall clarify in due course) is necessarily directed at the common good of the members (*SC* ii.3 [1], 59). Sovereignty is the absolute, indivisible and perpetual authority of the republic – in other words, the complete, singular and inalienable freedom of the body politic – to enact its general will into law. Rousseau stresses that this sovereign lawmaking power "can never be alienated" by the body politic to some distinct representative body (*SC* ii.1 [2], 57). Sovereignty can only be exercised by the people themselves in a general assembly: "Sovereignty cannot be represented … Any law which the People has not ratified in person is null; it is not a law" (*SC* iii.15 [5], 114).

A social contract, then, is a unanimous mutual promise or covenant before God to form a united people that has full authority to govern itself by enacting its general will into law. Much more needs to be said to clarify what this seems to involve for Rousseau. But an important preliminary question is: who is entitled to be a member of the republic? Who are the people with the right to vote in the general assembly? For Rousseau, the answer seems to be any male adult resident who owns enough property to support his family and equip himself to fulfil his military duties in defence of the country, provided that he is native-born, or, although foreign-born, has been given the franchise by special grant, or, otherwise, is a foreign-born son of either of these sorts of men. Rousseau may also approve of the practice at Geneva whereby only the native-born of these men are fully fledged citizens with the privilege of serving as magistrates.

He clearly rejects the idea that the body politic should be restricted to certain upper social classes on the basis of blood: he is against any form of aristocracy in that sense. Nevertheless, although commoners must be admitted along with nobles and royals (but not women or non-residents) as members of the republic, he seems inclined to insist on a property qualification that would exclude the poor. He applauds d'Alembert's recognition that "only two" of the four "orders of men" at Geneva "make up the Republic", for example (*SC* I.6 [10, note], 51). This excludes not only foreign-born residents and their sons, even sons born in Geneva, except when their membership is specially conferred by the government with the people's approval, but also any "bankrupt individuals" (d'Alembert 1960: 143). Similarly, he says that "the whole majesty of the Roman People resided only in the Comitia by Centuries", even though he admits that the poorest class of Romans, who did not "have a hearth", generally had no right to vote in that general assembly since they could not afford to equip themselves as soldiers (*SC* iv.4 [15–20, 34], 130–32, 135).

This restriction of the republic's membership to males who own a sufficient amount of property squares with Rousseau's narrative of men quitting the state of nature to form a republic. In moving to the civil state, he says, men transform "possession which is merely the effect of force or the right of the first occupant" into "property which can only be founded on a positive title" (*SC* i.8 [2], 54). A man's natural freedom to take whatever goods he thinks he needs to preserve himself and his family is converted into his "civil freedom which is limited by the general will", that is, his positive claim-right to own enough land to provide for his family's subsistence by "labor and cultivation" (*SC* i.9 [3], 55). True, each citizen completely surrenders his natural liberty and possessions to the state, and his positive property rights are then determined entirely by the sovereign people. But Rousseau makes clear that the people ought only to pass laws that recognize each citizen's equal claim to be able to support himself and his family by his own efforts. By implication, a general will must be a type of positive law that assigns equal claim-rights and correlative obligations of a certain content to all citizens. Moreover, it becomes easier to see how the alienation of any man's natural freedom and possessions to the republic is nevertheless to his advantage:

> What is remarkable about this alienation is that the community, far from despoiling individuals of their goods by accepting them, only secures to them their legitimate possession, changes usurpation into a genuine right, and use into property. Thereupon the possessors, since they are considered to be the trustees of the public good, since their rights are respected by all the members of the State and preserved by all of its forces against foreigners, have, by a surrender that is advantageous to the public and even more so to themselves, so to speak acquired everything they have given. (*SC* i.9 [6], 56)

By means of this alienation, any citizen is made more secure and "remains as free as before" (*SC* i.6 [4], 50). As a positive claim-holder, he can demand enforcement by the state of others' correlative obligations to make sure that he can support his family by his own labour and saving. As a member of the sovereign, he shares in the moral freedom of making the positive laws of property, which he and his fellows are obliged to obey.

This sounds quite similar to Locke's story, although it also blends some Hobbesian elements. But a probable objection to the imputed similarity is that Locke and Rousseau disagree sharply over the morally permissible degree of inequality in property holdings. Locke is often read as endorsing virtually unrestrained inequality after the introduction of money into the state of nature, an inequality that is then given positive protection in the Lockean commonwealth, whereas Rousseau is typically seen as an advocate of a far more egalitarian distribution of property determined and regulated by the sovereign people.

Perhaps Rousseau does dream of substantial equality of the sort found at Sparta for a considerable period, before glaring inequality emerged with the rise of the short-lived Spartan empire after the Peloponnesian War. Unlike Locke, he explicitly allows for socialistic arrangements made possible by the united people's acquisition of territory and possessions before the assignment of any positive titles to individuals. Men may begin to form a republic before they "possess anything" as individuals, he says. Acting together, they may "seiz[e] a piece of land sufficient for all" and then "they enjoy its use in common or divide it among themselves, either equally or according to proportions established by the Sovereign" (SC i.9 [7], 56). In this case, the general will enacted by the people would assign to each citizen positive claim-rights to own and cultivate equal plots of land, for example, or claim-rights to own some reasonable portion (sufficient for subsistence) of the fruits of the land that is itself owned and worked by all in common.

Nevertheless, whatever his ideal of distributive justice might be, Rousseau emphasizes that considerable inequality is compatible with a stable republic. The term "equality of wealth" must be understood to mean that "no citizen be so very rich that he can buy another, and none so poor that he is compelled to sell himself [into slavery]" (SC ii.11 [2], 78). To maintain a republic, the people should regulate the distribution of property to keep it within these rather broad limits: "to give the State stability ... tolerate neither very rich people nor beggars. These two states, which are naturally inseparable, are equally fatal to the common good; from one come the abettors of tyranny, and from the other tyrants" (SC ii.11 [2, note], 78). Thus, Rousseau and Locke may not differ much on the degree to which inequality of wealth is permissible within a republic or commonwealth.

Popular sovereignty and the general will

Given that sovereign legislative authority must be exercised directly by the people, Rousseau indicates that a republic should be small in size (SC iii.13 [6], 111–12), although he also suggests that the ancient Roman Republic illustrates the possibility of a working assembly numbering hundreds of thousands of people (SC iii.12 [3–4], 110]). In his view, it is only by participating in the sovereign authority that any member of the body politic becomes a genuine *citizen* as opposed to a merely passive *subject*. But to participate in enacting the general will into law, the citizen must have enough public spirit to cast his vote in the assembly for a proposal that he judges is *"advantageous to the State"* rather than *"advantageous to this man or to this party"* (SC iv.1 [6], 122, original emphasis). With the requisite public spirit, any reasonable citizen, being aware of his own fallibility as a human being, will endorse the majority (or perhaps super-majority) opinion of his fellow citizens as a better estimate of the general will than his own judgement alone can provide in cases of conflict:

> When a law is proposed in the People's assembly, what they are being
> asked is not exactly whether they approve the proposal or reject it,
> but whether it does or does not conform to the general will, which is
> theirs [as citizens]; everyone states his opinion about this by casting
> his ballot, and the tally of the votes yields the declaration of the
> general will. Therefore when the opinion contrary to my own pre-
> vails, it proves nothing more than that I made a mistake and that what
> I took to be the general will was not. If my particular opinion had
> prevailed, I would have done something other than what I had willed
> [as a participant in the sovereign authority], and it is then that I
> would not have been free.   (*SC* iv.2 [8], 124)

To the extent that they endorse the majority's judgement (even when it is contrary to their own personal judgement) of the general will and comply with laws
enacted on that basis, the citizens collectively can be called a self-governing
people with civil and moral freedom.

But what is the people's "general will"? Many answers have been suggested,
and much controversy remains. Rousseau indicates that it is "always upright and
always tends to the public utility", even though the people may not correctly
identify it (*SC* ii.3 [1], 59); that it assigns mutual obligations whose "nature is
such that in fulfilling them one cannot work for others without also working for
oneself"; and that it produces a "notion of justice" as "equality of right", which
is derived from "each one's preference for himself [*amour de soi*] and hence
from the nature of man" (*SC* ii.4 [5], 61–2). But what is meant by "public
utility" or "common good", and how is it compatible with "justice" and "equal
rights" based on each citizen's sense of his own basic interests as a man? Unfortunately, Rousseau is not as clear as he might have been about these central ideas,
largely, it seems, because he thinks they will be transparent to any honest man
who consults the dictates of his own conscience.

As suggested earlier, he seems to be saying that a "general will" of the people
is a type of positive law that assigns equal claim-rights and correlative obligations of a certain content to all citizens, where the content flows from the
people's best estimate of what the common good requires in their particular
social context:

> [T]he social pact establishes among the Citizens an equality such that
> all commit themselves under the same conditions and must all enjoy
> the same rights ... [E]very genuine act of the general will either obli-

gates or favors all Citizens equally, so that the Sovereign knows only the body of the nation and does not single out any one of those who make it up ... [Such] an act of sovereignty [is] ... a convention of the body with each one of its members: A convention which is legitimate because it is based on the social contract, equitable because it is common to all, and secure because the public force and the supreme power are its guarantors. So long as subjects are subjected only to conventions such as these, they obey no one, but only their own will.

(SC ii.4 [8], 62–3)

A general will might also oblige any citizen to surrender some of his property or risk his life for his country under certain extraordinary conditions, thereby placing general constraints on his positive claims to life, liberty and ownership. But it cannot single out particular individuals rather than others in order to apply itself to particular situations. It cannot specify which men will be chosen to risk their lives, for example, or which will be appointed to executive offices, or which will be punished for this or that crime. Particular acts of this sort involve the threat of force by some against others, and make up the distinct domain of the government as opposed to the sovereign people. Sovereignty is limited by general conventions that give the same bundles of positive titles to each citizen.

If I understand him correctly, Rousseau views a people's general will as that particular community's positive interpretation of a universal law of nature, or "principle of virtue", which is "engraven in the hearts" of all men by a divine creator. With respect to material goods, for example, an upright man's conscience or "moral sense" tells him directly, before he has reasoned about the matter, that each has a natural claim-right to be able to provide for the subsistence of his family through his own efforts. Although he instinctively recognizes these reciprocal natural claims in the state of nature, however, he cannot reasonably endorse them as genuine moral rights because he has no assurance that others will accept the correlative obligations as binding in the absence of external sanctions enforced by a common government. Lacking such assurance, every man reasonably dismisses all talk of moral obligations in the state of nature, as Hobbes insists, and employs his natural freedom to do whatever he thinks necessary for self-preservation. If he is so fortunate as to have become a citizen of a republic whose government is charged with executing the general will, however, that same man has promised his fellow citizens not only to consult his conscience but also to use his reason and judgement to decide how best to interpret and safeguard the rather abstract natural claim-right to property within the positive law of his particular community. Should the claim be spelled out in terms of a positive title to a plot of land sufficient to enable a man to provide for his family's subsistence by his own labour and cultivation? Or should it be specified in terms of a title to share equally in the produce of a territory jointly owned and worked by all in common? If the former, how much land should any citizen be given a positive right to cultivate, and under what terms and conditions? And so forth. Different sovereign peoples may answer these questions in different ways, depending on their distinctive territories, customs and other social circumstances.

On my interpretation, then, a given republic's general will is invariably an equal assignment of positive claim-rights and correlative obligations to all citizens, where the content of these positive rights reflects that particular people's best estimate of the *correct* way to specify certain underlying abstract natural rights so as to promote the common good of that particular community, keeping in mind that the natural rights are self-evident to any man who consults his conscience. Although complex, this idea of a people's general will is coherent, provided we accept the premise that human beings have certain basic rights to life, health, property and so forth, which any community must spell out in its own fashion.

It should also be noted that, by contracting with each other, any group of individuals, of whatever size, can voluntarily create reciprocal rights and obligations of a certain content, with which to achieve some common purpose. Thus, we may refer, as Rousseau does, to the "general wills" of associations that are not republics. Such voluntary associations, which may be as small as a partnership between two persons, can exist in the state of nature or even in the midst of warring governments, as well as in a republic. Moreover, a republican government is itself a smaller voluntary association within the republic. The members of the government contract with each other to carry out the executive functions entrusted to them by the people. A "corporate will" that is "general in relation to the Government" (as opposed to a sovereign will that is general in relation to the people) is apparently an executive convention or rule that distributes titles, privileges and duties to all holders of the supreme executive power, enabling them to appoint various subordinates as needed to effectively maintain the government and enforce the laws of the republic (*SC* ii. 2 [5], 87). Of course, any individual member of any of these associations might imagine and propose general wills for the relevant association, although that person's estimate of the general will may be mistaken. The members together must determine the best estimate, by consensus if not by majority voting.

No doubt men may become so corrupted by their desires for power and wealth that they can no longer hear the plain dictates of conscience, and will make no effort to discover a general will in any context. But a republic is impossible among such men. In this regard, we must keep in mind that Rousseau is not claiming that men always quit the state of nature in the way they ought. Rather, there is a legitimate way that results in a genuine republic, and an illegitimate way that results in a tyrannical government. In the one case, men unanimously contract to form a united people with sovereign power over the contiguous lands and possessions of the contractors, and each such people, besides respecting the borders of its neighbours and negotiating disputes with them as necessary, enacts general wills to regulate the use of its property for the common good. In the other case, ruthless leaders emerge to establish tyrannical governments that are more or less constantly at war, attempting to seize each others' territories and wealth. Which of these opposing paths is selected seems to be largely a matter of luck. It seems to depend for the most part on whether a great leader – a patriotic "lawgiver" rather than a vainglorious tyrant – appears at the right time to frame a government that can reasonably be expected to preserve the united people for an indefinite period.

Majority voting as an epistemic procedure

Although the divine law of nature is supposed to be immediately transparent to any man who consults his conscience, Rousseau admits that, even in a republic, most voters may not have enough public spirit to be genuine participants in the sovereign authority. He recognizes that, in the absence of the right motivation, the general will (although "indestructible") will cease to be visible because it is hidden under the partial wills of individuals and factions (SC iv.1 [6], 122). Partial wills must be understood here to mean wills directed against the equal rights of fellow citizens, and thus against the common good. But perhaps this problem of partial wills is not insurmountable, given that the people are not thoroughly corrupt. In addition to civic education in the rights and duties of being a citizen, he advocates abolishing all factions in the state or, if that is not possible, multiplying their number and equalizing their relative power: "if there are partial societies, their number must be multiplied, and inequality among them prevented, as was done by Solon, Numa, Servius" (SC ii.3 [4], 60).

Rousseau also admits that, even if they have the requisite public spirit, citizens will remain fallible and thus inevitably make errors in their deliberations about the general will. Nevertheless, it may be possible to minimize the cumulative impact of such mistakes. Under certain conditions, majority voting is properly viewed as an epistemic device such that the majority judgement serves as a maximum likelihood estimate of a correct judgement about what really constitutes the people's common good. Before outlining the conditions under which a straightforward version of this so-called Condorcet (1785) "jury theorem" holds, however, it is important to be clear about the objective common good that the majority voting procedure is being used to estimate.[3]

Recall that a people's general will is an equal assignment of claim-rights and correlative obligations of a certain content to all citizens. The general will is directed, by definition, at the common good because the common good includes that specific assignment of rights. But nobody knows for sure what the general will really is because nobody knows for sure which of many possible rights assignments, each involving rights of a distinctive content, really would promote the common good of that particular community.

Assume that the voters in the assembly do have the patriotism required to be genuine citizens participating in the sovereign power. Each citizen, asking himself "What is advantageous to the state?", will only consider proposed general wills, that is, proposed assignments of equal rights. Any other type of proposal will be dismissed out of hand. Any permissible proposal x differs from another y with respect to the specific content of the rights.

But every citizen, as an upright man who consults his conscience, does know something about the equal rights assignment that is best for his republic. He knows by instinct the universal law of nature, and the natural rights distributed by it. He knows, for example, that every man has a natural claim to be able to provide subsistence for his family by his own efforts. This natural knowledge is an objective element that is independent of the majority voting procedure. Strictly speaking, it seems for Rousseau to be a divine element, constraining human morality from beyond this world, since (like Locke) he views the law of nature as the voice of God. In effect, this element is a product of divine Reason. A beneficent god has implanted such knowledge in the human conscience so that human beings do not need to rely on their own fallible powers of reasoning to discover it.

By itself, any assignment of natural rights is inadequate for promoting the common good of any particular people. Such universal rights are too abstract and vague for that purpose. Indeed, an assignment of natural rights seems to be a "general will of the human race", the kind of general will advocated by Diderot but criticized by Rousseau as insufficient. It lacks an essential ingredient of any particular community's genuine general will, namely, the specific content that transforms the natural rights into positive rights suited to that particular people.

The citizen of any particular republic, when asking himself which equal assignment of positive rights is advantageous to his republic, must employ his own fallible human reasoning to judge how best to specify the content of the rights for the common good of his community with its distinctive territory, climate, traditions and so forth. He might judge that every citizen in his community should have a positive title to five acres of fertile land subject to easements and other public uses, for example, and a claim to keep the crops he cultivates, subject to 10 per cent taxation by the state. Yet he may be mistaken about this specific cultural ingredient of his people's general will. His judgement might not capture the content that would really promote the common good of his republic. Still, all is not lost. Under certain conditions, a maximum likelihood estimate of the optimal cultural ingredient can be constructed by a majority voting procedure. This estimate is contingent on the procedure, not independent of it.

It follows that a particular people's general will is in part constructed by the popular majority itself, and in part independent of the majority's opinion. The specific cultural content supplied by the majority is constrained to fill the abstract natural rights categories that are engraved by God in the human heart. The voice of the popular majority must supplement and complete as best it can the infallible voice of a beneficent god.

Under what conditions, however, does majority voting serve as an epistemic procedure of the sort required? Given that voters are sufficiently motivated by love of country to ask themselves the right question, the majority ranking of any pair of proposals x and y provides a best estimate of the correct ranking for the common good, if each voter is more likely than not to be correct about which proposal is "advantageous to the State", and if each votes independently of the way his fellows vote in the sense that each uses his own judgement rather than simply imitating how others cast their ballots. When these conditions are satisfied, the majority's probability of being correct increases rapidly as the number of voters in the majority increases and/or each voter's competence rises, under the following formula:

$$P_M = q^{\alpha-\beta}/(q^{\alpha-\beta} + r^{\alpha-\beta}),$$

where P_M is the probability that the majority is correct about the common good ranking of x and y, q is the probability (identical for all voters) that a voter is correct, r $(= 1 - q)$ is the probability that a voter is incorrect, α is the number of voters in the majority, and $\alpha + \beta = \eta$, the total number of voters in the assembly, in other words, the whole body politic. Thus, for example, if $q = 0.7$, $\eta = 1500$ (about the size of the body politic at Rousseau's Geneva) and a simple majority prefers x to y, then the majority's judgement that the content of the rights at x rather than the content at y is "advantageous to the State" is likely to be the correct judgement with probability $P_M = 0.85$. If the simple majority of 751 voters increases to a supermajority of 900 (60 per cent of the body politic), P_M is virtually unity.

Perhaps Rousseau anticipated Condorcet's results. He suggests that voters should independently cast their ballots in silence, for example, after retreating within themselves to consult their own conscience and judgement, as was apparently the practice in the popular assemblies at Sparta, Rome and Geneva. He also indicates that open ballots are preferable when most citizens are sufficiently motivated by public spirit but that secret ballots must be used when public spirit has been eroded by the spirit of faction and the republic is in decline (*SC* iv.4 [35–8], 135–6). Even if some discussion were permitted, the independence condition would be met as long as attempts to cajole or persuade others to vote in unison were ruled out. Moreover, it seems a fairly mild assumption that citizens (at least on average) are more likely than not to be correct about how to specify the content of equal basic rights for the common good of their community, if they are motivated to consider the question. Since these protect his own basic interests, every citizen has a strong incentive to think carefully about the "notion of justice" that is suited to his particular republic and its culture.

Some commentators doubt that Rousseau had Condorcet's approach in mind. Trachtenberg has argued, for example, that Rousseau endorses an ideal culture (*moeurs*) "that enforces the general will by encouraging citizens to make their own thinking depend on the thoughts of others" (1993: 231). The people would be relentlessly encouraged by their public education, arts and entertainments, and state religion to defer to their leading magistrates, it seems, and obey the prevailing laws and norms of the republic. But "the broad training citizens receive in the interest of conditioning them to obey the general will works against their ability to discover it … Rousseau's ideal culture makes citizens who are not capable of meeting Condorcet's conditions" (*ibid.*). If the general will is understood in terms of equal rights assignments, however, it is hard to see why the cognitive abilities required for Condorcetian estimation of it are discouraged by a culture that promotes fervent devotion to the very rights and correlative obligations that the majority enacts into positive law. The intellectual component seems to work hand in hand with the sentimental one to establish and sustain the community's "equality of right" and "notion of justice".

Republican government

Whereas sovereignty cannot be alienated by the citizens to legislative "representatives", Rousseau argues that executive power to administer the laws ought to be entrusted by law to a separate subordinate "moral body", namely, the "government" or "prince" (*SC* iii.1 [3–7], 82–3). There is no contract between the people and their government: "It is absurd and contradictory for the Sovereign to give itself a superior [or an equal] … There is only one contract in the State, the contract of association; and it, by itself alone, excludes any others" (*SC* iii. 16 [4, 7], 116–17). Rather, the popular majority enacts as it pleases a government of one form or another. By passing such a fundamental political law, the people establish this executive body's internal structure, including the various rights and duties attached to the chief executive office. The people should also create other bodies of magistrates apart from the regular government, Rousseau suggests, but more on that in due course.

Any form of government, whether democratic, aristocratic, monarchical or mixed, is a republican government so long as the executive trustees (the "magistrates") do not usurp the sovereignty of the people (*SC* ii.6 [9], 67). A government does not usurp the sovereign lawmaking power provided the magistrates apply all of the laws enacted by the citizens in assembly, including the laws passed by previous assemblies and left standing by the current one:

> Yesterday's law does not obligate today, but tacit consent is presumed from silence, and the Sovereign is assumed to be constantly confirming the laws which it does not abrogate when it can do so. Everything which it has once declared it wills it continues to will, unless it revokes it.   (*SC* iii.11 [4], 109)

To the extent that they exercise power beyond the limits of the laws enacted by the citizens, however, the magistrates usurp sovereignty, destroy the republic and establish a despotism in its place (*SC* iii.10 [6, 10], 107–8).

The sharp separation of the legislative power from the executive power, of the general will expressed by the citizens from the particular applications of it by the magistrates, is, however, more subtle than it may first appear. Rousseau explains that the magistrates also do not usurp sovereignty if, consistently with the laws, they issue executive decrees and regulations that the citizens leave standing despite having the power to overturn them in the assembly: "the commands of the chiefs may ... be taken for general wills as long as the sovereign is free to oppose them and does not do so. In such a case the people's consent has to be presumed from universal silence" (*SC* ii.1 [4], 57–8). This legitimate power of government to subject the members of the republic to rules and regulations issued by the magistrates imposes an important caveat on the requirement that all genuine laws must be ratified by the citizens. Without usurping sovereignty, the government can issue and enforce the bulk of what are legitimately taken to be the laws of the republic. Sovereignty would only be usurped if the magistrates prevented majorities in the assembly from enacting laws to nullify "the commands of the chiefs".

Far from spending their every waking hour in the assembly enacting all manner of legislation, however minor, the people may choose to confine their votes to major laws that distribute equal basic rights or modify them in important ways. Most of the everyday business of regulation could be left to the government within the limits set by the major laws, given that the people retain authority to nullify oppressive executive rules and orders by passing suitable legislation and might also establish auxiliary institutions with power to veto executive attempts to violate basic rights during the intervals between general assemblies. Of the major laws requiring popular ratification, the fundamental political laws may be termed the constitution, or framework of government, of the republic.

The lawgiver

Any proposed constitution ought to be drafted by a wise "lawgiver" on behalf of the people, in Rousseau's view, and the constitution most suited to one people with its particular circumstances and culture will typically differ from the constitution most suited to another people with different resources and traditions. The popular majority does no more than ratify the lawgiver's proposals in the assembly, and it will be something of a miracle if the lawgiver can persuade the majority to do even that much. There is nothing especially remarkable about this claim that a sage individual or group (as opposed to the people *en masse*) must draft a suitable constitution for the citizens to ratify. No doubt "gods" alone are sufficiently wise to know the truly *best* constitution "suited to each Nation" (*SC* ii.7 [1], 68–9). Yet men occasionally appear with qualities that allow them to pass themselves off as virtual gods. These men of "genius" possess not only the intelligence to design a constitution that the people could work to their common good for an indefinite period, but also the strength of moral personality required to persuade the people to accept such a constitution. True, even these great figures also need the good luck to live in times of relative peace and prosperity. But, however rarely, the right men sometimes appear in the right circumstances. Even if Lycurgus, Romulus, and Numa are mythical figures (as Rousseau himself suggests), historical examples of Rousseauian lawgivers include Solon at Athens, Dion and Timoleon at Syracuse, Calvin at Geneva, and Madison and his colleagues at Philadelphia.

More remarkable is Rousseau's claim that lawgivers must "honor the Gods with their own wisdom" in order to rally the people to ratify a proposed constitution (*SC* ii.7 [10], 71). Invoking divine authority is necessary "since the Lawgiver can use neither force nor reasoning" (*SC* ii.7 [9], 71). He cannot rightfully use force to enact the constitution without popular consent, nor can he rightfully compel anyone to obey his proposed rules. His office gives him neither legislative authority nor executive authority: "It is not magistracy, it is not sovereignty. This office which gives the republic its constitution has no place in its constitution" (*SC* ii.7 [4], 69). Thus, contrary to an influential view in the literature, "the spirit of Rousseau" is not compatible with a coercive lawgiver (Furet 1997: 178). By resorting to force, the lawgiver would usurp the people's sovereignty (by imposing a constitution without popular consent) as well as the government's executive power (by enforcing the rules against any individual), and thereby become a tyrant.

In this regard, there is an important distinction between "forcing someone to be free", by forcing him to obey a constitution or other major law that has been freely enacted by the people as a general will, and forcing the people to adopt or comply with proposals that the popular majority rejects. In the latter case, tyranny replaces republican freedom. Unlike a tyrant, a genuine lawgiver welcomes popular ratification of his proposed constitutional provisions because he proposes certain equal basic claim-rights, including equal rights to vote in the assembly, for all citizens. The lawgiver recognizes that ratification by the popular majority is essential for identifying, and inspiring popular devotion to, the specific constitutional structure and positive rights that are advantageous for that particular community. Neither the lawgiver nor some council of legislative "representatives" can perform this complex task for the people, in Rousseau's view. Rather, each citizen must have a vote in the assembly, not only to express his preference (*amour de soi*) as to how best to protect his own vital interests that are rightfully protected by virtue of human nature, it seems, but also to facilitate a popular *majority* judgement (as opposed to a popular minority judgement) as required for a maximum likelihood estimate of what is truly advantageous for the community. Thus, if most are publicly spirited, the test of popular ratification helps to check tyrants who, masquerading as lawgivers, wish either to deny equal basic rights or, perhaps less malevolently, to legislate and enforce equal rights whose content has not been endorsed by the people. Once the people have ratified a proposed constitution as a general will, however, each citizen (strictly, each resident of the republic's territory) is obliged to obey the law and respect the relevant positive rights, and each may legitimately be forced to do so by the magistrates.

Similarly, there is a distinction between legitimately forcing an individual to obey executive laws and commands that cohere with major laws in a way tacitly accepted by the people in so far as the people have let the executive measures stand after having had an opportunity to strike them down, and illegitimately forcing the people to adopt and comply with proposals that the popular majority has neither freely enacted nor ever had an opportunity to reject. A republican government confines itself to the legitimate use of force, whereas a tyrant exercises force illegitimately. But a genuine lawgiver is precluded from using force at all.

Not only is he precluded from using force, the lawgiver also cannot rely on human reasoning to persuade the people to enact the constitution because most new citizens have not yet developed the intellectual and moral capacities needed to appreciate or comply with sound fundamental political laws: "each individual, appreciating no other scheme of government than that which bears directly on his particular interest, has difficulty perceiving the advantages he is supposed to derive from the constant privations required by good laws [i.e. general wills]" (*SC* ii.7 [9], 70–71). These ordinary citizens are not necessarily burdened with corrupt habits as a result of previous immersion within the customs of an illegitimate state ruled by some vain tyrant often at war with others of his stripe. Rousseau's theory allows that citizens may have largely avoided such corruption by living in a state of nature free of the influence of oppressive governments. Even so, they cannot be expected to replicate the "sublime" moral reasoning of the wise lawgiver. Yet they always have a natural conscience or "moral sense" by virtue of their humanity. Thus, under the right conditions, any citizen can always gain access to the god-given law of nature engraved in his heart. The lawgiver's appeal to divine authority might tap into that divine element in the hearts of citizens, such that most are persuaded to adopt a constitution not by human reasoning but by fear of a beneficent god, whom they believe has bestowed reciprocal natural rights on all men.

It should not be thought that the lawgiver's inability to rely solely on reasoning to persuade the people to adopt a constitution implies that the new citizens are typically incompetent to judge which positive rights and correlative duties are advantageous for their community. True, the moral element, that is, the impartial recognition and respect for universal natural rights, is rooted in religious awe rather than rational calculation. Once that moral component is in place, however, it may not be implausible to suppose that citizens are typically more likely to be correct than incorrect about which specific positive interpretations of such natural rights are advantageous for their community. After all, each person's judgement on this matter can be based solely on his reasoning about how best to protect his own vital interests as positive rights. There is no contradiction between the personal qualities required for ratifying or amending a constitution and those required by Condorcetian estimation.

Provisional democracy

Once a form of government has been ratified, the popular majority then goes on to nominate and elect "the chiefs who will be entrusted with the established Government" (*SC* iii.17 [3], 117). This act of appointment is not an exercise of sovereignty, however, since it is not a general will but rather a particular executive act that names particular individuals to fill senior government posts. After noting the puzzle of "how there can be an act of Government before the Government exists", Rousseau explains that the puzzle is resolved "by a sudden conversion of Sovereignty into Democracy; ... the Citizens having become Magistrates pass from general to particular acts, and from the law to its execution" (*SC* iii.18 [5], 117–18). The popular legislative assembly spontaneously transforms itself into a provisional democratic government, in which the citizens serve as chief magistrates acting by majority vote in a grand executive council. This "provisional Government either remains in office if such is the form that is adopted, or it establishes in the name of the Sovereign the Government prescribed by law" (*SC* iii.17 [7], 118). Thus, the provisional democracy might establish an aristocratic form of government, in which chief executive authority resides with a minority of citizens, by nominating and electing to office the relatively few citizens who are to be the ruling elite.

Aside from its "distinctive advantage" for establishing the form of government enacted by the popular majority, however, and for electing the members of the chief executive office (as well as other magistrates such as tribunes, censors and temporary dictators) under terms and conditions set out in electoral laws, a "genuine" democratic government holds no attraction for Rousseau. He says that democracy corrupts the general will by fusing chief executive power with sovereign legislative power in the majority of citizens. These two kinds of power ought to be kept separate. Otherwise, popular majorities with both powers will inevitably be led to pursue their particular interests at the expense of the common good: "A people which would never misuse the Government would not misuse independence either; a people which would always govern well would not need to be governed" (*SC* iii.4 [2], 91). Except as a provisional government for limited functions, democracy is undesirable and, indeed, impossible among men, even in a small republic. "If there were a people of Gods, they would govern themselves democratically. So perfect a Government is not suited to men" (*SC* iii. 4 [8], 92).

Elective aristocracy

Instead, in addition to his preference for a small republic, Rousseau prefers an "elective" aristocratic form of government to execute the laws ratified by the people. Strictly speaking, he endorses a "mixed form of government" because the ruling aristocracy is elected on the basis of merit or wealth by the provisional democratic government consisting of the whole body of citizens, who (sitting as provisional chiefs) elect by majority vote from among their own number the few chief magistrates who will lead the regular government established by law.

He says that all feasible governments are strictly mixed forms in any case, because executive power is always distributed across multiple bodies, including larger and smaller councils as well as a head of state, "with this difference" that sometimes power is relatively concentrated at one end of the distribution, sometimes at another, and even "at times the distribution is equal" (*SC* iii.7 [1–2], 99). Rousseau can maintain that executive power is always dispersed in this way consistently with his view that *sovereignty* is never located in the government.

The election of the ruling elite should take place according to laws passed by the citizens in assembly, he emphasizes. If there is no electoral law so that the government is permitted to choose when or if elections will take place, the inevitable result is an "hereditary" aristocracy, which is "the worst of all Governments" (*SC* iii.5 [4], 93). In this case, the ruling elite inherits supreme executive authority through blood connection without being confirmed to office by the citizens according to a law that fixes regular dates of election. Such a hereditary aristocracy is incompatible with republicanism because the governors are regularly appointed by the noble families rather than by the sovereign people.

Once elected by the assembly, the elite council would typically appoint, or otherwise second the assembly's election of, some further number of subordinate magistrates, including, perhaps, a singular head of state or even multiple heads (such as the two elected "consuls" of Rome). A titular head office of this sort would give the government a partly monarchic aspect, just as the general assembly of the citizens gives it a partly democratic aspect. Whether or not any such head office is created as part of the government, however, supreme executive power in a predominantly aristocratic "elective" mixed government ordinarily rests with the elected few in an upper council or senate.

An elective monarchy or, strictly speaking, a predominantly monarchic "elective" mixed government in which supreme executive power is entrusted by the people to a single chief, remains conceivable. But it is far too dangerous even in a large republic where it has most to recommend it, since there is a strong tendency for the monarch to become a tyrant (*SC* iii.6 [4–5], 95). Even if he has the self-restraint to prevent himself from usurping sovereignty, the elected monarch will need ministers to help govern the state. But he will almost certainly appoint "fools" incapable of exercising the executive authority entrusted to him by the citizens (*SC* iii.6 [6–8], 96). In any case, an elective monarchy must face the intractable problem of instability associated with electoral competition for the throne upon the death of a sitting king. The attempt to remedy this problem by establishing a hereditary monarchy offers no adequate solution since it merely substitutes regencies for elections. Hereditary monarchy is also dangerous to the republic in much the same way that hereditary aristocracy is. The royal family may seize sovereignty by ignoring the need for regular popular ratification of the king or, more precisely, the royal nominee for the chief executive office. Despotism is virtually guaranteed, Rousseau seems to believe, since a king born to rule can hardly be expected to confine himself to applying laws that are enacted or at least tacitly accepted by the people (*SC* iii.6 [10–16], 97–9).

Separation of powers

Rousseau prescribes a complete separation between the people's lawmaking power and the government's executive power such that when one is active the other must be passive: "The instant the People is legitimately assembled as a Sovereign body, all jurisdiction of the Government ceases, the executive power is suspended, and the person of the last Citizen is as sacred and inviolable as that of the first Magistrate" (*SC* iii.14 [1], 112). His idea seems to be that the government should draft major pieces of civil and criminal legislation apart from the constitution, and present these proposed general wills to the assembly for the people's consideration. The executive body should also be responsible for issuing more or less minor legislation required to fill in the details of the major laws and apply them, subject to override by the assembly if the popular majority grows highly dissatisfied with the way the government is doing this. For their part, the people enact or reject the government's proposals but do not amend or redraft them, and also override any standing executive rules and regulations that provoke the majority's displeasure. Presumably, the majority should freely override executive "legislation" as it sees fit, whether or not any magistrate initiates the proceedings.

The people should typically leave the drafting and redrafting of civil and criminal general wills, even ones of fundamental importance, to senior government officials, just as the drafting of the constitution itself is left to the lawgiver. In the "Epistle Dedicatory" for his *Discourse on Inequality*, Rousseau is clear that "the power to propose new Laws … [should] belong to the Magistrates alone" in a well-constituted republic (Rousseau 1997a: 116). He also seems to prefer that most discussion of proposals should take place outside the assembly, an indication of his desire for the votes to be cast independently (*SC* iv.1 [7], 122). As Cranston points out, this was still the practice at Geneva when Rousseau was writing: the citizens "had the vote, but no right to speak or initiate legislation" in the "General Council" (1989: 422). Yet this does not imply that discussions should be confined to the upper councils of the government. Consistently with a Condorcetian perspective, the people may freely discuss the laws outside the assembly. Rousseau even suggests that citizens should have time between assemblies to debate proposals: a proposed general will need not be voted upon at the same assembly in which it is first introduced (*SC* iv.4 [31], 134).

The Rousseauian version of separation of powers implies that the government has legitimate power to check the people by refusing to enforce any "iniquitous decrees" that are not genuine laws because they deny some citizens their equal rights or exempt a few from their equal obligations. The popular majority also has power to check the government by refusing to enact proposals that are not general wills, and by nullifying any regulations issued by the executive that violate the equal basic rights of citizens. To exercise this control over the government, the people must be free to assemble regularly at dates that the majority itself establishes by law: "there must be fixed and periodic assemblies which nothing can abolish or prorogue" (*SC* iii.13 [1], 111).

These regular assemblies should always "open with two motions ... which ought to be voted on separately": *"whether it please the Sovereign to retain the present form of Government"* and *"whether it please the People to leave its administration to those who are currently charged with it"* (*SC* iii.18 [6–8], 119–20, original emphasis). If a new lawgiver proposes to amend the constitution or even to replace it altogether, for example, the popular majority may decide to enact his modified form of government. If the current magistrates have displeased the people by repeated abuses of executive authority, the majority may decide to elect new magistrates without necessarily altering the constitution. There is no reason to suppose that the people must confine attention to candidates nominated by the outgoing magistrates, who are suspected of abusing their trust. Any candidate with significant popular support should be free to run for office in these (hopefully rare) situations. Otherwise, there would be no credible threat of throwing the abusers out of office, in which case there would be no check against tyranny.

By this device of fixed and periodic assemblies, Rousseau makes it possible for the sovereign people to effect periodically a lawful revolution. In contrast, Locke seems to have expected that the popular majority would arise against unjust government more or less spontaneously, perhaps with some leadership from prominent men in the community, only after a long train of repeated abuses. Whereas a Lockean revolution signals constitutional chaos and a state of war between the people and their rulers, Rousseau offers a more peaceful and regular alternative.

Checks and balances

Rousseau is evidently aware of the need for precautions to help maintain the proper balance between the popular sovereign and the government. To keep the sovereign within its proper sphere, he recommends educating the people about their rights and duties as citizens, including their duty to consider, vote for and enact only general wills. Since factions are inevitable, he prescribes multiplying their number so as to moderate the influence of any of them on the majority's judgement. But no citizens should be excluded from the assembly. At the same time, to keep the government within its proper sphere, he recommends educating magistrates about their rights and duties as magistrates, including their duty not to usurp the lawmaking power from the people. Since usurpations are inevitable, he proposes periodic assemblies whereby the people regularly review their form of government and the conduct of its chiefs. Again, no citizens (including the current magistrates) should be excluded from the assembly.

Nevertheless, the danger remains that executive and legislative power will become fused in the hands of some faction at the head of the government. So Rousseau suggests that the people should take further steps to create a rather sophisticated system of countervailing powers. One step is to "divide the Government", in other words, disperse the supreme executive power across multiple councils and require each council to agree before the government can act. By contrast, in an undivided government, the chief executive power is lodged in a single council or individual magistrate. Dividing the government in this way *weakens* it if one magistrate or a small council had formerly exercised the supreme executive command (*SC* iii.7 [4], 99). But the same step *strengthens* the government if its supreme force had formerly been lodged in a numerous council, as in a democracy (*SC* iii.7 [6], 100).

Another step he prescribes is for the people to "temper" the government, in other words, create "intermediate magistrates who, leaving the Government whole [undivided], merely serve to balance the two Powers and to uphold their respective rights" (*SC* iii.7 [5], 100). These intermediate magistrates include tribunes or ephors, and censors. They are not part of the government since they "merely serve to balance" the executive power rather than exercise any of it. The tribunes have authority to veto particular government acts or executive "legislation" when the assembly is not in session, for example, and thereby help to prevent executive magistrates from encroaching on the sovereign lawmaking power or violating basic individual rights embedded in positive law. The tribunes also have authority to nullify "iniquitous" acts of the people, however, and thereby help to prevent a popular majority faction from interfering with the government or trampling on individual rights.

Similarly, the censors have authority to discourage both the people and the government from usurping each other's legitimate power or violating basic individual rights recognized in the positive law. The censors issue public declarations of the republic's cultural norms (*moeurs*), with a view to persuading ordinary citizens and magistrates to engage in particular actions and refrain from others. For purposes of illustration, Rousseau directs attention to his *Lettre à M. d'Alembert*, in which he argued that the Genevans should not import Parisian theatre into their city because such entertainments, although perhaps suited to a decadent and corrupt absolute monarchy like France, were not suited to the *moeurs* of a genuine republic. Geneva needed its own brand of theatre, more generally, arts and entertainments that celebrated the Genevan people, the history of their republic, and their distinctive way of life. But the censors, like the tribunes, have no authority to enact laws or employ coercive force themselves.

Rousseau might have gone on to prescribe that these special magistrates should have power to compete with government magistrates by drafting and proposing different general wills to the popular assembly. This would tend to reduce the government's control over the legislative initiative, and perhaps give the people a wider variety of proposals from which to enact laws. But he seems unfriendly to this possibility. He recognizes that the tribunes at Rome did seize power to draft and propose legislation to the assemblies, for example, but he apparently views it as illegitimate and accuses the tribunes of "usurping some of the rights of the Senate" (*SC* iii.15 [8], 115). Indeed, these special magistrates are so likely to usurp both executive and legislative authority for partial ends, he fears, that their number should be multiplied (as it was at Rome) so that one tribune is more likely to veto another's abuse of power. Moreover, the tribunate as a whole should be periodically suspended by law, he says, so that its authority to "prevent everything" is not continuously in play (*SC* iv.5 [3–8], 136–8).

Rousseau does propose that the people should pass a law permitting the election of a temporary dictator to deal with extreme emergencies threatening the very life of the republic. Such a dictator does not have sovereignty during his one "very brief" fixed term in office (six months at Rome). At most, this "supreme chief … silences all the laws [including the constitution] and provisionally suspends the Sovereign authority" in order to save the people. His "suspension of the legislative authority does not abolish it; [he] cannot make it speak, he dominates it without being able to represent it; he can do everything, except make laws" (*SC* iv.6 [4], 138–9).

Church and state

Beyond recommending a rigorous public education and censorship to preserve the *moeurs* of the republic, Rousseau argues that the people should establish a "civil religion", the "dogmas" of which men would be compelled by law to affirm in public as a condition of becoming a citizen or even remaining as an inhabitant of the republic's territory. The "positive dogmas" are the "existence of the powerful, intelligent, beneficent, prescient, and provident Divinity, the life to come, the happiness of the just, the punishment of the wicked, the sanctity of the social Contract and the Laws" (*SC* iv.8 [33], 150–51). The one "negative dogma" is "intolerance": a citizen is not permitted to follow any theology, including strict versions of Roman Catholicism and Calvinism, that refuses to tolerate any religion except itself. Rather, "one must tolerate all those [religions] which tolerate the others insofar as their dogmas contain nothing contrary to the duties of the Citizen" (*SC* iv.8 [35], 151).

Rousseau insists on this "purely civil profession of faith" because, in his view, a man cannot be "either a good Citizen or a loyal subject" unless he believes in the dogmas of the civil religion: "the Sovereign may banish from the State anyone who does not believe them; it may banish him, not as impious but as unsociable, as incapable of sincerely loving the laws, justice, and, if need be of sacrificing his life to his duty" (*SC* iv.8 [32], 150). He goes so far as to recommend the death penalty for any citizen who "behaves as if he did not believe" these dogmas "after having publicly acknowledged" them.

It follows that, for Rousseau, atheists, and those who believe in a maleficent god that rewards the wicked and punishes the just, are "unsociable" and thus incapable of participating in the sovereign authority. Such men cannot "sincerely love" the general will, the "equality of right", and the "notion of justice" essential to a republic. They cannot be trusted to estimate or obey the republic's general will because they do not believe in a "beneficent Divinity" or, therefore, in the divine law of nature that distributes the natural rights underlying and constraining a general will's assignment of positive rights. The claim that basic rights ultimately have some such divine source accounts for Rousseau's view that faith in a beneficent deity is essential to civil morality.

The claim that a well-constituted republic must impose this theology on its citizens as part of public morality falls short of the more advanced liberal outlook of thinkers like Thomas Jefferson and James Madison. In addition to its intolerance of atheists and worshippers of evil gods, the claim opens the door to far more intolerant religious establishments. Nevertheless, Rousseau's view is no less liberal than Locke's on this score.

Conclusion

In *The Social Contract*, I have argued, Rousseau holds out the ideal of a small-scale liberal republic whose citizens directly enact into positive law certain equal basic rights that the popular majority judges are advantageous to that particular community, given its distinctive circumstances and traditions. These positive rights are more concrete and detailed elaborations of underlying natural rights, whose reality is undeniable, he suggests, to any upright man who consults his conscience and hears the voice of a beneficent god therein. The government of this ideal state or genuine republic is entrusted with force to execute these laws and thereby protect the equal rights of all citizens. But it also issues the bulk of the quotidian legislation with the tacit consent of the people. It is preferably aristocratic in form, in the sense that its supreme force is entrusted to an elite council of a few senior magistrates. Yet there is also a fairly sophisticated system of countervailing powers designed to keep the sovereign people and the government in their proper respective spheres, and thus prevent the emergence of tyranny. True, tyranny will eventually have its way – "If Sparta and Rome perished, what State can hope to last forever?" (*SC* iii.11 [1], 109) – but Rousseau implies that, with a bit of luck, a liberal republic of the sort he recommends can at least endure for a long time. He evidently thinks it is the sort of model that any prospective lawgiver might study with profit.

It may well seem that Rousseau's ideal is no longer relevant. Our advanced large-scale societies are hardly likely to be reorganized any time soon into various confederations of small independent states, it may be objected, and most voters simply do not have the time or inclination (even if they have the intellectual capacity) to become informed about the many complex issues requiring legislation in the modern setting. Yet large-scale Rousseauian republics are no longer inconceivable, in light of the advent of computer networks that make possible electronic assemblies of large bodies of citizens. Moreover, it is not a compelling objection to his theory to insist that voters would never have the knowledge or time to pass all of the laws or oversee the government. He allows that the government should issue the bulk of legislation, with the tacit consent of the sovereign. The people should confine their attention to major legislation and executive commands, bearing in important ways on basic rights.

In an ideal large-scale Rousseauian "electronic republic", the people would not spend their days and nights assembled at their computers, surrounded by piles of books and documents, voting continuously and trying frantically to catch up on the issues. Rather, they would assemble periodically to enact or reject major legislation proposed by the government, and to nullify any existing executive rules and regulations that the popular majority judges to be incompatible with basic rights. In the spirit of Rousseau, the people would be aided in the latter task by intermediate institutions like a supreme constitutional court with power to review and nullify "iniquitous" executive measures as well as invalid decrees passed by the assembly itself.

But perhaps there is no hope that voters in a large polity will develop the intense public spirit required by Rousseau's ideal. As he indicates, a genuine republic presupposes genuine citizens who are motivated to specify a public conception of the common good (including "equal justice") for their community, and also fairly competent when it comes to judging how best to protect their own vital interests as human beings. He is evidently aware that, if voters are not properly motivated, the republic will tend to dissolve into warring factions and tyranny. Indeed, he never denies that a genuine republic will be a rare phenomenon. They were certainly scarce in his day, and in 1764 he apparently concluded that even his native Geneva no longer fit the bill. It is hard to believe that he would be more optimistic today, given such factors as population growth and the widespread decline of faith in a beneficent god. Whether we should be more optimistic is an open question. To the extent that a genuine republic becomes impossible for want of genuine citizens, however, any reasonable observer can only share Rousseau's apparent longing to return to the early state of nature as he depicts it, where the individual can live in accordance with his natural conscience because of his relative isolation from other men. Such a desire to withdraw into private life is perfectly understandable when public life has fallen so far from the republican ideal.

Notes

1. Henceforth, *SC* i.1 [1], 41, indicating Book I, Chapter 1, first paragraph of *Social Contract*, with the relevant page of Gourevitch's English translation (Rousseau 1997b: 39–152) immediately after the comma.

2. An individual's claim-right correlates to obligations in other people. If the individual has a claim-right to own private property, for example, or a right to be free from slavery, then others have corresponding duties to, respectively, refrain from interfering with his use of his property and refrain from enslaving him. A claim-right may be contrasted with a liberty-right that does not correlate to obligations in others. The individual may have a liberty-right to compete with others for a single available job, for example, but others have the same right to compete rather than any duty not to compete. Rousseau seems to be arguing that there are natural claim-rights and correlative natural obligations that cannot become genuine legal or moral claims and correlative obligations until men jointly contract to form a republic.

3. An epistemic device is an instrument for discovering or filling in the truth about something that we have reason to suppose exists independently of the instrument. A telescope is an epistemic device for acquiring knowledge about the planets. According to the Condorcetian view that I am suggesting was anticipated by Rousseau, majority voting is an epistemic procedure for acquiring the best available information about any particular community's common good. For Rousseau, the common good includes distributions of equal positive claim-rights whose content is constrained to some extent by underlying natural rights that exist independently of the majority voting procedure. Majority voting fills in the truth about those natural rights for the community by

generating a maximum likelihood estimate of the particular positive interpretation of them that really is most advantageous for that particular community.

Bibliography

d'Alembert, J. le Rond 1960 [1757]. "Geneva". In *Politics and the Arts: Letter to M. D'Alembert on the Theatre*, J.-J. Rousseau, A. Bloom (ed. and trans.), 139–48. Ithaca, NY: Cornell University Press.

Cohen, J. 1986a. "Reflections on Rousseau: Autonomy and Democracy", *Philosophy & Public Affairs* **15**, 275–88.

Cohen, J. 1986b. "Structure, Choice, and Legitimacy: Locke's Theory of the State", *Philosophy & Public Affairs* **15**, 301–24.

Condorcet, J. 1785. *Essai sur l'application de l'analyse à la probabilité des decisions rendues à la pluralité des voix*. Paris: L'Imprimerie Royale.

Cranston, M. 1989. "Jean-Jacques Rousseau and the Fusion of Democratic Sovereignty with Aristocratic Government", *History of European Ideas* **11**, 417–25.

Dent, N. J. H. 1988. *Rousseau: An Introduction to his Psychological, Social and Political Theory*. Oxford: Blackwell.

Estlund, D. with J. Waldron, B. Grofman & S. Feld 1989. "Democratic Theory and the Public Interest: Condorcet and Rousseau", *American Political Science Review* **83**, 1317–40.

Furet, F. 1997. "Rousseau and the French Revolution". In *The Legacy of Rousseau*, C. Orwin & N. Tarcov (eds), 168–82. Chicago, IL: University of Chicago Press.

Gildin, H. 1983. *Rousseau's Social Contract: The Design of the Argument*. Chicago, IL: University of Chicago Press.

Grofman, B. & S. Feld 1988. "Rousseau's General Will: A Condorcetian Perspective", *American Political Science Review* **82**, 567–76.

Ladha, K. 1992. "The Condorcet Jury Theorem, Free Speech, and Correlated Votes", *American Journal of Political Science* **36**, 617–34.

Riley, P. (ed.) 2001. *The Cambridge Companion to Rousseau*. Cambridge: Cambridge University Press.

Rousseau, J.-J. 1960. *Politics and the Arts: Letter to M. D'Alembert on the Theatre*, A. Bloom (ed. and trans.). Ithaca, NY: Cornell University Press.

Rousseau, J.-J. 1964 [1762]. *Du contrat social*. In *Oeuvres completes*, vol. III, B. Gagnebin & M. Raymond (eds), 347–470. Paris: Bibliotheque de la Pleiade.

Rousseau, J.-J. 1997a. *The Discourses and Other Early Political Writings*, V. Gourevitch (ed. and trans.). Cambridge: Cambridge University Press.

Rousseau, J.-J. 1997b. *The Social Contract and Other Later Political Writings*, V. Gourevitch (ed. and trans.). Cambridge: Cambridge University Press.

Trachtenberg, Z. M. 1993. *Making Citizens: Rousseau's Political Theory of Culture*. London: Routledge.

Young, H. Peyton 1988. "Condorcet's Theory of Voting", *American Political Science Review* **82**, 1231–44.

Further reading

Victor Gourevitch's edition of *The Social Contract* (Rousseau 1997b: 39–152) is among the most helpful for English-speaking students. The pages of his translation are conveniently cross-referenced to those of *Du contrat social* in the third volume of the Pleiade edition of Rousseau's *Oeuvres completes* (Rousseau 1964: 347–470).

Index

Abstract (Hume)   167, 173, 177
actions   52
affects   51–2
afterlife   95
agnosticism   3
Alembert, Jean d'   194, 217
Amsterdam   37–8
analytic philosophy   83
animals   96, 127–9, 185
appetite/appetition   52, 68–9, 70, 72
Aquinas, Thomas   89, 121
aristocracy   107, 197
   elective   212–14
Aristotle   90, 93, 111, 134, 162
   influence   3, 6, 69, 70, 89, 121
arithmetic, as paradigm of reasoning   96
Arnauld, Antoine   169
associations   178, 203
astronomy   90
atheism   3, 47, 58, 98, 218
atomism   63–5, 68, 83, 89, 92
atoms   92
attributes   40
Ayer, A. J.   174

ballots   206
Bayle, Pierre   169–70
behaviour, motivations behind   93–4
belief   4, 16–17, 117, 120, 132–3, 182, 186–7
   perceptual   187–8
   philosophical   187–8
Berkeley, George   x–xi, 4, 134, 137–65, 169, 178
   as an empiricist   5, 7–8
   on God   142–6, 148–50, 153–4, 163
   life   137, 143
Berkeley's Master Argument   159–62
Bible   109–11
body   9, 22–3, 27, 40, 48, 65, 68, 72, 92, 186
   relationship to mind   22, 29–34, 47, 56, 72–4
body politic   197–8
Bonnot, Etienne   193
Borges, Jorge Luis   84
Boyle, Robert   102, 169
Bradley, F. H.   83
brain   92–3, 94–5; *see also* mind
bravery   100
Butler, Joseph   169

calculus   61
Calvinism   218
cannibalism   119
Cartesian Circle   25–6
Cartesian dualism *see* dualism
Catholicism   62, 111, 218
causes   43–4, 46, 48, 68–9, 71, 90
   and effects   180–85
   Hume on   174, 179, 180–81, 184–5
censors   216
change   66–7
Charles II, King   109
children   125
   unwanted   118–19, 194
Christianity   2–3, 99–100, 111; *see also* God
church
   definition   110
   and state   109, 217–18
Cicero   55
circles   90

citizens 195
  public spirited 200, 204
  rights and duties 215–16
Clarke, Samuel 169
Cogito, ergo sum 19
coherence 187
commonwealth 105–9
  Christian 109–10
  justification for 111
communication 96
compatibilism 95
Compendium to Hebrew Grammar (Spinoza) 38
conceivability 178, 184
Condorcet, Marquis de 204, 206–7, 211, 214
Conduct of the Understanding (Locke) 115
consciousness 124
constancy 187
continental philosophy 84
contingency 77
contracts
  in founding of states 105–8
  social 103–4, 105–7, 197–200
contradiction, principles of 75
Copy Principle 173, 175–6
corruption 203
cosmological argument 24, 28, 80
Cranston, M. 214
creation 23–4, 43, 74, 80, 81, 82
  natural and non-natural 65–6
Critique of Pure Reason (Kant) 117
Cromwell, Oliver 111
curiosity 97

De Cive (Hobbes) 90
De Corpore (Hobbes) 90
De Veritate (Herbert) 118
democracy 2, 107, 197, 211–12
Descartes, René ix, 3, 15–36, 66, 71, 121, 135,
    137, 178
  on God 9, 24–6
  influence 38, 40, 42, 48, 84, 95, 116, 118, 122–
    3, 169
  philosophical strategy 16–17
  as a rationalist 5–6, 8–9
  as scientist 5, 16, 27, 29
despotism 214
determinism 44, 83–4
dictatorship 106, 217
Diderot, Denis 194, 205
Discourse on Inequality (Rousseau) 195, 214
"Discourse on Metaphysics" (Leibniz) 61
Discourse on Political Economy (Rousseau) 194
Discourse on the Sciences and Arts (Rousseau)
    194
disease 81
"Dissertation on the Passions" (Hume) 168
dissolution, natural 65
doubt 16–17
dreams 17–19, 94, 147–8
dualism 22, 29–34, 47–8, 137; *see also* mind
duration *see* time
duties 111, 215–16

education 194, 207, 215–16
egoism 54, 100, 105
elections *see* voting
Émile (Rousseau) 194
emotions 51–2, 55, 93
  impact on behaviour 93–4, 97
empiricism 5, 94
energy 71–2
English Civil War 90, 101, 111
Enlightenment 1–3, 11–13
Enquiry Concerning Human Understanding
    (Hume) *see Treatise of Human Nature*
    (Hume)
Enquiry concerning the Principles of Morals
    (Hume) 168
entelechies 69–70
Epilogue to the Satires (Pope) 190
equality 100–101, 199
Erasmus, Desiderius 4
Essay Concerning Human Understanding (Locke)
    x, 115–39
  origins of 115–16
  structure and style 116–18
Essays and Treatises on Several Subjects (Hume)
    190
eternity 54, 56, 75
Ethics (Spinoza) ix–x, 37–59
  format and structure 39–40
Euclid 90–91
eudaimonia see happiness
evil 26–7, 81–2, 97
Examination of Malebranche (Locke) 115
existence 174
  Descartes on 19–23
  of ordinary objects 152–3
  thinking as proof of 19–21, 23
existentialism 84
experience 6
extension 47, 121
external world 187

fairies 111
faith 129, 133–4
fatalism 2
fear 91
feeling 174
Fogelin, Robert 172
Four Dissertations (Hume) 168
freedom 2, 83–4, 108, 195, 196, 210
  free will 26, 50, 95–6
  Leibniz on 77–9
Frege, Gottlob 125
French Revolution 11, 194, 197

Galileo Galilei 3, 90, 94, 102
Gassendi, Pierre 116, 127
Geneva 193–6, 198, 206, 209, 214, 220
geometry 90–91
ghosts 111
God 4, 6, 26–7, 31, 34, 38, 40–47, 75, 99, 104
  anthropomorphizing of 42, 44–5
  Berkeley on 142–6, 148–50, 153–4, 163

existence of 24–8, 41–2, 80, 99, 133, 142–6
  Hobbes on 99, 104, 108–9, 111
  as an innate idea 119–20
  knowledge of 54–5
  Leibniz on 79–83
  nature and attributes 40, 44–6, 47, 50, 54, 58, 79, 81
  Rousseau on 197–8, 209, 218
  Spinoza on 39, 40–47, 58
  as unique substance 40–42
  see also Christianity; creation
gods 99
good 26–7, 97, 201
government 89, 91
  foundation of 105–6
  justification for 111
  operation of 207–9
  separation of powers 214–15, 216
  tyrannical 195, 196–7
  see also republics; state

happiness 47, 56, 58
Harvey, William 90
hate 53
Henry VIII, King 109
Herbert of Cherbury, Lord 118
Hobbes, Thomas x, 10, 11–12, 89–113, 127, 134, 169, 178, 193
  autobiography 91
  base view of human nature 11–12
  inconsistent with traditional Christian views 93, 98–9
  similarities to Rousseau 199, 202
Hooke, Robert 102
human nature 10–12
  as self-centred 91, 100–101, 105
  Hume on 171–2
  science of 171
  as social 93
  see also nature, state of
humans, distinct from animals 96, 99, 105, 127–9
Hume, David xi, 3, 84, 95, 125, 145, 167–92, 194
  as an empiricist 5, 9–10
  influences on his work 5, 169–70
  life 16, 173, 190
Hume (Stroud) 172
Husserl, Edmund 84
Hutcheson, Francis 169–70

idealism 4, 138–41, 147; see also immaterialism
ideas 120–22, 139, 141–2, 148
  abstract 154–5, 178–9
  association of 124–5
  clear and distinct 25–8, 29, 71
  complex 120, 122–4
  conception of 159–62
  existence of 146
  Hume on 174–5
  innate 118–20
  knowledge of 131–2
  relationship to minds 141–2
  signified by words 125–9

simple 120–21
  transparent 157
identity 124, 129, 186
  personal 188–9
idolatry 111
imagination 94, 147–50, 187
immaterialism 137–42, 147–64; see also idealism
impressions 174, 183
indiscernibility 75
indivisibility 64–5
induction 172
inertia 94
inference 172, 174, 179
infinity 40
innatism 118–20, 134
intentionality 95
intuition 129–30, 189

Jefferson, Thomas 218
Johnson, Samuel 138
joy 52–3
Judaism 37–8, 99
justice, in state of nature 102

Kant, Immanuel 1, 4, 83, 117
Kemp Smith, Norman 170, 172
knowledge 5, 94, 97–8, 117
  degrees of 129–30
  Descartes on 17–18
  innate 118–20
  Locke on 129–34
  types of 49–50, 54–6

language 96–7, 103, 126, 155–6; see also words
Language, Truth and Logic (Ayer) 174
Last Judgement, mortalist view of 98
Lavasseur, Thérèse 194
lawgivers 209–11
laws 2, 106–8, 195–6, 201, 214, 219
  of nature 102–5
  of science 102
Leeuwenhoek, Antoni van 74
legislation see law
Leibniz, G. W. x, 3, 61–87, 178
  influence on later philosophers 83–4
  influences on his work 39, 61, 69, 70
  life 61–2
  as mathematician 61
  philosophical system 61–2
  as rationalist 5–6
  as scientist 5, 68, 76
Letter to M. d' Alembert (Rousseau) 194, 217
Leviathan (Hobbes) x, 89–113
  as commentary on the Bible 109–11
  frontispiece 91–2
  method 90
  origin of title 89–90
  references to the Bible 90
  as work of science 90
liberalism 11–12, 197
liberty see freedom
life, object of 56

Locke, John   x, 12, 115–36, 138, 139, 178, 193, 197
   attacked by Berkeley   154, 157
   belief in God   3–4
   as an empiricist   5, 7
   influence of science on his work   5, 122
   influence on later philosophers   134–5, 169–70
   life   116
   similarities to Rousseau   199–200, 215, 218
logic   3, 18
Louis XV, King   196
love   52–3, 56, 82

Machiavelli, Niccolò   2
Madison, James   209, 218
magistrates   208, 210, 212, 213–19
Maimonides   56
Malebranche, Nicolas   139, 145, 169–70, 178, 185
marriage   203
materialism   89, 98, 137, 152, 158
   atomistic   89, 92, 94–5
   see also immaterialism
mathematics   2, 5, 21, 28, 61, 94
   beliefs about   17–18
matter   73
   existence of   137–9, 155–6
   nature of   63–4
medieval philosophy   3
Meditations on First Philosophy (Descartes)   ix, 15–36, 169
memory   72, 74, 94, 174
microscopes   74
Mill, John Stuart   125, 145
mind
   Descartes on   22, 29–34, 95
   empiricist theory of   120–25
   existence of   139–40
   Hume on   171, 174, 185, 187–90
   identity with brain   92–3, 94–5
   Locke on   132
   materialist view of   92–5
   relationship to body   3, 22, 29–34, 47, 56, 72–4
   relationship to ideas   141–2
   relationship to matter   137–8, 140
   see also dualism; innatism
miracles   46, 58, 68, 74, 110
modes   40, 43, 122
modus ponens   18
momentum   72
Monadology (Leibniz)   x, 61–87
   style   62–3, 83–4
monads   3, 63–84
monarchy   107
   elected   213
   hereditary   213–14
monotheism   99
morality
   subjectivist   97, 103
mortalism   98
motion   66–8, 71–2, 90, 94
Murray, Gilbert   2–3
My Own Life (Hume)   167–8
mysticism   2

names   96, 126–7
nativism   118
naturalism   171–2, 182, 186
nature
   and God   44–7, 50, 205
   laws of   102–5, 108–9, 204
   relationship to human life   50–51, 54
   state of   10, 92–4, 100–105
necessity   44, 77
Netherlands   38, 57–8
Newton, Isaac   3, 61, 102, 169, 171
Nietzsche, Friedrich   84
nominalism   96, 127
Norton, David Fate   169
number   122

Ockham, William of   127
ontological arguments   28
opinion   129

pain   32
Pascal, Blaise   169
passions *see* emotions
Passmore, John   168
peace   103
perception   70–72, 74, 120, 141, 156–8, 175
   and belief   187–8
   complex and simple   175–6
   distinct from imagination   146–51
   of ideas   138, 146–7
   receptivity assumption   146–7
   as source of knowledge   130–31
perfection   80
phenomenalism   173–4, 175, 188
phenomenology   68, 84
Philosophy of David Hume (Kemp Smith)   172
philosophy, definition of   1
physical world
   existence of   29, 139
   proof of   17–18
physics   68, 76
Plato   1
plenum   66
Political Treatise (Spinoza)   38
politics   10–13, 57–8, 89, 91
   as a science   90, 92
Pope, Alexander   190
power
   desire for   97–8, 203
   separation of   214–15
   of the sovereign   105–7
Prince, The (Machiavelli)   2
Principles of Human Knowledge (Berkeley) *see*
   Treatise Concerning the Principles of Human Knowledge (Berkeley)
Principles of Nature and Grace, The (Leibniz)   62
Principles of Philosophy (Descartes)   19, 38
property, distribution of   199–200, 202
Protestantism   4, 62
psychology   92, 102, 124
punishment   97, 107, 108
qualities, primary and secondary   121–2

realism
  direct 187
  representative 139–40, 140, 159, 162
  sceptical 174
reality 68
reason 2–6, 46, 75, 82, 186
  as a cause 186
  demonstrative 180–81
  Leibniz on 74–9
  and sensory perception 49–50
  sufficient 75, 76, 77, 79–80
receptivity 146–7
reflection, as source of knowledge 120
Reformation 100
Reid, Thomas 172–3
relations
  natural 177
  philosophical 177, 180, 183
religion
  and belief 132–3
  as cause of war 90
  civil 196
  features of 99–100
  harmful effects of 170
  Locke on 118
  relationship to philosophy 3–4, 90
  and the state 109, 217–18
  as social phenomenon 98–100
Renaissance 2
representative realism 139–40, 140, 159, 162
republics 196, 197, 200, 207–11; see also govern-
    ments; state
revelation 109, 133
rights 2, 12, 103, 203, 205, 207, 215–16, 218–19
Rijnsburg 38
Robespierre, Maximilian 194
Rome 206, 217
Rousseau, Jean-Jacques xi, 10–11, 193–222
  influence 219–20
  life 193–5
Royal Society 122
Russell, Bertrand 83

sadness 52–3, 55
Sartre, Jean-Paul 84
scepticism 16, 17, 137, 171, 172–4, 182, 186
scholasticism 15, 16
science 2, 3, 4, 5, 29, 90, 102, 122
Search After Truth (Recherche de la Vérité)
    (Malebranche) 169–70
secularism 2–3
security, drive for 91
Selby-Bigge, L. A. 168
self 21, 22, 188–9
semantics 3, 125–9, 155
Seneca 55
senses 21, 22–3, 29–34, 49–50, 94, 138, 141
sensory perception 146–8, 175–7, 179, 184
  and existence 152–8, 163–4
  as source of knowledge 120–22, 130–31
"Short Treatise on God, Man and His Well-Being"
    (Spinoza) 38, 39, 44

sight 21, 130
signification 125–9
sin 81–2
slavery 200
sleep 70
Smith, Adam 12
Social Contract, The (Rousseau) xi, 193–222
social contracts 103–8, 197–200
society 10
Socrates 107
soul 3, 119
  Aristotle on 69–70
  immortality of 38, 48–9, 56–7
  Leibniz on 72–4
  nature of 40, 51, 189
sovereignty 109, 110, 111, 197–8, 202, 208
  checks on 215–16
space 75, 122–3, 174
Sparta 195, 199, 206
speech 92
  as uniquely human 96–7
Spinoza, Baruch (Benedict) de ix–x, 3, 37–59, 178
  influence on later philosophers 37, 61, 84
  influences on his work 38, 40, 42, 48, 55–6
  Judaism and excommunication 37–8, 42
  life 37–8, 57–8
  politics 57–8
  as a rationalist 5, 6–7, 37–59
Spinozism 37, 47
state 197
  creation of 105
  ideal 10–12
  as "mortal God" 89–90
  and religion 109, 217–18
  size 200, 218
  types of 107
  see also government; republics
Stillingfleet, Edward, Bishop of Worcester 115,
    129
Stoics 55
Stroud, B. 172
subjectivism, and morality 103
substance 3, 40–42, 65, 73, 75–7, 122–3, 132
  and change 66–8
  Leibniz on 63–9
supernatural 74
survival, as primary concern of human nature 100

technology 13
theodicies 26–7
Theodicy (Leibniz) 62, 76, 81
Theological-Political Treatise (Spinoza) 38, 39, 58

thinking 47, 120, 174
  as proof of existence 19–21, 23, 28
Thirty Years War 90, 101
Three Dialogues between Hylas and Philonous
    (Berkeley) 137, 138, 143, 147–51, 160, 164
time 75, 122, 174
totalitarianism 12
Trachtenberg, Z. M. 207
Tractatus Logico-Philosophicus (Wittgenstein) 83

Treatise Concerning the Principles of Human Knowledge (Berkeley) x–xi, 137–65, 169
Treatise of Human Nature (Hume) xi, 167–92
  influences 169–70
  failure 190
  nature of the project 170–74, 190
  scope and structure 167–8, 185
"Treatise on the Emendation of the Intellect" (Spinoza) 38
tribunes 216–17
truth 27, 76–8
Two Treatises on Government (Locke) 116
tyranny 106, 200, 203–4, 219–20

Uniformity Principle 181
universals 127

virtue 54, 172, 186

vivacity 175, 182–3, 185, 187
void 66, 174
Voltaire 81, 194
Voorburg 38
voting 206, 210, 212, 220
  as a duty 216
  as a right 198–9

wars 90, 101, 107, 111
will 52
  general 195–6, 201, 204–5
William the Conqueror 111
Wittgenstein, Ludwig 83
women, excluded from voting rights 198
words 155
  as signs 125–9
  see also language
worlds, possible 81